FORD MADOX FORD
AND ENGLISHNESS

Edited by
Dennis Brown and
Jenny Plastow

Rodopi

Amsterdam - New York, NY 2006

The Ford Madox Ford Society

Acknowledgements

The editors would like to thank John Mole for permission to publish his poem 'Fordie' for the first time. Especial thanks, too, to Mick Brookes for his time-consuming and expert work in co-ordinating the formatting of contributions; also to Sam Worsfold-Brown for facilitating editorial liaison.

Cover illustration: Ford Madox Brown, *The Last of England*, watercolour on paper (1864-6).
© Tate, London 2006

Title page illustration: Ford c.1915, pen and ink drawing.
© Alfred Cohen, 2000

ISBN-10: 90-420-2053-9
ISBN-13: 978-90-420-2053-5
©Editions Rodopi B.V., Amsterdam - New York, NY 2006
Printed in The Netherlands

International
Ford Madox Ford
Studies
Volume 5

For information about the Ford Madox Ford Society,
please see the website at:
www.rialto.com/fordmadoxford_society

Or contact:
max.saunders@kcl.ac.uk
or:
Dr Sara Haslam S.J.Haslam@open.ac.uk
Department of Literature, Open University,
Walton Hall, Milton Keynes, MK7 6AA, UK

IFMFS is a peer-reviewed annual series. Guidelines for contributors, including
a full list of abbreviations of Ford's titles and related works, can be found by
following the links on the Society's website. Abbreviations used in this volume
are listed from p. 287

FORDIE

John Mole

Your links are a No Man's Land
beyond the clubhouse, history's
dead ground, declivities
dissolved through mist to a pantomime
of ghosts, their plus-fours
marching in step. A metronome
keeps pace, its narrative
constrained by time.
                        But break
rank, Fordie, your rogue swing
a musical phrase, your aim
risking it all. When the mist clears
see how the land lies, how the sun
like a burnished pendulum
gilds the fairway. Make it new
in the raising of your game
and your handicap brought down
to a figure of speech
in easy conversation.
                        Look,
the flags are out all over England
and here on the course
you celebrate the last of it
with a sturdy drive, not yet
the master of your fate
but holding ground
and, as the distance redefines
our measure, keeping faith.

CONTENTS

GENERAL EDITOR'S PREFACE

Max Saunders

Ford Madox Ford has as often been a subject of controversy as a candidate for literary canonization. He was, nonetheless, a major presence in early twentieth-century literature, and he has remained a significant figure in the history of modern English and American literature for over a century. Throughout that time he has been written about – not just by critics, but often by leading novelists and poets, such as Graham Greene, Robert Lowell, William Carlos Williams, Gore Vidal, A. S. Byatt, and Julian Barnes. His two acknowledged masterpieces have remained in print since the 1940s. *The Good Soldier* now regularly figures in studies of Modernism and on syllabuses. *Parade's End* has been increasingly recognized as comparably important. It was described by Malcolm Bradbury as 'a central Modernist novel of the 1920s, in which it is exemplary'; by Anthony Burgess as 'the finest novel about the First World War'; and by Samuel Hynes as 'the greatest war novel ever written by an Englishman'.

During the last decade or so, there has been a striking resurgence of interest in Ford and in the multifarious aspects of his work. As befits such an internationalist phenomenon as Ford himself, this critical attention has been markedly international, manifesting itself not only in the United Kingdom and the U. S. A., but in Continental Europe and elsewhere. Many of his works have not only been republished in their original language, but also translated into more than a dozen others.

The founding of the International Ford Madox Ford Studies series reflects this increasing interest in Ford's writing and the wider understanding of his role in literary history. Each volume will normally be based upon a particular theme or issue. Each will relate aspects of Ford's work, life, and contacts, to broader concerns of his time. Thus the first, *Ford Madox Ford: A Reappraisal*, explored his less familiar books. The second investigated *Ford Madox Ford's Modernity*. The third, *History and Representation in Ford Madox Ford's Writings* traced his interest in history throughout his career, with specific emphases on the Tudor trilogy, the first world war, and the 1930s. The fourth, *Ford Madox Ford and the City*, explored the ways in which the city – mainly London, but also Paris, New York, and others – figures in his writing from his earliest poetry to his last essays, some of which (on American cities) were published in this series for the first time.

This fifth volume considers Ford's work in relation to the concept of 'Englishness', which has received particular attention recently, especially in response to multiculturalism, globalization, devolution, and the expansion and development of the European Community. Readers of Ford's best-known novels of modern British life will be aware of his intense attention to ideas of Englishness. Yet Englishness emerges from this volume as a central preoccupation throughout his *oeuvre*, in his poetry, historical fiction, discursive books, and literary editing, as much as in *The Good Soldier* or *Parade's End*. What's more, Ford emerges as pioneering in his discussions of Englishness, especially in his trilogy *England and the English*: pioneering not only chronologically, because these books anticipate the Edwardian run of 'Condition of England' literature; but also critically. Ford's account stands out strikingly as eschewing most of the characteristic attitudes of the Edwardian discourse of Englishness: nationalism and imperialism; the identification of nation with race, and the concomitant eugenicist anxieties about degeneration and decline; and the construction of historical myths of English supremacy. Instead, he focuses on Britain's multi-racial and multi-cultural history, in ways which anticipate debates about contemporary British society, history and culture.

England and the English appeared in an omnibus edition in Britain for the first time in 2003, when Sara Haslam's valuable edition for Carcanet brought it back into circulation. (The three volumes had originally been published separately in the U.K., and had only appeared under the collective title in the U.S.A. in 1907.) The trilogy is necessarily a reference-point for many of the chapters here, and is central to one third of them. Two essays (by Sara Haslam and Andrzej Gasiorek) concentrate on it. Two (by Karen McDermott and Donald Mackenzie) discuss it in relation to Ford's other trilogy, the novels comprising *The Fifth Queen*. Another two (by Nick Hubble and Christine Berberich) read *The Good Soldier* alongside *England and the English*.

Ford's thinking against the grain of national ideology has much to do with his ambivalent personal relation to Englishness: both as the son of a German father and English mother; and as a bohemian in a society whose official culture seemed resistant to artistic modernity. Such status, as at once insider and outsider, is of course directly related to how he presents the English in his fiction. (Thus several contributors touch on the extraordinary scene, described in *The Spirit of the People*, of a grotesquely reticent English 'goodbye' which seems to have provided the 'germ' for the story of *The Good Soldier*.) But the point is not so much that his attitudes were symptomatic of his familial and cultural heritage, than that his representation of Englishness is inflected by what he called 'the Critical Attitude'. Englishness is something he diagnoses, presents with an analytic depth perhaps only possible for someone with such dual positioning. In short, he takes an ironic attitude to Englishness, and it is this which makes his account of it most modern. This attitude continues through his career. Those writing here on his later books, produced once he had left England and was increasingly identifying himself as a French and American author, bring out the ways in which he was still contemplating Englishness even while even further distancing himself from it.

The focus on Englishness in this volume brings a new intelligence and sophistication to an important aspect of Ford studies. This in turn reveals the depth of Ford's contribution to what we now call cultural studies; and how here too he was a pioneer, considering mass culture and its relation to literary tradition long before George Orwell, *Scrutiny*, or Raymond Williams. From another point of view, though, as the editors explain, the work here also develops the project established in earlier volumes of the series, of reappraising Ford's engagement with modernity, history, and the city. It shows some of the ways in which Ford was responsive to, even prophetic of, major social transformations of his age. As such it also looks forward to future volumes, which are planned on his responses to cultural transformations, his contacts with other writers, and his work as an editor working to transform modern literature.

The series is published in association with the Ford Madox Ford Society. Forthcoming and projected volumes will be announced on the Society's website, together with details of whom to contact with suggestions about future volumes or contributions. The address is: www.rialto.com/fordmadoxford_society

INTRODUCTION

Dennis Brown and Jenny Plastow

The theme of Englishness permeates Ford Madox Ford's work overall, and it is most directly articulated in his trilogy *England and the English* (1905-7).[1] As many comments and references in the contributions to this book indicate, the early years of the twentieth century – the moment of transition between late Victorian and Edwardian culture – are characterised by a literary preoccupation with the contemporary state of the nation. And it was one of Ford's friends, C. F. G. Masterman, who memorably encapsulated this phenomenon in the title and subject-matter of his book *The Condition of England* (1909).[2] Long after its publication, the phrase 'condition of England' became a critical genre-term to categorise such disparate novels as H. G. Wells's *Tono-Bungay* (1909), E. M. Forster's *Howards End* (1910) or D. H. Lawrence's *Women in Love* (1920), with Ford's own *Parade's End* (1924-8) having a strong claim for inclusion in the genre. At the same time Ford's editorship, from 1908, of *The English Review*, indicated his commitment to a contemporary Englishness, even though, as Jason Harding's chapter indicates, the title also enabled him to smuggle in much excellent international writing, while devoting his editorials to largely national issues. Ford's early writing on the English theme, in fact, was situated within a large context of various and developing discourses about national identity – a turn of the century collective negotiation of ideas about nation conducted largely through narration.[3]

Ford's *The Spirit of the People* (1907) endeavours to create a kind of synthesis between the shock-thesis of *The Soul of London* (1905) and the traditionalist antithesis of *The Heart of the Country* (1906). From the perspective of the new millennium, it appears now as idealistic myth rather than even an 'impressionistic' version of contemporary social reality. It also constructs a vision which seems essentially middle-class, male-oriented and largely evocative of South East life and culture – and, for all its disclaimers, participates in the very English 'optimism' and 'self-deception' (257) which Ford notes. England, he says, is 'generally humane beyond belief' (237): it is a 'hospice on the long road to a western Atlantic' (263); it believes in muddling through (267), that 'God is good' (289), that the accused always deserves the 'benefit of the doubt' (302), that contentious 'things' should be omitted from social discourse (312) and that to 'play the game' (316) is essential to the good life. Perhaps unnecessarily, Ford seems ambivalent about his own national status – 'a nationality that is more or less my own' (244), or 'the nation that gives me shelter' (311). Yet, as some of the contributions below indicate, this may be dictated by his own attractions to Germany, France and the United States, and hence the direction of his own future loyalties rather than a genuine sense of an outsider's role (the name of Hueffer notwithstanding). However, his final tribute in this trilogy to England and Englishness is as positive as the most perfervid patriot might hope to wish, especially from an exponent of the 'arts':

> ... if these people be not the chosen people, this land will always be one that every race would choose for its birthings and its buryings until the last Aaron shall lead the last of the conquering legions across the world. (326)

As is evident in many of the chapters below, such sentiments are expressed and tested in Ford's many works, whether in fiction, expository prose or poetry. Rooted in the early twentieth-century 'moment' as they are, they connect his writing to the preoccupations of his contemporary colleagues, and also with those of one hundred years later. For, after the 'finest hour' of 1940-2 and the slow dissolution of Empire in the post-war years, and in the midst of recent devolution-politics, a revival of literary interest in England and Englishness has been going on. Nationalism, in itself, has been much discussed: English history reworked for a newer generation,[4] TV programmes and journalistic reassessments have made the topic of Englishness of the moment again.[5] A successful chain of shops opened in response to the British desire to buy nostalgia, *Past Times,* has a video collection almost identical with that available for the British expatriate community in Kampala's British Council library; back numbers of British television series, Agatha Christie's *Poirot* and *Miss Marple,* Evelyn Waugh's *Brideshead Revisited; Upstairs Downstairs, Jewel in the Crown, Tenko;* all soft-focusing perceptions of what Englishness was, at home and abroad. At the same time, writers such as Peter Ackroyd (with *The Soul of London* in mind) have focused on the metropolis, novelists have drawn on the countryside as backdrop for everything from romantic idyll to murder mysteries, and poets such as Glyn Maxwell (*The Breakage*, 1998), George Szirtes (*An English Apocalypse*, 2001) or Geoffrey Hill (*The Orchards of Syon*, 2002), have taken Englishness as a major motif. Indeed, in his preface to the *Apocalypse* collection (2001), Szirtes, a Hungarian 'refugee', describes an England very close to Ford's evocation:

> England, for me, for all of us, was the place where Nature, and by extension, the World, grew cultivated and inhabited: however despoiled it might have become, it embodied a gentle but imperial dream of enlightened subduing.[6]

It has become established that 'England' is an 'imagined' or 'imaginary'[7] community rather than a historical entity. And the issue has become complicated (as anticipated in Ford's work) by the 'special relationship' with America and the inclusion of the nation within an expanding European Union. Perhaps, then, it is no accident (as they say) that the revival of interest in Ford's writing – emblematised and stimulated by the University of London Ford Madox Ford conference of November 1996 – should have roughly corresponded with the renewed interest in Englishness. Yet when the editors first mooted a book about Ford in this context, it was difficult to imagine what the response from contributors might be – especially from American and European academics. However, the Ford Madox Ford Society's conference in Manchester in December 2004 provided an answer to this, and most of the essays in this volume were first aired there, with many stimulating ideas on Ford and Englishness and the range of Ford's work emerging as a genuinely international collocation. At the time, the contributions seemed to organise themselves into an interconnected selection on specific topics – and this contributed to the structure and opportunities for discussion of a successful event.

However, for the purposes of this book, the editors have preferred to adopt an approximately chronological organisation. This was partly because thematic structure, in cold print, tends to rather arbitrary classification which restricts the scope of argument in any one chapter and may be felt to be reductive by contributors. More positively, it is hoped the chronological arrangement will help readers identify particular periods and texts of interest within the large Ford canon. In addition, it serves to demonstrate Ford's ongoing meditations on England and the English, from earlier years, through the Great War experience and into national exile.

The book commences with Philip Davis's urbane and wide-ranging consideration of Ford as representative of an English 'remnant' – the 'invisible church', as it were, of national identity and integrity. Ralph Parfect's essay then embeds the topic in terms of Ford's placement within a literary tradition of adventure writing, immediately followed by Sara Haslam's expanded and adapted version of her Introduction to the valuable republication of *England and the English* – Ford's quite early and direct indication of the central issue, with reference to London, the country and the spirit of Englishness.[8] This is followed, in turn, by Andrzej Gasiorek's 'Ford Among the Aliens' which has stimulating things to say about *The Soul of London* in particular and Ford's importance as an early proponent of multiculturalism. Karen McDermott and Donald Mackenzie write about *The Fifth Queen* trilogy and its importance in rendering a key era of change in the formation of Englishness (the reign of Henry VIII) – discussions which are then given a different perspective by Peter Easingwood's examination of Ford in relation to literary myth and history-writing.

Jason Harding's contribution marks a brief period of Ford's apparent centrality in modern letters as editor of *The English Review*, a time when he contrives to make international modernism a factor in contemporary English sensibility. Nick Hubble on the 'English' trilogy and *The Good Soldier* indicates how the experimentalism of *The Good Soldier* is connected to the sociological insights of the books on national identity, while Christine Berberich works a similar point concerning the idea of the gentleman in the best-known modernist texts. This brings the book's chronology to the phenomenon of the Great War. Anurag Jain's essay shows how Ford the novelist and poet lent his talents to nationalist propaganda in this struggle. Jenny Plastow examines the theme of 'work' in Ford's distinctive notion of national consciousness, including soldiering-as-work, while Austin Riede reminds us that, despite the international catastrophe of the war, there are important links between *The Good Soldier* and Ford's post-war masterpiece *Parade's End*. At this point, Jörg Rademacher's demonstration of the problems involved in translating Ford's war tetralogy into German is a salutary reminder that even the 1914-18 clash of nations should be placed within a wider context of international literary culture – *Parade's End* reconsidered, as it were, in the language of Thomas Mann's *The Magic Mountain*.

In the post-war period, Ford – like several other English writers – eventually left England. After some years in Paris, for a while he taught in America, and Robert McDonough's chapter on *The Rash Act* and *Henry For Hugh* indicates Ford's ongoing negotiation of Anglo-Saxon 'doubling' in terms of English and American identities. At the same time, Christopher MacGowan's essay on *Great Trade Route* casts light on Ford's fantasy of a 'real England' (like the 'remnant') embodied in the USA and connected up by the seaways and highways of global civilisation. The book concludes with a more general essay, where Dennis Brown endeavours to cover Ford's specifically 'English' poetry from 1893 to 1921.

The contributions, then, address the main part of Ford's literary career – most particularly the years when he lived in England and was committed to its cultural health. In his later years, Ford moved to Paris, where his founding of *The Transatlantic Review* promoted international modernism rather than the native tradition. At the same time, his great war-sequence, *Parade's End*, constituted a modernist version in writing of 'The Last of England' – the title of a famous painting by his grandfather, Ford Madox Brown. However, his imagined Englishness survived his retirement abroad, and beyond specific fictions is evidenced in the memoirs and essays he wrote later. Both in America and, towards the end in Provence, Ford's thinking about national identity and international culture is both implicit and explicit in his writings, and in the very reminiscent, 'amateur' style he used to represent a life. It is, one might suggest, a very English trait to look back at one's experience of native life in meditation rather than plan some revolutionary alternative.

Considering the various chapters overall, it is noticeable to the 'postmodern' mind how much Ford's various renderings of Englishness manifest the inherent constructedness of the term, and of other related terms such as 'nation', 'identity' or indeed 'gentleman'. Not only this, but the writings are inherently self-aware of such re-presentational constructedness. Here Ford's use of irony, impress-ionism and hyperbolic anecdotage invite, as Max Saunders's bio-graphy suggests, a reconsideration of Ford's earlier reputation as fantasist, exaggerator or even liar. Ford's progressive texts indicate and enact within themselves, all the issues of relativistic viewpoint, false-memory syndrome and the inevitable subordination of 'real' world to artificial word (the 'linguistic turn') which are a common-place of contemporary cultural intelligence.

Put more sceptically, Ford's self-knowing literary rhetoric subtly suggests that there can be no Englishness-as-essence, only an imagined community conveyed by imaginative language – a view that should blunt the polysyllabic self-confidence of our current 'theorists' of nationalism. Further, his work insists on the historical relativity of specific Englishnesses. Or, as Robert Colls and Philip Dodd put it, 'Englishness has had to be constantly reproduced'.[9] Ford does this by focusing on what he finds to be critical periods in the making of Englishness – for instance, the Protestant revolution (*The Fifth Queen*), the cultural remnants of 'Dutch William's' Glorious Revolution (*Parade's End*), turn of the twentieth century modernity (*England and the English*) and the Great War and its aftermath (*When Blood is Their Argument, The Marsden Case, Parade's End, The Rash Act* etc). Englishness, Ford shows, is not a stable and unitary concept but a changeable ideal, always dependent (in the era of print-hegemony at least) on the kind of language used. In that sense, this book is a specific successor to the previous volumes in the International Ford Madox Ford Studies series – *History and Representation in Ford Madox Ford's Writings,* edited by Joseph Wiesenfarth, and *Ford Madox Ford and the City*, edited by Sara Haslam.[10]

One thing that might be hoped for, however – a preliminary definition of 'Englishness' – is deliberately absent. In this sense, the book is critically descriptive rather than analytically theoretical in the manner of, say, Krishan Kumar's interesting *The Making of English Identity*.[11] Its aim is to show how Ford, by a variety of literary means, addresses and, somewhat sceptically and impressionistically, represents a multi-dimensional Englishness-in-the-making, with its inevitable backdrop:

> ... the air is thick
> with the noise of the past, so it is hard to see
> what it is made of, what all this rhetoric
> is actually about.[12]

NOTES

1   References, here, are to Ford Madox Ford, *England and the English*, ed. Sara Haslam, Manchester: Carcanet, 2003.

2   As noted in Dennis Brown's contribution (below), Masterman also organised literary propaganda for the War Ministry – to which Ford contributed.

3   See Homi K. Bhabha (ed.), *Nation and Narration*, London and New York: Routledge, 1990.

4   There are ample references in the contributions below. Perhaps the most illuminative texts would be Ernest Gellner, *Nations and Nationalism*, Ithaca: Cornell Press, 1983, the 'European' perspective of Norman Davies's *The Isles: A History,* London: Macmillan, 1999, and Simon Schama's mainstream television series *A History of Britain* and the trilogy that followed.

5   See, for instance, Jeremy Paxman, *The English: A Portrait of a People,* London: Michael Joseph, 1998; Simon Heffer, *Nor Shall My Sword: The Reinvention of England*, London: Phoenix/Orion, 2000; and Andrew Marr, *The Day Britain Died,* London: Profile, 2000.

6   Preface to George Szirtes, *An English Apocalypse*, Highgreen: Bloodaxe, 2001, p. 11.

7   See Benedict Anderson, *Imagined Communities: Reflections on the Origins and Spread of Nationalism*, London: New Left Books, 1983, Eric Hobsbawm, *Nations and Nationalism Since 1780: Programme, Myth, Reality*, Cambridge: Cambridge University Press, 1990 and Salman Rushdie's *Imaginary Homelands: Essays and Criticism 1981-1991,* London: Granada/Penguin, 1992.

8   i.e. *The Soul of London* (1905), *The Heart of the Country* (1906), *The Spirit of the People* (1907). The composite book was published, at the time, only in America, with an 'Author's Note': *England and the English: An Interpretation*, New York: McClure, Phillips and Co., 1907.

9   *Englishness: Politics and Culture 1880-1920*, ed. Robert Colls and Philip Dodd, Beckenham: Croom Helm, 1986, p. 299.

10 *History and Representation in Ford Madox Ford's Writings*, ed. Joseph Wiesenfarth, Amsterdam-New York: Rodopi, 2004. *Ford Madox Ford and the City*, ed. Sara Haslam, Amsterdam-New York: Rodopi, 2005.

11 Krishan Kumar, *The Making of English National Identity*, Cambridge: Cambridge University Press, 2003.

12 Szirtes, 'Jerusalem', *An English Apocalypse*, p. 115.

THE SAVING REMNANT

Philip Davis

'Englishness' has often been an easy option to adopt in the past and, equally, is nowadays an easy target at which to aim. Alienation is not so difficult a position to occupy, at least in academe. But nothing in Ford, that hybrid figure of paradoxes and disguises, is straightforward. My subject here is thus ambivalence – the ambivalence of those who do still want to be at home, but do not feel truly at home in the modern society or country or world in which they find themselves. Consequently, this essay is for those interested in predicaments such as that of Ford's Tietjens. I am concerned with those figures who think, moreover, that their isolation may not be simply personal but, rather, representative of something lost and forgotten that nonetheless could still be found again – recallable, in part perhaps, even through themselves and their own life-efforts. For such figures, history is something lost – the lost potential of a race's ancient thoughts – or something which, if retained, is retained only as hidden within the individual's memory, in the latent mixed-up store of inherited things that seem nonetheless utterly and personally instinctive. Such half-buried retention means that, even so, there is the possibility of resonant things coming through to us, like half-recognised *forward* memories, demanding development, seeking re-incorporation and adaptation in the persons and times they find.

I want to begin with three quite separate images of such things – three events of resonant thought, which seem to me to belong together in relation to my subject-area. My passages come from three books at the heart of English reading traditions.

My first is taken from Genesis, the story of God's threatened destruction of Sodom and Gomorrah, lands that have broken their covenant and fallen away from their promise. Here is the protest of one man, faced by that threat of punishment:

> But Abraham stood yet before the LORD.
> And Abraham drew near, and said, Wilt thou also destroy the righteous with the wicked?

Peradventure there be fifty righteous within the city: wilt thou also destroy and not spare the place for the fifty righteous that are therein?

That be far from thee to do after this manner, to slay the righteous with the wicked: and that the righteous should be as the wicked, that be far from thee: Shall not the Judge of all the earth do right?

And the LORD said, If I find in Sodom fifty righteous within the city, then I will spare all the place for their sakes.

And Abraham answered and said, Behold now, I have taken upon me to speak unto the Lord, which am but dust and ashes:

Peradventure there shall lack five of the fifty righteous: wilt thou destroy all the city for lack of five?

And he said, If I find there forty and five, I will not destroy it.

And he spake unto him yet again, and said, Peradventure there shall be forty found there. And he said, I will not do it for forty's sake.

And he said unto him, Oh let not the Lord be angry, and I will speak: Peradventure there shall be thirty found there. And he said, I will not do it, if I find thirty there.

And he said, behold now, I have taken upon me to speak unto the Lord: Peradventure there shall be twenty found there. And he said, I will not destroy it for twenty's sake.

And he said, Oh let not the Lord be angry, and I will speak yet but this once: Peradventure ten should be found there. And he said, I will not destroy it for ten's sake. (Genesis 18.22-32)

Not fifty, not forty five, not thirty, not twenty, and perhaps even ten is negotiable. This is the ancient comic spirit of Jewish *chutzpah*, a loyally defiant and ruefully plucky cheek – 'I have taken upon me to speak unto the Lord; Oh let not the Lord be angry' – when the creature tries to put his Creator back on the tracks worthy of Him. It celebrates a world saved by ten or two or even merely one of the just, the righteous, the remnant who hold open possibility still for the race. Thus in its seriousness it belongs to the tradition of moral haggling in the great Jewish argument with God. For here, as in the story of Noah and the Ark, is the founding idea of a People's Saving Remnant, of those who are dissidents facing two ways in their dissent. For, firstly, like the patriarch Abraham, they argue against God for the sake of God and in the name of His own righteousness. Secondly, they also represent in whatever small number a hidden society within Society, against but within Sodom: a loyal oppositional memory of what that false Society truly should be and a memory of that from which in its falsity it has fallen. In the words of the prophet, Isaiah: 'Except the Lord of Hosts had left unto us a very small remnant, we should have been as Sodom, and we should have been like unto Gomorrrah' (Isaiah 1:9); 'For though thy people Israel be as the sand of the sea, yet a remnant of them shall return' (Isaiah 10.22). To reassure you of my relevance here, I shall want to refer at the end of this article to those disguised, risky and contrasting Modern Prophets and Saving Remnants, Ford's Tietjens and Lawrence's Birkin – where, for all the risks of Romantic vaingloriousness in assuming the role, prophet means not simply one who foretells the future, but one who is as a living memory or reminder of the originating spirit of a people and a purpose forgotten and distorted in the later days of the mere letter of its meaning.

But let me turn to my second image, this time not from the Authorized Version of the Bible but from Shakespeare – to be precise, from act 4 scene 1 of *Henry V* when, on the eve of battle, the young King Harry visits his own people, the common soldiers on the ground, in disguise. What follows is a dispute over the king's moral responsibility for the death of his troops:

> *Michael Williams:* But if the cause be not good, the King himself hath a heavy reckoning to make, when all those legs and arms and heads chopped off in a battle shall join together at the latter day, and cry all, 'We died at such a place' – some swearing, some crying for a surgeon, some upon their wives left poor behind them, some upon the debts they owe, some upon their children rawly left. I am afeard there are few die well that die in a battle, for how can they charitably dispose of anything, when blood is their argument?[1] Now, if these men do not die well, it will be a black matter for the King that led them to it – who to disobey were against all proportion of subjection.

> *King Harry (in disguise):* So, if a son that is by his father sent about merchandise do sinfully miscarry upon the sea, the imputation of his wickedness, by your rule, should be imposed upon his father, that sent him. Or if a servant, under his master's command transporting a sum of money, be assailed by robbers, and die in many irreconciled iniquities, you may call the business of the master the author of the servant's damnation. But this is not so. The King is not bound to answer the particular endings of his soldiers, the father of his son, nor the master of his servant, for they purpose not their deaths when they purpose their services. Besides, there is no king, be his cause never so spotless, if it come to the arbitrament of swords, can try it out with all unspotted soldiers. . . . If they die unprovided, no more is the King guilty of their damnation than he was before guilty of those impieties for the which they are now visited. Every subject's duty is the King's, but every subject's soul is his own. (*Henry V* 4.1 133-76)[2]

In the Middle Ages in certain kingdoms, rulers appointed top officials to go about incognito, or even went themselves disguised as the poor and the ordinary, to find out what was going on in the lower reaches of their administrations. Within that secret tradition, superman going incarnate as everyman, Harry revisits his kingdom, takes his idea of it in him down into its reality, partly to check that idea, partly again to inform and reinvigorate that reality.

Not so much Henry V, but Harry it is then who finds in himself, disguised as one of the king's subjects, the translation of all that he stands for as king. This is not just Harry making veiled excuses. Nor is it that the feudal order here is simply, artificially rigid: rather, it maps onto an equivalent mental order which, within the ordinary subject he imitates, allows for an extraordinarily mobile capacity for coherent yet finely complex distinctions within interlocking orders of being – the roles of the People, the King, the Lord above, and what responsibility is owed and due at each level. Thus distinguished are particular endings within general causes; political necessities and yet individual destinies; the language of duty and the language of soul – yet all held together so that even disagreements are not finally between different and incompatible world-views but within different parts of the same world-view, the same *country*, as viewed from different aspects. The subject's soul is at once both within the king's command and wholly above and beyond it.

Out of such disguised visits as this, Harry can re-create, as if for the first time again, England itself as the age's version of a collective, of a new blood-brotherhood, *transcendent* of the class order (father/son, master/servant) which comprises it – because in physical battle, as in the death it may lead to, all are also mortally equal:

> We few, we happy few, we band of brothers.
> For he today that sheds his blood with me
> Shall be my brother; be he ne'er so vile
> This day shall gentle his condition.   (*Henry V* 4.3 60-63)

Out of such visits, I repeat, Harry can make English history and tradition not a thing of the past but something willed into being in the very present, as an action about to make a memory and, indeed, a remembered future for itself:

> He that shall see this day and live t'old age
> Will yearly on the vigil feast his neighbours
> And say, 'Tomorrow is Saint Crispian.'
> Then will he strip his sleeve and show his scars
> And say, 'These wounds I had on Crispin's day.'
> Old men forget; yet all shall be forgot,

> But he'll remember, with advantages,
> What feats he did that day . . .
> And gentlemen in England now abed
> Shall think themselves accursed they were not here,
> And hold their manhoods cheap whiles any speaks
> That fought with us upon Saint Crispin's day.   (*Henry V* 4.3 44-67)

Remembering with advantages: that isn't just about the easy targets of Churchillian rhetoric, or mythological distortion, or sentimental exaggeration. It is about the added emotion necessary to make something happen before it can; thereafter, the emotion is earned as a reward for what later will seem achievedly great which at the time was strugglingly uncertain and frighteningly mundane. It seems very unlikely that we here today could celebrate whatever went into the spirit of Agincourt; but that is what literature does: it makes ostensibly alien history into memory-potential again, and memory into re-imagination. Literature is itself, I am saying, the equivalent of the Saving Remnant: the root-language which keeps the authentic memory alive from the moment of its happening, and not the distorted thing it later becomes in a more degenerated language. Again, I list in passing some relevancies to Ford here: Tietjens, the believer in an old English feudal order, all the more aware, even so, of living in an increasingly modern, pluralist world; the army in the First World War as a last, renewed latter-day version of feudal family order, with painful responsibilities falling upon a reluctant yet necessary commander; Tietjens, the intellectual superman whose intellect so often serves to keep him detached, finally forced down even so into the realities amidst which there is no space for overview (if a man could stand up!); no overview, moreover, for a man whose mentality is now shot, disturbed and tested as if merely ordinary; the superbrain in danger of forgetting by shell-shock all it has stored.

The Bible, Shakespeare, and finally another scene of the English abroad amidst the violence of France, as taken from Charles Dickens. Here from *A Tale of Two Cities* (1859)[3] is the self-confessed wastrel Sidney Carton about to change places in prison with his double, Charles Darnay, the man loved by Lucie Manette in preference to himself, now awaiting execution. Earlier, Carton had stood before a mirror, looking at the change he has made to himself, in comparison with Darnay, a man who 'shows you what you have fallen away from', and what you might have been', a man with whom he wishes then to 'change places' and gain Lucie's love (Book 2 Chapter 4). But when

Carton confesses this love to Lucie, he says he cannot change, can 'never be better than I am' without her and yet she cannot love him. Now in Darnay's jail, changing places means something different. The visitor Carton makes the prisoner Darnay write for him, whilst he waits for the drug concealed in a vial inside his tunic to kick in, allowing Darnay to be taken away in Carton's place and Carton to be left behind in his:

> Pressing his hand to his bewildered head, Darnay sat down at the table. Carton, with his right hand in his breast, stood close beside him.
> 'Write exactly as I speak.'
> 'To whom do I address it?'
> 'To no one,' Carton still had his hand in his breast.
> 'Do I date it?'
> 'No.' . . .
> '"If you remember,"' said Carton, dictating, '"the words that passed between us, long ago, you will readily comprehend this when you see it. You do remember them, I know. It is not in your nature to forget them."'
> He was drawing his hand from his breast; the prisoner chancing to look up in his hurried wonder as he wrote, the hand stopped, closing upon something.
> 'Have you written "forget them"?' Carton asked.
> 'I have. Is that a weapon in your hand?'
> 'You shall know directly. Write on; there are but a few words more.' He dictated again. '"I am thankful that the time has come, when I can prove them. That I do so is no subject for regret or grief."' As he said these words with his eyes fixed on the writer, his hand slowly and softly moved down close to the writer's face.
> The pen dropped from Darney's fingers on the table, and he looked about him vacantly.
> 'What vapour is that?' he asked. (Book 3 Chapter 13)

But Carton won't let him stop, he carries on dictating what is actually to Lucie: 'If it had been otherwise, I never should have used the longer opportunity . . . If it had been otherwise, I should but have had so much the more to answer for. . . . If it had been otherwise . . .' – but then the pen trails off from that incomplete alternative if-life and falls from Darney, unconscious.

My third motif is that of sacrificial scapegoat, but not simply that. Otherwise, why, so very oddly, did Carton need his last letter to Lucie to be in Darnay's hand, rather than his own? It isn't just Romantic heroism. There has always been a raw element of competition in Carton's relation to Darnay and here it is as though it is that element which must be transmuted and not merely set aside. Carton needs Darnay's future life with Lucie – achieved only through Carton's death – to be the life that Carton wanted and never had, to be a second life of Carton's own. Yet the way in which he has become Darnay here, his better self, is not merely selfish either. Selfish? selfless? self-despair? self-indulgence? None of these separately: the love for Lucie that Carton shares with Darnay is what makes the sacrifice truly possible as neither simple vicariousness nor self-sacrifice, alone.

Moreover, the sacrifice had to be done abroad, in disguise and anonymity, and away from home, in order to restore the possibility of home elsewhere. It may look as though the motif of the scapegoat here is very different from that of the Saving Remnant I discussed first of all. Carton is, he knows, just one individual fallen man, his life a life wasted that can afford to be cast away in a good cause since already cast away in a bad; whereas the nation's Saving Remnant are the righteous, the nucleus of the future race returning out of exile, who save and are saved at once. Yet this is the way it must happen – shifting places, back-to-front – if the damned are to do in their own way what the saved do more straightforwardly: the damned cannot incorporate the saving goodness in themselves but must take themselves away from the salvation they leave behind, even by incorporating all that is bad in their own destruction. That is the only way in which the individual in Carton can stand for more than himself, can recreate the people, and imagine a future son of Darnay and Lucie bearing and redeeming his name. At the scaffold Carton's unspoken thoughts are no longer that he can 'never be better than he is' without Lucie, but that 'it is a far, far better thing that I do than I have ever done' (Book 3 Chapter 15). That is to say, remarkably, he converts a passive death-by-execution into a last-second action of his own.

But the disguise is not just Carton disguised as Darnay. It is final loving goodness won out of the appearance of suicidal evil, its opposite; it is something more than individual secretly disguised within, and silently bequeathed by, the sacrifice of the individual himself. In Ford's *The Rash Act* there is a secret metaphysical relief at once wonderful and terrible when at the last, beyond despair, Henry Martin finds that he has nothing more personally to lose, nothing more to barter with – momentarily knowing, more than was ever possible before, the gain of a creature's free life even through its last surrender and final loss. It is in this very area that Tietjens is thinking when in *No More Parades* he nonetheless finally rules out suicide and accepts continuance precisely because 'the problem will remain the same whether I am here or not. For it's insoluble. It's the whole problem of the relation of the sexes'.[4] The motif of the sacrifice, precisely by not being allowed, is part of the dynamic of such perseverance, on the rebound.

At any rate, in *A Tale of Two Cities* the sacrifice made is emphatically English and Protestant. For it is not only set against the revolutionary rationalism of France, it is also set against the whole Catholic tradition of centralization that Matthew Arnold envied for maintaining the nation's culture, even as Dickens was writing. The English way, here, is defined as more individual, more off-centre, more local or provincial or unpredictable and unexpected in its location – the meaning not held explicitly in central offices of government or religion but in hidden pockets, in dispersal, wherever the Word, democratically translated, spreads and establishes itself. And in that looser, shifting and more contingently flexible context for the People, the three motifs I have here given – the Saving Remnant, the disguised leader and the hidden gain of sacrifice – are all secret versions of each other, disguises to rescue a future for the present by means of a suddenly transformed past.

This historical difference between the greater variability of English Protestantism and the greater coherence of French rational Catholicism explains why, within the tradition of Protestant English history, even Matthew Arnold had to be content with something other than centralization. Instead, within each class in England, says Arnold in *Culture and Anarchy* (1869), there are 'a certain number of *aliens*, if we may so call them, – persons who are mainly led, not by their class spirit, but by a general *humane* spirit'.[5] Yet these aliens, which Coleridge in an earlier generation had called the clerisy, were not alienated but assimilated: without being *of* them, they worked *in* the structures they sought to change. At the very onset of the processes of modern institutionalisation, the Victorian prophets worked, paradoxically, within the institution to get beyond institutionalisation, within the form of books to get to that real life outside them which was the books' own subject-matter, within the middle class to get beyond the confines of class. They were agents, a small and scattered counter-society within society. In a lecture entitled 'Numbers' on his 1884 tour of America, Arnold himself spoke of these cultural agents as the remnant, the chosen few, as opposed to the majority, the sheer weight of numbers whom they sought to save from within. We may be knee-jerk tempted to call this elitism or paternalism; but to Arnold, it was what he called the social idea, the idea of equality, the agent bringing to everyone out of the whole of cultural time what the society at the present time had forgotten or was denying them, in the blind processes of mass industrial democracy. This, at any rate, was a secular version of the parish priest. Back in 1821 the Revd Thomas Chalmers, for example, had argued in his *Christian and Civic Economy of Large Towns* that the social situation in the newly emergent large cities could only be personalized by turning the cities back into smaller local rural districts, each with its own minister, on the Scottish Presbyterian model of the country parish. The minister was to occupy, with what Chalmers called the kindly influence of the mere presence of a human being, the otherwise huge and unfilled space interposed between the classes of high and the low. For Tietjens, however, that influence is retained only in the memory held in books, the tradition embodied in George Herbert, in Samuel Johnson.

But now think of the world that Tietjens inherited. By 1905, writing in *The Soul of London* in *England and the English*, Ford saw the great mass city as the site of Modernity – huge, impersonal, unhomely, ungraspable yet absorbingly assimilative; leaving individuals dizzyingly de-individualized and de-centralized in their unconfident sense of their smallness in the scale of things, in the loss of a sense of roots and local feelings, in the mere relativism of their realizing so many others to be of as little import as themselves. Yet by the time Ford writes *The Spirit of the People*, there is another variation on this awesome power of assimilation, in time as well as space. England is also Shakespeare's island set separately and safely within encircling seas; it has become, says Ford, a place of geographically natural Sanctuary for all the world, wherein as from a melting-pot there emerges a people so contingently mixed and experimentally compounded of Romans, Britons, Anglo-Saxons, Danes, Normans, Scotch, Huguenots, Irish, Jews that England becomes the humane testing-ground of pragmatic liberal tolerance, where people may be able to live together, forming new combinations, in large masses.

I simply want to say that it is in this roomy experimental *territory* lodged between assimilation as destructive and assimilation as hospitable that Tietjens is called into being as the great, hidden internal test-case for the nation. *Parade's End* is itself the English melting-pot, or the testing-ground staked out between the simple initial opposites of lonely Tietjens as irrelevant alien relic or missionary Tietjens as Saving Remnant. The man representative of the sixteenth or the seventeenth or the eighteenth century is thus put into the twentieth, like an embodied microcosmic test of history, without a clear sense of whether the experiment is to bring the past forward again or leave it finally behind. Yet actually, the art has always to do with something struggling *in between* those initiating but over-simplified dialectics, which Tietjens calls 'illuminative exaggerations' (*PE* 454). The work that results from between those large alternatives is the literary-historical equivalent of a chemical or biological mix. For Ford, only art, only literature, has a language – the quintessentially English language evolving over time – thus subtle enough to investigate the fine shades, the shifting levels, the complex combinations that go on in this test of history. Only literature can test the borderlines between true and false versions of the thing. And, equally in the country and the society, only literature can find a discourse that goes across the set categories that otherwise leave the study of 'politics' and 'history' too remotely distinct from the surprise of sudden emotional experience and imaginative involvement – the surprise of individuals suddenly finding themselves in areas they had not known they could respond to as a potential part of them still.

Here, for example, is what is thrown up from the crucible of such a test – a vision from a moment within the battle of the Somme described in Ford's *No Enemy* (in many ways a first draft of parts of *Parade's End*), amidst the scarred mud of the battlefield:

> It came like one of those visions that one's eyes, when tired, will see just before one falls asleep. There was a rhomboid of deeper, brighter green, of a green that was really alive, beyond the grey-green of the field they were in [. . . .] It hardened and brightened, took shape as a recumbent oval, like eighteenth century vignettes [. . . .] And it didn't connote any locality . . . It was just country – but perfectly definite [. . . .]
>
> Possibly that little vision of English country, coming then, was really a prayer. (*NE 35, 37*)

This is, I take it, what Ford gestures towards in *The Heart of the Country*, in *England and the English*: that such green refuges, even when more thoroughly literal and definite, are also mentally metaphors of a lost home in the world, of a secret prayer for a natural place, that is actually nonetheless, says Ford, a hope grown 'intangible' (*HC 113*). 'Intangible' does not mean that these natural places are not real to touch or sight, but that they also stand for more than themselves.

And that is why Englishness itself may not be simply dismissible as a fiction or a myth, but is rather a metaphor that holds on to some hidden truth that abides within all our shifting contexts. But what do I mean by that, or by suggesting that there is something to be gained in thinking of Englishness as metaphor?

I turn here to one of the great figures behind *Parade's End*, Edmund Burke – where in his *Reflections on the Revolution in France*, he speaks against the *a priori* rationally planned French creation of a new enlightenment society and in favour of more mysteriously gradual processes of unplanned assimilation, of quasi-biological modification over time. In the economy of the English evolutionary model, it is not a problem to find the same basic thing cropping up at different levels and in different formations, translated first into this shape and then modified into that. For thus, says Burke, 'To be attached to the subdivision, to love the little platoon we belong to in society is the first principle (the germ as it were) of public affections'.[6] That is to say, that little platoon may first be the private-seeming family, may extend into the village or the communal purpose of a club or institution, before it becomes the region or the country; yet in all of its appearances, even in the most narrow, it is a potential version of the social principle itself, of the sense of belonging to something more than oneself. Sometimes the model of the world you belong to looks as though it could be serially progressive and expansive – from the love of family, to a larger love of tribe or country, to the still larger love of mankind. But at other times, when that progress has become merely notional, the lower or earlier or smaller version has to re-emerge like a Saving Remnant to stand against the larger and higher in which it is lodged, in order to reclaim the founding germ. Crucially then, we don't always know the size of world we belong to, of the home-land that is the extent of our proper or effective concern.

Then, whatever the scale in which they are found, the question is whether Tietjens and Birkin are, in their different ways, those memory-germs, those hidden prophets, those disguised individuals of the remnant – even in the midst of the personal flaws and lonely inadequacies that may make them also seem such cranks and egoists, false imitators of Christ instead. It is as it is for Daniel Deronda faced by the spectacle of Mordecai in George Eliot's novel of an English world in emotional and spiritual decline: 'Reduce the grandest type of man hitherto known to an abstract statement of his qualities and efforts, and he appears in dangerous company: say that, like Copernicus and Galileo, he was immovably convinced in the face of hissing incredulity but so is the contriver of perpetual motion'.[7] I am interested in the shapes of thought thrown up in such borderline individuals, the significant variations of thoughts which *must* have come from somewhere else because they are virtually incomprehensible to contemporaries. When Tietjens speaks as follows to Levin, Levin cannot make it out:

> Tietjens said:
> 'It's an encouraging spectacle, really. . . . There are enormous bodies of men . . . Seven to ten million. . . All moving towards places towards which they desperately don't want to go. Desperately! Every one of them is desperately afraid. But they go on. An immense blind will forces them in the effort to consummate the one decent action that humanity has to its credit in the whole of recorded history; the one we are engaged in. (*PE* 453-4)

The War is itself bungled, and all the rest that men do outside it is commonly petty and often discreditable. But still when Levin exclaims, '*What* a pessimist you are!', Tietjens replies, 'Can't you see that that is optimism?' It is not to do with success or failure: there are two sides and, in abstract, you could have been born on either side: 'If we lose, they win . . . then they provide the success instead of ourselves. But the thing is to be able to stick to the integrity of your character' (*PE* 454). If a man could stand up, then mentally at least he could see both sides: 'Let us, for God's sake, talk of the gallant enemy. We have got to plunder the French or millions of our people must starve; they have got to resist us successfully or be wiped out' (*PE* 174). The thing is that having seen both sides and the arbitrariness between them, Tietjens still returns to his own side, even *after* having given up on simply the winning or the losing. It is like that moment which Matthew Arnold thought one of the greatest touchstones in human thinking, when near the end of his *Thoughts on French Affairs*, Burke imagines some future date in which his position against the Revolution which seems to him 'resolute and firm and right' may turn out after all to have been on the other side of the borderline, 'perverse and obstinate and wrong'. That says Arnold is Burke's great disinterested 'return upon himself'[8] – even though, and especially since, he must remain true nonetheless to the position he still believes in, whatever it may turn out to have been later.

So it is with Tietjens in *Parade's End* or with Private Bourne in that great First World War novel by another of the writers discovered by Ford's *English Review*, Frederic Manning in *Her Privates We*. For in both, an intellectual with an overview refuses to be a brain in this war but returns to enlist below his status, disguised and assimilated as a body, a part, within it all instead; one amongst the immense crowd of men, with separate thoughts, *in* them yet not fully *of* them, in some extreme crisis-version of democracy. It is a human *shape*, I want to say, instinctively descended from the three motifs with which I opened: the saving remnant, the disguised leader, the hidden sacrifice, all versions of the germinal society-within-society which might redeem the memory of Englishness – and all this, without the position being tied in advance to abstract definitions of being either left or right wing.

I want to end with two shapes of experience that should make you feel why there must always be equivalents of both old testaments and new lands.

This time they are taken from within Lawrence's *Women in Love,* in the configuration of which the sort of Christianity that Tietjens represents has gone dead, has gone into the bullying selflessness of father Crich. The order in which the following two movements take place is important. The first is this:

> 'Humanity itself is dry rotten really. There are myriads of human beings hanging on the bush – and they look very nice and rosy, your healthy young men and women. But they are apples of Sodom, as a matter of fact, Dead Sea Fruit, gall-apples. . . .
> I abhor humanity, I wish it was swept away. It could go, and there would be no *absolute* loss, if every human being perished tomorrow. The reality would be untouched. Nay, it would be better. The real tree of life would then be rid of the most ghastly, heavy crop of Dead Sea Fruit . . .'
> 'So, you'd like everybody in the world destroyed?' said Ursula.
> 'I should indeed. . . . It is the most beautiful and freeing thought.'
> [But] Ursula saw that, all the while, in spite of himself, he would have to be trying to save the world. She hated the Salvator Mundi touch.'[9]

This vision of the destruction of what has become all too human and deadly is not simply, in the midst of the First World War, a mad wish for something even worse than that conflagration. Nor is it the twentieth-century fascism that Lawrence is sometimes unjustly taken to support. Rather, it is a memory of purgation, of the lost necessity of *somehow* getting to start afresh. For deep within it lies the radical idea that life shouldn't just go on – and on and on. Such mass-destruction or mass-suicide is only available to Birkin as a vision of a lost tradition too dramatic for the modern world: it is left in him as no more and no less than a mental metaphor. And with it, Birkin *is* indeed tempted to forego the back-breaking responsibility of trying to salvage something. But a second movement shows him unable to leave the world and abandon what he calls 'the old, old effort at serious living', having instead to recommit himself to it again – through marriage:

> 'We won't care about *anything*,' she said.
> He sat still and laughed.
> 'And we'll be married, and have done with them,' she added.
> Again he laughed.
> 'It's one way of getting rid of everything,' she said, 'to get married.'
> 'And one way of accepting the whole world,' he added. (Chapter 26)

While to Ursula marriage is precisely the way of getting out of the world, of being just two alone together, Birkin himself now replies that actually marriage is a way of re-joining the world via the smallest platoon, redeeming the idea of marriage itself or what Tietjens called 'the whole problem of the relation of the sexes'. Even if there is no one else to witness the redemption, the thought is that getting it right, re-creating the tradition with fresh spirit, may be a way of saving the world:

> 'See what a flower I found you,' she said. . . .
> 'Pretty!' he said, looking at her with a smile, taking the flower.
> Everything had become simple again, the complexity gone into nowhere.
> (Chapter 23)

In Tietjens, this becomes that austere ardour involved in finding a way for two people – himself and Miss Wannop – really to *talk* again, intimately and truly.

In short then, when I read *Daniel Deronda*, *Parade's End* and *Women in Love*, or when latterly I read John Berger's *A Fortunate Man* or Doris Lessing's *The Making of the Representative for Planet 8*, I think it may be a most grievous category-error to dismiss the individual efforts in such places as merely the mistakenly heroism of a belated Romanticism. The saving of meaning could go on again within any part of the world we *can* incarnately influence – even within the English language, even inside English studies.

NOTES

1   This is of course the source for the title of Ford's first book of wartime propaganda: *When Blood is Their Argument*, London: Hodder and Stoughton, 1915.
2   Shakespeare, *Henry V*, New Cambridge Shakespeare, ed. A. Gurr, Cambridge: Cambridge University Press, 1992 – henceforth *Henry V*.
3   Parenthetic references to *A Tale of Two Cities* are to the Everyman Dickens edition, ed. Norman Page, London: Dent, 1994.
4   Ford, *No More Parades*, in *Parade's End*, Harmondsworth: Penguin, 1982 – henceforth *PE*; p. 491.
5   Arnold, *Culture and Anarchy and Other Writings*, ed. Stefan Collini, Cambridge: Cambridge University Press, 1993, p. 35.
6   Edmund Burke, *Reflections on the Revolution in France*, 1790, ed. Conor Cruise O'Brien, Harmondsworth: Penguin, 1970, p. 135.
7   George Eliot, *Daniel Deronda*, ed. Barbara Hardy, Harmondsworth: Penguin, 1986, Chapter 41.
8   See Arnold's 'The Function of Criticism at the Present Time' (1864) which appeared in his *Essays in Criticism* 1865.
9   D. H. Lawrence, *Women in Love*, Harmondsworth: Penguin, 1960, Chapter 11.

ROMANCES OF NATIONHOOD:
FORD AND THE ADVENTURE STORY TRADITION

Ralph Parfect

In 1924, thinking back to the origins of his novel *Romance*, Ford declared: 'Why the writer should ever have thought of writing of pirates, heaven knows'.[1] In spite of this disclaimer, Ford does in his memoirs provide several clues, some perhaps misleading, as to not only why but also how he came to write a work of adventure fiction, drafting the prototype novel 'Seraphina' in 1898, and, over the next five years, in collaboration with Conrad, revising and adding to the text and changing its title to *Romance*. Among the contradictory reasons Ford gives for 'writing of pirates' are: firstly, that Edward Garnett made the suggestion, pointing Ford towards the historical records of Aaron Smith, the last person to be tried for piracy at the Old Bailey in 1824;[2] secondly, that Ford himself had come across an account of Smith's grim adventures while researching for his book on Ford Madox Brown – of spotting the article in Dickens's periodical *All The Year Round*, Ford wrote that 'certain subjects will grip you with a force almost supernatural' (*JC* 13); and, finally, that '*Treasure Island* was terribly to the fore then' – perhaps an admission that Ford wished to conform with popular taste (*RY* 195). In this essay, I would like to consider a further probable reason for Ford's turn to the adventure tradition, namely that it provided him with a fresh and productive means of exploring one of his key interests: Englishness. As the concordance for *Romance* reveals, the word 'English' occurs in the novel over a hundred times, and the word 'Englishman' twenty times.[3] I will put this linked interest of Ford's in Englishness and adventure into literary and biographical context, and consider how Englishness is constructed and interrogated through the figures of, firstly, *Romance*'s John Kemp, a reconstructed English adventure hero, and secondly of Katharine Howard in *The Fifth Queen* trilogy, in whom traces of the adventure tradition are again reconfigured, particularly in terms of gender.

The adventure tradition in Western literature can be traced back over many centuries – in English writing to Defoe's *Robinson Crusoe*

(1719) and beyond, and in classical literature to the narratives of Odysseus, Jason and the Argonauts, and other such voyaging heroes. Late Victorian commentators such as Andrew Lang made precisely these kinds of connections, thereby establishing a pedigree for an often disparaged genre.[4] But I am taking the term more narrowly here to denote a broad strand of nineteenth-century fiction in English, often by Scottish writers, its best-known early-century progenitor being Sir Walter Scott, and its mid-century followers including Captain Marryat and R. M. Ballantyne. A late-century flowering of the adventure tradition was stimulated in part by Stevenson's *Treasure Island* (1881), and further nurtured by writers such as H. Rider Haggard, Rudyard Kipling, G. A. Henty and Sir Arthur Conan Doyle, who together contributed to the 'romance revival' of the 1880s and 1890s.

Among the notable spokesmen for this revival was W. E. Henley, an influential figure early in Ford's career, albeit one to whom Ford remained ambivalent. In *Thus To Revisit* (1921) Ford writes of Henley helping to initiate a change of tone in literature at the fin-de-siècle: 'Henley and his school', Ford remarks, formed 'a vocal and combative body', one which 'admired physical force, lawlessness, piracy, the speed of motor-cars, and the deftness of linotype machines', and which 'studied words from the Authorised Version and Sir Thomas Browne'.[5] This latter feature of the romance revival, its attraction to archaism and overt stylisation, was one that alienated the proto-modernist Ford, who complained elsewhere of 'the semi-biblical over-emphasis of Stevensonian word-jugglery' that the school supposedly espoused (a deft caricature of Stevenson's prose, though one that hardly does justice to its actual heterogeneity, economy of style, and playfulness).[6] Ford's friend Stephen Crane, in reaction to reading one particular sentence by Stevenson, made a similar claim, one that Ford endorsed, namely that Stevenson 'put back the clock of English fiction fifty years'.[7] Stylistically Ford thus saw himself as far beyond more than one key player in the romance revival, and on a personal level he found Henley's school, as he writes in *Ancient Lights*, 'strange and rough' and 'unreasonably boisterous and too loudly cocksure' – hence too extreme an antidote for 'the hot-house atmosphere of Pre-Raphaelitism' that Ford wished to escape (*AL* 196). Yet at the same time Ford did share with the revivalists a taste, which followed him from childhood, for adventure and action narrative. In *Ancient Lights* he tells us how, as a child, in reaction to 'being trained for the profession of a genius' by his Pre-Raphaelite forbears, 'I used to lock myself in the coal-cellar in order to read *Dick Harkaway* and *Sweeney Todd the Demon Barber* and other penny dreadfuls' (*AL* 228-9). He also produces a quasi-Stevensonian account of prepubescent fantasy and daring:

> Thank God, having been an adventurous youth whose sole idea of true joy was to emulate the doings of a hero of a work called *Peck's Bad Boy and His Pa*, or at least to the lesser glories of *Dick Harkaway*, who had a repeating rifle and a tame black jaguar and who bathed in gore almost nightly – thank God, I say, that we succeeded in leading our unsuspecting cousins into dangerous situations from which they only emerged by breaking limbs […]' (*AL* 103).

Before we examine romance and adventure in Ford's writing, some distinction needs to be made between these two overlapping terms. Common features of romance fiction include an idealised or at least feudal or semi-feudal setting, a quest narrative, and a courtly love motif derived from the original romances of medieval France. Adventure fiction often shares the first two of these features, and can also incorporate subplots resembling courtly love narratives, but its key characteristic, not always present in romance, is a strong focus on action and danger: what Stevenson described as 'the problems of the body and the practical intelligence'.[8] Ford's fairy stories of the 1890s, *The Feather*, *The Brown Owl*, and *The Queen Who Flew*, have been classified as romances and analysed as such by Timothy Weiss, since all involve feudal settings, and quest narrative and courtly love are present in some if not all.[9] Adventure also infuses these stories – *The Queen Who Flew*, for example, sees its protagonist through a series of hair's-breadth escapes. Yet action and danger are sufficiently subordinated to the romantic plots for these tales not to qualify as adventure per se. Ford and Conrad's novel *Romance*, on the other hand, in which the hero John Kemp is assaulted, kidnapped, involved in piratical acts and repeatedly called on to use violence while protecting his noble and beautiful cousin Seraphina, whom he eventually marries, can (despite its title) clearly be categorised as adventure fiction.

There is a notable Anglocentrism within Ford's romance and adventure fiction. *The Queen Who Flew*, in spite of its idealised semi-feudal setting, alludes wryly to the English past and present by taking as its premise the heroine's Queen Elizabeth-like resistance to marriage, and by describing her kingdom as 'the most prosperous and

contented nation in the world', a possibly ironic view of Ford's
England at the time of writing.[10] Many recent critics have examined
late Victorian and early twentieth century adventure fiction for its
nationalist ideologies. Andrea White, for example, has argued that, via
the encounter with otherness that most adventure narratives involve,
national identity is able to define itself – often, in English adventure
fiction of the period, in supremacist and imperialist ways.[11] White
argues, like many other critics, that Conrad both taps into and
questions this supremacism. Yet her argument ignores Conrad's
collaboration with Ford, *Romance*, in favour of the more canonical
Heart of Darkness and *Lord Jim*, contributing to a relative neglect of
Romance by Conrad and Ford scholars alike. I would like to suggest
that *Romance* deserves greater attention for its staging of imperial
ideology than it has so far received.

How, then, do the romance and adventure elements of *Romance*
represent and question notions of Englishness? Unusually for Ford's
fiction, this occurs to a large extent through action. Action is of course
not the only means, nor is it the first that strikes us. Without the first-
person narrator's attention to self-description and self-analysis, for
example, we would not learn, as we do in the opening chapter, that
John Kemp is by background a quite typical English adventure hero,
the product of a quiet, disciplined, rural and domestic upbringing,
much like Defoe's Robinson Crusoe, Marryat's Peter Simple, or
Stevenson's Jim Hawkins. Self-narration also reveals John Kemp's
nobility (he is the grandson of an Earl), this being a further trait
common to many English adventure heroes, such as Leo Vincey in H.
Rider Haggard's novel *She* (1887). First-person narrative generally is
of course crucial to Ford and Conrad's practice in *Romance* of
impressionism – the Modernist focus on a focalising self's subjective
perception of the outside world. Yet although action is narrated impressionistically in *Romance*, it contributes significantly to the construction of an idealised, heroic Englishness. Through numerous
scenes of kidnapping, piratical invasion and physical struggle, John
Kemp is forced to demonstrate qualities that include valour, self-
reliance, and physical dexterity. The plot hinges on the fact that he
also believes in the fair fight, even when this puts him in terrible
personal danger. His very involvement in Caribbean politics and piracy, after two quiet years of planting in Jamaica, is hastened when he
strikes a British official, who, Kemp feels, has unfairly assaulted a
political enemy. Later he twice refrains from killing his own enemies

when they are at his mercy: firstly the corrupt Irish judge O'Brien, and subsequently the psychopathic Spanish pirate Manuel-del-Popolo. Kemp believes it unfair and dishonourable to kill in cold blood; of his struggle with O'Brien, he declares: 'I shall force him to come out and fight fair – and kill him as an English gentleman may'.[12] When Kemp himself is held captive, as occurs several times in the novel, further adventure hero qualities are displayed: an unflinching defiance of and even contempt for his pirate captors, such as is also seen in novels like Ballantyne's *The Coral Island* (1857) and Stevenson's *Treasure Island*; and, in the powerful and disturbing episode of prolonged entrapment in a cave without food or water, great physical endurance, stoicism, and self-control.

Although none of these qualities is inherently 'English', all are nevertheless framed in the novel within a discourse of Englishness, the chief mouthpiece for which is Kemp's Spanish relative Carlos Riego. Carlos, whom at the start of the novel Kemp helped flee England, is Anglophile to a perhaps intentionally comical extent. Not only does he repeatedly link Kemp's courage and nobility to his nationality; more generally he believes, as he phrases it when persuading Kemp to marry and protect his cousin Seraphina, that 'English things last forever – English peace, English power, English fidelity. It is a country of much serenity, of order, of stable affection' (*Romance* 150). As Kemp comments, '[Carlos] had on him the glamour of things English' (*Romance* 150).

The evidence so far points towards *Romance* being limitingly monologic, one-sidedly inscribing an idealised view of Englishness. However, the novel is more complex than this. Adventure fiction, with its highlighting of difference and otherness, allows Ford and Conrad to construct Englishness dialogically and dynamically. In stark contrast to Carlos with his fetishisation of Kemp's national character, Carlos's maimed companion Tomas Castro has a wholehearted contempt for the English; they are 'foolish and wrong-headed' (*Romance* 48). The supposed impartiality of the English legal system, by which Kemp himself is almost hanged for piracy at the end of the novel, is for Castro coldly ignoble and 'savage' (*Romance* 126). Above all, Kemp's restraint in refusing to kill O'Brien and Manuel-del-Popolo in cold blood, is not merciful but instead proud and selfish in that it releases them to do further evil: 'Are all you English like princes that you should never think of anybody but yourselves?' Castro asks, before indeed being killed horribly through the freed Manuel's devices

(*Romance* 306). Kemp sees Castro's ruthlessness as 'benighted and primitive' (*Romance* 306); yet Kemp too had wondered after earlier letting O'Brien go free: 'Had I acted like an Englishman and a gentleman, or only like a fool satisfying his sentiment at other people's expense?' (*Romance* 258). O'Brien himself further adds to the dialogism of the novel's representation of Englishness. An embittered Irish rebel, turned colonial renegade, he is virulently, ideologically anti-English. 'These English', he tells Kemp, 'I've seen them spit the child on the mother's breast. I've seen them set fire to the thatch of the widow and childless' (*Romance* 470). Kemp is seemingly uninterested in the iniquities of English colonialism in Ireland – his pragmatic approach is to stop at the thought: 'I was an Englishman. He hated me' (*Romance* 202). Yet through O'Brien's presence in the novel Ford and Conrad's staging of the traditional English adventure hero, far from being straightforwardly romantic, is complicated and politicised.

What further complicates the romanticisation of Englishness in the novel is the self-consciousness to which the very concept of romance is subjected. Not only does Kemp repeatedly muse on what romance is; he also perceives that Carlos's anglophile exoticisation of Englishness is exposed as subjective via his own idealisation of Carlos's Spanishness. The two positions comically mirror and thereby destabilize one another, as romanticisation and hero-worship emerge as wholly relative, and both fictions begin to unravel. In line with this self-deconstructing tendency within the novel's discourses of nationhood, the overriding quality that it in fact pins to its English hero is the anti-romantic quality of disillusionment. Although the novel has a happy ending, with Kemp and Seraphina safely married, and Kemp benignly musing on romance, it is energised by a constant tension between his insistence that his adventures have constituted romance, and his intense narration of the subjective experience of suffering, disgust and disappointment. Ford's agenda (shared with Conrad) to question romance and adventure for the benefit of English letters, is made explicit in his memoir *Thus to Revisit*. Stephen Crane, Ford tells us, had complained that the English had treated literature as 'one immense, petty, Parlour Game [. . . .] Even our adventure stories, colonial fictions, and tales of the boundless prairie were conducted in that spirit' (*TR* 119). Ford concurs that 'Anglo-Saxondom' is regrettably divided between those who idealise gentility and those who idealise heroism, whether it be in war, or physical endeavour, or the struggle against poverty. 'The probability is', Ford proposes, 'that Heaven on Earth is to be found only in the kind hearts of kindly men who have known disillusionment' (*Romance* 120). John Kemp ultimately emerges as this very figure – the adventure narrative has allowed his heroic English virtues to be tested and vindicated, yet in his narrative a sense of disillusionment is never far away.

The disillusioned English adventure hero is arguably a type that also makes an appearance in Ford's *The Fifth Queen* trilogy, albeit with the full disillusionment coming only in the final pages. That hero, or heroine, is the idealistic Katharine Howard. To dub Katharine an adventure hero is certainly to stretch the term; even to label the trilogy 'romance' (as Ford subtitled the third volume) requires qualification, since as historical fiction it deals less in romance than in politics. It is clearly more than a romance novel; as Herbert Howarth has shown, it is an adaptation and development of a popular genre, the new turn-of-the-century historical novel of writers such as Maurice Hewlett and Baroness D'Orczy, in which Ford found attractive the entertaining rapidity of narration and the period language that Hewlett called 'pothouse realism'.[13] Katharine is more than a romantic heroine. As Howarth argues, Ford's representation of Katharine, quite at variance with the sexually forthright figure of more recent historiography, challenges the genre and lends it a new seriousness by making Katharine a Catholic martyr. This is a tactic that Howarth rightly defends. It enables Katharine's story to work at the level of myth, in a way that is all the more compelling for its transparency. If the reader knows that Ford is whitewashing Katharine's reputation, this does not necessarily obviate the pleasurable suspension of readerly disbelief. In spite of the pseudo-sanctification of Katharine, however, she does at crucial moments in the narrative engage in physical action, and displays many of the necessary qualities of the adventure hero, such as nobility, courage, and physical dexterity.

The trilogy's link with the adventure tradition is reinforced by its first novel's dedication to Joseph Conrad. Furthermore, Katharine's story is essentially a quest narrative, her grail being of course the undoing of King Henry's break with Rome. Her disillusionment comes in the final chapter when she confesses: 'I was of the opinion that in the end right must win through. I think now that it never shall – or not for many ages – till our Saviour again come upon this earth with a great glory'.[14] Up to this point, Katharine devotes every effort to her mission, one that involves, like John Kemp's, both physical action and the negotiation of national identity. Misleadingly, Katharine's first appearance, in which she is guided by her cousin and would-be lover Thomas Culpepper through a riotous sectarian brawl to the safety of the King's garden, is inauspicious. 'A woman', we are told, 'covered to the face in a fur hood and riding a grey mule, was hit on the arm by the quarterstaff of a Protestant butcher [...] because she wore a crucifix round her neck. She covered her face and shrieked lamentably' (*FQ* 36). It is left to the enraged Culpepper, who at this point seems more the adventure hero type than his cousin, to '[strike] his dagger through the butcher's throat' (*FQ* 36). By the end of the first novel, however, Katharine is ensconced in the palace as a maid to the Catholic Lady Mary, and is beginning to take on more adventurous roles: she has carried a treasonable letter written in invisible ink, and has shown herself capable of self-defence, stabbing the spy Throckmorton with the sharpened point of her crucifix to evade capture. Ford's narration of action in this scene is as immediate and direct as anything in Stevenson:

> A great burst of sound roamed, vivid and alive, from the distant stairhead. She started and cried out. Then there came the sound of feet hastily stepping the stair treads, coming upwards. A man was coming to lay hands upon her!' (*FQ* 218)

The second novel in the trilogy, *Privy Seal*, in spite of its suggestive subtitle *His Last Venture*, is more concerned with conspiracy than with action, yet, as with the novel that preceded it, the climax gives Katharine a role in violent transactions, this time through her failed plea for the stay of execution of her political enemy Thomas Cromwell. Significantly, her heroic quality here is that of restraint, of holding back the hand of violence, just as with John Kemp's mercy towards O'Brien and the pirate Manuel – restraint being a quality identified there with Englishness. The third volume of the trilogy, *The Fifth Queen Crowned*, climaxes in Katharine's own execution, but before this she again works towards her ends through physical action, in the scene where the embarrassing arrival of her drunken cousin in her bedchamber leads her to asphyxiate him, an act which the unwary reader might initially take as a murder attempt, whereas, more subtly than this, it is merely intended to silence him. All of the action on Katharine's part in the trilogy is highlighted by its contrast with the unheroic acts and the misadventures of the male characters in the novel, especially King Henry with his vacillation, and Culpepper with

his lovelorn degeneration into drunkenness and desperate venge-
fulness. Through Katharine, Ford effectively regenders the adventure
hero, even if physical action is only a relatively marginal part of her
adventurous journey.

Katharine's mission to reunite England with Rome involves her
in a very different construction of Englishness to that found in
Romance. Whereas in that novel various perceptions of established
national identities were brought into conflict, in the *Fifth Queen*
trilogy national identity is perceived as being unstable, with religion as
the great undecided factor. In both novels, Catholics and Protestants
are pitted against one another; but whereas in *Romance* religion
divides along national lines, in the trilogy the English themselves are
shown to be religiously divided. What contributes further to the fluid
sense of Englishness in the trilogy is that the contested sources of
religious and intellectual identity are largely imported: the Church of
Rome; German Protestantism; Katharine's cherished Greek and Latin
'New Learning'; and medieval European scholasticism. In Thomas
Cromwell's adherence to Machiavellianism there is a further foreign
system of thought against which no effective alternative 'English'
political method is offered in opposition. Only Katharine, the 'virtue
mad Queen' (*FQC* 519) and occasional action heroine, emerges as a
counterweight to Cromwell's cynical *realpolitik*, and even Katharine
eventually must resign herself to defeat.

Ford's reworkings of romance and adventure story elements
allow him in both *Romance* and the *Fifth Queen* trilogy to dramatize
conflicting notions of Englishness. In *Romance*, the English heroic
character, incorporating both a readiness for and a restraint from
physical action, is perceived as being stable, yet is differently
interpreted and judged by friends, enemies, and the hero himself,
through his modernist narratorial mode of nuanced disenchantment. In
the *Fifth Queen* trilogy, Englishness is in flux, and the quest narrative,
at times involving physical action, is one of struggle over the very
foundations of national identity, a struggle that leads not only to
disillusionment but to defeat for the hero. Ford's ambivalence towards
the romance and adventure materials available for fiction in English
would later feed into the anti-romanticism of the subject-matter of *The
Good Soldier* (1915), in which the supposed chivalric hero becomes a
philandering anti-hero. The earlier novels borrow from a nineteenth-
century adventure tradition that *The Good Soldier* would reject, but in

so doing they also reinterpret and refashion that tradition in ways that both highlight and question notions of Englishness.

NOTES

1   Ford Madox Ford, *Joseph Conrad: A Personal Remembrance* – henceforth *JC*; London: Duckworth, 1924, p. 14.
2   Ford, *Return To Yesterday,* London: Gollancz, 1931– henceforth *RY*; p. 195.
3   Todd K. Bender and James W. Parins, *A Concordance to Conrad's Romance*, New York: Garland, 1985.
4   See Andrew Lang, 'Realism and Romance' 1886, reprinted in *The Fin de Siècle: A Reader in Cultural History c. 1800-1900*, ed. Sally Ledger and Roger Luckhurst, Oxford: Oxford University Press, 2000, pp. 99-104: 'The "Odyssey" is the typical example of a romance [...]. Are we to be told that we love the "Odyssey" because the barbaric element has not died out of our blood, and because we have a childish love of marvels, miracles, man-eating giants, women who never die, "murders grim and great", and Homer's other materials. Very well' (p. 102).
5   Ford, *Thus To Revisit*, London: Chapman and Hall, 1921, p. 35.
6   'The Work of W. H. Hudson' (1909), reprinted in *Ford Madox Ford: Critical Essays*, ed. Max Saunders and Richard Stang, Manchester: Carcanet, 2002, p. 69.
7   Ford, *Ancient Lights and Certain New Reflections* – henceforth *AL*; London: Chapman and Hall, 1911, p. 52. Ford misleadingly renders the sentence as simple narrative dressed up in florate language: 'With interjected finger he delayed the motion of the timepiece' (*AL* 52). The cue for Ford's comment is no doubt Stevenson's murder story 'Markheim', and its metaphorical description of the murderer's remorse: '[N]ow, by his act, that piece of life had been arrested, as the horologist, with interjected finger, arrests the beating of the clock'. See R. L. Stevenson, 'Markheim' (1885), in *The Merry Men and Other Tales*, London: Heinemann, 1924, pp. 87-106, pp. 96-97.
8   R. L. Stevenson, 'A Gossip on Romance', 1882, reprinted in *R. L. Stevenson on Fiction*, ed. Glenda Norquay, Edinburgh: Edinburgh University Press, 1999, pp. 51-64, p. 54.
9   Timothy Weiss, *Fairy Tale and Romance in Works of Ford Madox Ford*, Lanham, Maryland: University Press of America, 1984, pp. 19-37.
10 Ford, *The Queen Who Flew*, London: Bliss, Sands and Foster, 1894, p. 5.
11 See Andrea White, *Joseph Conrad and the Adventure Tradition: Constructing and Deconstructing the Imperial Subject*, Cambridge: Cambridge University Press, 1993.
12 Joseph Conrad and Ford, *Romance* (1903); London: Dent, 1923, p. 365.
13 Herbert Howarth, 'Hewlett and Ford Among Renaissance Women', *Journal of Modern Literature*, 5:1, February 1976, pp. 79-88, p. 80.
14 Ford, *The Fifth Queen* trilogy (1906-8), London: Bodley Head, 1962 – referred to in the text as *FQ*; p. 590.

ENGLAND AND ENGLISHNESS: FORD'S FIRST TRILOGY[1]

Sara Haslam

Ford Madox Ford produced his most concentrated exploration of England and Englishness between 1905 and 1907. The trilogy *The Soul of London, The Heart of the Country* and *The Spirit of the People* (published together in America as *England and the English*) formed part of a contemporary wave of texts dedicated to a more or less factual examination of London in particular – Walter Besant's *A Survey of London* (1902-12), for example. Ford's subtitle for *The Soul of London* was *A Survey of a Modern City*, but he did things very differently from his fellow Edwardian authors. In his style and substance, according to Alan Hill's introduction to *The Soul of London*, Ford offered the 'clearest signs' to be found of early modernism.[2] More unusually still, and as I hope to show, conservation and innovation are both integral to Ford's project.

The signals of early modernism are perhaps mainly to do with Ford's impressionism. The trilogy in fact eschews superficially factual history and instead shares characteristics with novels of the time – Ford's and others'. (Ford says he's trying to 'get the atmosphere of London' rather than to provide an encyclopaedic record; *SL* 3.) In addition, the influence on these texts of a range of visual art forms, including the Impressionism of Whistler and Monet, has been recently debated; Ford initially saw the first volume of his project as a 'collaboration' with artist William Hyde.[3] But the clear signs of modernism are to do with structure too. A recurrent language in all three books is that of the perfumer and/or musician. 'Notes' from different times and locations are placed together for the harmony or arresting discord that they produce. The past, as the 'ground-bass', resounds regularly, punctuating the present throughout even the first of the trilogy, a book designed to celebrate modernity in the city. This jostling of tenses is less marked though in the later two books. *The Heart of the Country* looks in general to rural places, older than cities, while the *Spirit of the People* travels further back still. 'For the

Country was before the Town', Ford writes in the introduction to the 1907 American edition of the trilogy, 'but, before either ... was the People itself'.[4]

On publication of *The Soul of London*, on 2 May 1905, the *Daily Mail* called it, 'the latest and truest image of London, built up out of a series of negations, that together are more hauntingly near to a composite picture of the city than anything we have seen before'.[5] It devoted a full column to the book, recognizing in its interest both something of the zeitgeist, and Ford's brilliant, painterly, technique. Such praise was mainly to do with the way Ford might be said to have echoed contemporary fascination with threats to Englishness: notions of urban chaos or flux, degeneration and decline.[6] H. G. Wells' *Tono-Bungay* (1909), one of his most successful novels, is a good example of this trend, and *The Soul of London* also exploits it to a degree. The other two volumes of the trilogy represent the necessary concomitant escape to the country version of Englishness, one which is also, as I have indicated above, a flight into the past (though true to Ford's modernism, the present and the future still make their presence felt). Yet *The Soul of London* is primarily excited about the modern varieties of vibrant Englishness that only the city can provide. London is 'illimitable', 'kaleidoscopic' and resonates with the voices, experiences, memories and aspirations of its countless inhabitants.

The contemporary context

Books, like Ford's, which debated Englishness, were in vogue when he published them for several reasons: perhaps most obviously because of the focus afforded and encouraged by the turn of the century. The act of looking forward also involved looking back. Readers of the 1890s, state Michael Neve and Mike Jay, were 'positively engulfed with imaginative constructions of the next century'.[7] When these included such plans as those for a Channel Tunnel, Englishness was perceived as under threat, and in need of re-evaluation and support. Linked to the Channel Tunnel project, 'invasion literature', novels and pamphlets that envisioned the defilement of the island, enjoyed record sales figures from a fascinated and appalled population during the years 1900 to 1914.[8] In a nice variation on this theme, Ford also sees similar invasive forces at work from within the country, as a result of industry. Hostile forces inflict a mortal blow on the 'natural' – what existed before their incursion. Whereas the 'river is a natural way [...], railroads tunnel through hills

[...] and crash through the town itself, boring straight ways into the heart of it with a fine contempt for natural obstacles' (*SL* 38). (The sexual imagery implicit in the Channel tunnel, and in railway tunnels, is significant too: fears of miscegenation went with those of invasion.[9])

The second Boer war (1899-1902) was another important factor in fuelling the debate on Englishness, because as Linda Colley has noted, national identity depends in order for its construction on an obviously hostile Other, against which it can range and define itself.[10] Reflection on this war, and contemporary notions of a weakening urban workforce – showing the decline from a pastoral English ideal represented by George Eliot's Adam Bede, say – actually fed into one another, because of the scrutiny under which the (largely male working class) fighting population was put. Sir William Taylor, the Surgeon-General, wrote in 1904 of the 'alarming proportion of the young men of this country, more especially among the urban population, who are unfit for military service on account of defective physique' (*1900* 290). If England was to be physically strong, the message seemed to be, that strength would come not from industrial centres, but from rural havens. Ford mentions reading an 'organ of advanced thought' propagating such theories at the outset of *The Heart of the Country* (*HC* 120). Worryingly, he reports that by 1906, in the opinion of this journal, 'country stock' is considered to be too different from the city type and thus, his reader infers, incompatible for regenerative purposes. Even when men were looked for in rural areas for such purposes, however, they were not necessarily there. According to Alun Howkins, the forced migration of the 1870s-1890s had worked 'only too well', and he states somewhat dramatically that 'there were no men left on the land'.[11] For the popular conception of Englishness – one reliant on theories of hereditary urban degeneration, or 'Physical Deterioration' as Ford describes it in *The Soul of London* – to be satisfied, they had to be persuaded to return.[12]

For related and additional reasons, what Martin Weiner calls a 'suspicion of material and technological development and [...] exclusion of industrialism' in England fomented around the end of the century and encouraged a polarised perception of England as either 'workshop' or 'shire' (and think here of the recent popularity of Tolkein's *Lord of the Rings*).[13] Ideas of progress associated with the one, came up against the nostalgia fundamental to the other. This kind of polarity was popular, and effective, in literature, and not just with those like William Morris who were known for their utopian dream visions. Thomas Hardy, Rudyard Kipling and Edward Thomas had all contributed to its success, and would continue to do so. Writers like Ford, and also James and Conrad, were more equivocal in their analysis of the polarity of city versus country, and Ford's trilogy bears this out. In their representations of rural and urban landscapes, one was not necessarily superior to the other: both could be seen to have their place in the modern literary conception of Englishness.

The modern context

In our own time, a second wave of new books questioning English (and sometimes by extension British) identity has provided the best possible context for re-examination of Ford's contribution to the debate. Examples from the recent turn of the century include Norman Davies' *The Isles*, John Redwood's *The Death of Britain*, Jeremy Paxman's *The English*, Simon Heffer's *Nor Shall my Sword*, Roger Scruton's *England: an Elegy* (in which England is referred to in the past tense throughout), and numerous works of fiction, such as those mentioned below. Renewed focus has been placed on Englishness once again, and it seems as though this has occurred for reasons similar to those of a century before. In 2000, the Falklands had been the most recent war fought in the interests of British sovereignty, and elements of the media coverage of this event left little doubt as to its catalytic function regarding ideas of nationhood. Indeed, there were those who claimed that the war was intended to shift energies away from domestic discontent in this way.

In addition, as shipyards, mines and steelworks closed in the last quarter of the twentieth century, difficult questions about technology and industry, and progress, were being asked. Such closures, and other factors such as those mentioned above, helped to create the impression that notions of Englishness were shifting again – this was the message of some of the publications that emerged. Those notions that were foregrounded could easily be mapped onto ideas from the fin-de-siècle, for, in a final example of an echo of the past, debates have arranged themselves around the same polarity as those of a hundred years ago. One reader of Scruton's *Elegy* pointed out the 'absence of urban England, let alone immigrant England' in the book – which means, curiously enough, that Ford's text would read as more current in some ways.[14] By page twelve of *The Soul of London*, Ford is discussing all the nationalities that are involved in creating a composite photograph of 'the Londoner' which he also names 'the Modern'.

In a review of Christopher Hart's novel *The Harvest*, in June 1999, D. J. Taylor writes of a 'new movement in English fiction', that he identified due to the publication of this and other linked novels. He describes this new movement (and in a way the adjective seems hardly to be justified) as 'provincial, if not rural, focused on an older England outside the urban sprawl, and symptomatic of a revolt against literary London's gargantuan obsession with the western postal districts and, ultimately, itself'. Re-vivifying Hardy, *The Harvest* is set on the borders of contemporary 'Wessex' – this virtual place still being one of the clearest ever examples of the literary contribution to the construction of Englishness. But meanwhile, at this new turning point, there was the predictable and opposite polarity with which to contend. Martin Amis in *London Fields* (the dust sheet of the hardback says that in his focus on a richly diverse part of London Amis 'dissects the nature of a society as it hurtles towards the end of the millennium'), and *The Information*, Peter Ackroyd's biography of London, the enormous success of Zadie Smith's *White Teeth*, provided evidence of a continuing celebration of all that is quintessentially modern in urban life. Waterstone's Booksellers capitalised on this mirror image of Taylor's 'new movement' by publishing a *Guide to London Writing* in 1999. It was advertised with a quotation: 'England is a small island. The world is infinitesimal. But London is illimitable'. In a tribute to its roots, the quotation came not from these new millennial writings, but from *The Soul of London*.

Ford's trilogy can profitably be read against this backdrop. City and country both feature strongly in the record of his impressions of England and the English. These impressions both represent still-felt cultural needs regarding the mythologies of the English countryside (the idea that, in Stanley Baldwin's phrase, 'England is the country, and the country is England'[15]), and challenge them with the kaleidoscopic word-pictures that project aspects of London with a breathless excitement borne out of the modernist project. For these reasons, it is important that each book is read in the light of the others – relatively. Ford's representation of the 'town' is necessary to build that of the 'country' against it, but it's also much too simplistic to see Ford as simply adding to the pile of urban degeneration literature.

Biographical matters, and publication of the trilogy

The way in which Ford constructs, and views, London 'from a distance' at the outset of the trilogy – a crucial characteristic of his authorial stance – may well have something to do with his conception of his own personal and critical distance from the English life and lives he was setting out to record. The fact of his German father may be the most obviously relevant one here, but he goes so far as to describe himself as 'a man of no race and few ties – or of many races and many ties' in *The Spirit of the People* (*SP* 325). Consciousness of his mainland European heritage and roots infuses his writerly persona in more books than these, and he travelled, partly in order to invigorate and maintain these roots, from a young age. He lived in some of the great cities of the world throughout his life, including London, Paris and New York. (He was in London as he began to write the trilogy, however; born on its outskirts, and having lived there for periods already, he moved back in January 1904.)

Ford was related by birth to Christina and Dante Gabriel Rossetti, and his early contacts as a writer included this famous family as well as a number of other distinctly 'un-English' figures whose influence also shaped his perspective and development to greater or lesser degrees: David Soskice and other Russian émigrés known to the Garnetts; Stephen Crane; Henry James.[16] The most important man in Ford's writing life would be listed here too. Edward Garnett introduced Ford to the Ukranian-born, sea-faring Joseph Conrad in 1898. This was the beginning of a period of collaboration between the two writers which resulted in joint novels, but more significantly in the development of literary impressionism, the technique Ford uses to such brilliant effect in this trilogy – *The Soul of London* represented Ford's first literary success. Perhaps this particular combination of familial and professional influences leads, at least in this instance, to the tension at the heart of Ford's impressionism: the way in which the writing is both an expression of personality and a much more extensive, critical, human vision.

Continuing the organic imagery in the titles of the volumes, *The Heart of the Country* was published the year after *The Soul of London*, on 9 May, and also received good reviews. Dedicated to Henry James, the volume bespeaks Ford's debt to this other companion author who was fascinated by Englishness from the position of outsider. James's essay, 'London', published in 1888, which I discuss below, had also possibly provided more direct inspiration for Ford in his current project. (More immediately, Ford heard James was planning a book on London as he was writing *The Soul of London*; a letter from James in April 1904 reassures Ford that his project was 'relegated to a dim futurity'.[17]) Max Saunders, Ford's most recent biographer, places the trilogy from *The Heart of the Country* onwards in the developing 'Edwardian preoccupation with a folk-culture that was rapidly disappearing'. This may be one reason for the attention paid to its publication by Edward Thomas, C. F. G. Masterman and Edward Garnett, among others.[18] Thomas published a book in 1906 (several months after *The Heart of the Country* appeared) called *The Heart of England*, and coined the phrase 'the south country' in a poetry collection published later than Ford's trilogy, in 1909; the phrase recurs in literature of and about the time as a way of encoding the rural vision of Englishness. According to Robert Colls, there was indeed what he calls a 'revival' of interest in 'folk studies' and local archaeology around this time. He puts this down to a sense of social and political unrest, both domestic and international, which caused a flight into the nation's 'racial and rural essence'.[19] As one expression of this flight, chapter 5 in *The Heart of the Country* is called 'Utopias'; rather than being a 'no-place', Ford's initial image of utopia is an agricultural variety that he knows exists.

The Spirit of the People appeared in 1907, and had a less happy birth than the previous two volumes. This was due to a combined failure in relationships, Ford's with his agent, and with his publisher too. It didn't cause a stir as had the others, a fact that Ford miserably put down to a lack of effort on behalf of his publishers, Alston Rivers. Perhaps less easy to market too, in terms of the contemporary atmosphere, this volume is less focussed than its partners, and ranges widely in history, psychology, religion and politics. In its analysis of the English character, however, it discusses sexual repression in a way that reveals a germ of the story of his greatest book, *The Good Soldier* (1915).

Technique
Key terms, describing various techniques, appear in the trilogy, some of which relate to Ford's modernist credentials, and to his collaboration with Conrad, and others to contemporary imagistic fashions. Overall his style is similar to a series of 'moments of vision', joined by sections of prose which build up to these plateaux, and which allow for Ford's form of making a case. Often part of this case

making is structured along the lines of 'I know someone who...', 'I met a woman who...'. An example comes in *The Heart of the Country*, as Ford discusses field labourers that he has known, building them towards a final image of 'Every-man, this final pillar of the state' who is, for Ford, the 'heart of the heart' of the country (*HC* 197-8). This anecdotal style can be wearing, unless one bears in mind that it is part of a philosophy that privileges the ordinary encounter, the individual meeting and sharing of minds, and makes it representative. It's not an uncommon way of constructing 'travel writing', or that devoted to cultural observation. Henry James adopted it in his essay on London, and in many other examples of his travel writing (an editor of *English Hours* writes how James 'never missed an opportunity to exchange a few words with beggars he met, or with peasants, farmers, shepherds'[20]). In one of the most famous examples of books about Englishness, H. V. Morton's *In Search of England* (1927), the same technique can be observed. Morton meets, for example, the 'last bowl turner in England', who reveals to him the secrets of his rural trade.

One of the techniques that Ford practises throughout is alluded to a number of times in the first pages of the text (and I mentioned it briefly at the outset of this chapter), in the repetition of the word 'impression'. Consideration of the extent of self-consciousness necessary to a writer's professional existence caused a debate that predated Ford. It raged in the later half of the nineteenth century, thanks to Matthew Arnold, amongst others, but in the years before the First World War it became an essential part of literary life. [21] On one side of the divide were the avowed impressionists, derided by Irving Babbitt as 'the last effete representatives of romanticism'.[22] Michael Levenson characterises impressionism 'as both a precise rendering of objects and an unrepentant subjectivising': as attention to detail, in other words, in what one saw, *and* in what one felt/remembered.[23] Opposed to the impressionists, on the other side of the divide, were those, like Babbitt, for whom art was primarily about self-transcendence. Most relevant in discussion of fiction, perhaps, the impressionist debate is played out, as we shall see, in all writing of the period. It is an impressionist approach that Hilaire Belloc describes in 1900 as he begins his book on Paris:

> There comes, I suppose [he writes in the preface], to every one who has felt keenly the modern impression of a place he loves, a desire to know its

changing past, the nature and experience that it draws from the centuries, and the platform upon which there can be constructed some little of that future which he will never see.... [A man] will end by making a record that is as incomplete and fragmentary ... as are the notes and letters we keep to remind ourselves of absent friends [....] This book belongs, then, to that kind of history (if it can be called history at all) which is as superficial and as personal as a traveller's drawing or as the notes of a man's diary.[24]

Ford found himself very much on the side of the impressionists, and argued that the techniques he developed with Conrad were above all Impressionist. With grim humour he relates the potential cost of this preference: 'Impressionists were considered to be bad people: Atheists, Reds, wearing red ties with which to frighten house-holders'.[25] Nonetheless, impressionism, which distrusted facts when it came to representing human experience, and instead embraced the multiple truths of how something seemed, and looked and felt, was important enough for them both to take the professional risk.

For Ford, impressionism was, above all, about the ability to 'make you see'; it was about using layered perspectives, of time, as well as of space. So he isn't that interested in facts (he doesn't want to tell us about the '720 firms of hat manufacturers employing 19,000 operatives'; *SL* 3), he's interested in how those facts are experienced, in showing what things look like and feel like from different angles, through different lenses, with different focal points. It is no coincid-ence that a favourite image in the trilogy is the 'composite photo-graph', by which he means the overlaying of visual images in ways which meant each retained its essence but which contributed to a multiple whole. It wasn't so long before that the new art of photo-graphy had been spat upon as a 'democracy of the portrait', a descrip-tion which helps further to contextualise Ford's interest in everyday, ordinary, experience.[26] Sometimes he uses the composite photograph as a way of representing and preserving typical characters (see *SP* 270), and sometimes to illustrate the interweaving of past and present time (see *SP* 266). His use of this image is a key example of the way in which innovation and conservation meet and merge in these books.

Rendering is another key term in the trilogy, and one closely related to impressionism. Ford uses to it to mean the opposite of telling how something definitively is. It goes with impressionism because it's about suggesting, with emphasis in artistic terms on the act of representation, on the approach and re-approach to the experience of the object or event in question. Together, these issues help to indicate Ford's contribution to modernism – one that is, perhaps, most evident in the first volume of the trilogy where the chaos and complexity of the city demands such literary treatment.

Related to the visual intent and impact of Ford's technique in this trilogy, is the nature of the imagery that he employs. One of the most extraordinary, and bizarre, examples of this imagery is the body of the country, complete with organs, blood, and spiritual dimensions. Country roads and hedgerows, for example, are the vessels which pump the blood from the heart of the country: market days are 'pulse days' (*HC* 146-9). Most powerfully, though, Ford focuses on this body's digestive powers, locating those firmly in the region of the capital city, using the phrase 'modern juices' to describe London's ability both to erase the differences between its inhabitants, and to re-define them, on the other side of digestion, as it were (*SL* 12). Striking as this is, it is not entirely original to Ford. Such organic imagery was popular at the time, and Henry James's famous essay on London (first published in 1888) provides a possible model for the hungry beast that Ford depicts at times in his trilogy.[27] James describes London as 'like a mighty ogress who devours human flesh', needing the nourishment to maintain her levels of vivacity and to do her 'work'.[28] Ford develops his image, however, if he was aware of it, because James's is a faintly Darwinian vision, in which it is the weak who are 'gobbled up' as fuel. In *The Soul of London*, it is all of those who go to make up the Modern Spirit that are oozed over, and turned into London's own, before their individual memories and perceptions are allowed to re-assert themselves in Ford's celebration of difference.

In the final section of this essay, I want to say something about each of the books individually. This will involve assessing their contribution to Ford's depiction of Englishness, sometimes in comparison with that of other contemporary writers.

The Soul of London

True to Ford's impressionist ethos, there are many pictures of the city offered here, some of which seem to contradict each other. The tension between the city as a place that fosters individuality, and one which takes it away is not resolved. The 'immense crowd' of the city, to which Ford refers from time to time, has much in common with Gustave le Bon's dystopic depiction of primitiveness and savagery when large numbers of individuals congregate and agitate, and fill the lone watcher with fear.[29] The enormous range of individual sights, of one's fellow human beings and their experiences of life, that Ford takes such pains to represent, can be 'nerve-shattering', because there are simply too many to respond to and recognise (*SL* 90). (One is reminded of George Eliot's 'roar which lies on the other side of silence' that she uses to describe the ability to be 'aware of all ordinary human life', an overwhelming ability because of the frequency of ordinary tragedy.[30]) Partly what we are experiencing here is the result of Ford's own terrible encounters with agoraphobia and nervous illness, serious episodes of which began in 1904, but in the excitement propagated by the city there is always the fear of chaos if such excitement goes 'too far'.

In general, however, the 'kaleidoscope' of human experiences, to which the city gives the receptive writer access, is to be celebrated as one of the truths of modern existence. Living in the city is related to a journey by train, during which you see a variety of landscapes: geographical, emotional and psychological. All human life is there; the other side of the 'nerve-shattering' plurality is the way in which 'London holds us' – by this Ford means 'fascinates/enthrals' – as she shows us 'many things' (*SL* 79). The final pages of the book construct an optimistic vision of a 'London of the Future' that continues to preserve the stories of the Past.

In terms of contributions to the debate on Englishness, *The Soul of London* and the *Spirit of the People* both provide Ford's perspective on what became known as the 'Great Man cult', part of a debate established by the Victorians. In an essay on the rivalry between champions of Wellington and Napoleon (both of whom are mentioned on several occasions in the trilogy), Iain Pears relates the rise of this cult to the 'arrival of the Victorian worship of self-discipline'. In the earlier volume, Ford laments the passing of the Great Figure due to the way in which sheer numbers in London prevent towering figures from asserting themselves (*SL* 94). In contrast, in *The Spirit of the People*, he develops the theory of the 'Great Man of his type' in a retrospective historical analysis, beginning with Thomas Cromwell (*SP* 271), whom he credits with 'welding England into a formidable whole'. The Great Man may have retreated in modern life, but he is essential to Ford's historical vision of Englishness.

The Heart of the Country

Existing criticism of this trilogy focuses for the most part on *The Soul of London*, but the second and third volumes have much both to recommend and to distinguish them, especially in a consideration of Ford's depiction of Englishness. The utopian theme is strong in the second volume (and the 'country' that we find here is mainly that of Kent). There's no doubt that, above all, the country is supposed to be seen as a corrective to city living, a place from which regenerative strength can be drawn when the excitement proves too much. Ways into and through the countryside are a focal point in this text: web-like structures that show and create the links between the communities and individuals that make up its population. Bloodlines, and, crucially for Ford, thoroughfares for gossip, they connect the village cottages that compete with the country labourer for Ford's depiction of the 'heart of the heart of the country'. It is the village aspect of the countryside that is often called on elsewhere to illustrate Englishness; H. V. Morton states that 'the village that symbolises England sleeps in the sub-conscious of many a townsman'.[31] George Sturt illustrates the kind of mythical organic community that proliferated in literature, as he laments the loss of Englishness. Unsurprisingly, his focus is 'a village', one 'inhabited by Peasantry: rounded in by its own self-sup-porting toil, and governed by its own old-world customs'.[32] Convinced by the benefits of such toil (though he places emphasis on the 'Every-man' field-labourer and the more limited community of the cottage), Ford contributes to the sense of country people being tougher than town-dwellers in this text, also because, in a manner similar to Hardy, he depicts the importance of the relationship between character and place. Divorce from one's roots is impoverishing, and it is the natural base of those roots that provides most strength in the face of a changing world. Despite evident temptation, Ford manages to avoid sentimentality in his depiction of the countryside. Though he presents the positive aspects of country living, the effects of lack of comfort, poor diet, and ill-education, are shown too.

The many images of the tramp in *The Heart of the Country* are significant in Ford's depiction of Englishness. In Roy Porter's *Myths of the English*, an essay is devoted to the rise of the 'romantic and sentimental tramp of the Edwardians';[33] Henry James is seduced by the 'romantic attractiveness' of the same construct in *English Hours* (Porter 100). This primarily literary figure – no-one did much sociological research into vagrant life at the time – symbolised the rejection of authority and the 'encroachments of business and city life' (Porter 99, 106). A rural figure in fantasy, the tramp guarded primitive secrets and country codes; Ford's tramps have 'gone back into the heart of the country and have become one with the ravens, the crows, the weasels, and the robins' (*HC* 135). They inhabit a different world even from those who live in the country, and offer a commentary from their perspective as outsiders (Ford's tramps are very well-travelled) that is of value to Ford – and other writers of the time – because of what Porter calls their 'innocuous anarchy' (Porter 5). They represent the old ways, old knowledge, and can be called up as repositories of Englishness, but offer no real threat to the status quo. That ability belongs to the 'Grim Reaper' that Ford conjures up in 'L'envoi' – the auctioneer that presides over enforced and painful change due to the death or bankruptcy of local inhabitants. But even he isn't able to vanquish the ploughman, with whom Ford leaves us (*HC* 227), one who seems to walk straight out of Ford and into Hardy's 'In Time of "The Breaking of Nations"' nine years later, without changing at all.

The Spirit of the People

This is the book in which Ford uses the image of the composite photograph to such productive effect. He finds it a useful tool because of its ability to illustrate the merging of times as well as of spaces/objects, as he ranges throughout history in his discussion of the English character and spirit. Building on the idea of the Great Man Cult, Ford develops that of the representative type of an age, one that can be compared with other types from other ages in the search for similarities and differences, in physical as well as emotional ways. He refers to a composite photograph that he has had made of some of Holbein's sketches of the 'typical Englishman' of his day (*SP* 270). Curiously (and humorously) enough, the result reminds him of W. G. Grace, as well as of a type of character he seems to recognize from contemporary 'English rural districts'. In opposition to this robust portrayal of the English character, Ford explores further the theory of degeneration (*SP* 265), and finds some evidence to support it in both the declining birth-rate and the movement of the population of the countryside to the town. Here, he also assesses the characteristics that make up the typical Englishman. Unsurprisingly, as he tries to impose a narrative, things can become fairly confused, especially in his attempts to discuss race and the relationship between 'Englishness' and 'Britishness'. In general, however, the pictures he paints are lucid ones, though perhaps provocative, and are especially stimulating in his forays into Protestantism versus Catholicism, and the law. Furthermore, the book comes into its own when the theme is repression.

The crowd, already discussed in the *Soul of London*, re-emerges in Ford's consideration of society here. It does so less symbolically (and perhaps less neurotically) than in the earlier volume, because, with sociological intent, he wants to compare the English crowd with those of other nations. On the other hand, he displays the same nervousness at the thought of large numbers of people congregated together and the power of this mass – as well as an impressionist style in his discussion – that we encountered before. Brutal behaviour of policemen figures in Ford's analysis of the crowd. He wants to acknowledge it even as he dismisses it as uncommon, but thus lends a distinct flavour to this volume of the trilogy (*SP* 245-6), linked both to what Clive Emsley calls the resulting 'disquiet among many individuals of liberal and left-wing sympathies', and the concerns of many of his contemporaries about Englishness.[34]

Finally, as the book draws to a close, Ford takes us back to the beginning of the trilogy with his celebration of the variety that makes up the English character. This is the 'type of the future' (*SP* 322) not in any narrow jingoistic sense, but in the sense that, throughout its history, this type has been forged by the encounter with new and different perspectives. Unable to resist the call of myth in his final sentences however, Ford resorts to a beautifully written passage about the way in which it is England that has made the English, and those qualities that constitute Englishness. Ford's England is green, tranquil and fertile, and exerts its influence over the chaotic city on which it nevertheless depends for its literary construction, and for its fame.

NOTES

1   An earlier version of this essay appeared as the introduction to my edition of Ford's *England and the English*, Manchester: Carcanet, 2003. This revised version appears here with the kind permission of Michael Schmidt. Unless otherwise indicated, all references are to this edition of the trilogy.
2   Ford, *The Soul of London*, ed. Alan G. Hill, London: Everyman, 1995, p. xix.
3   Nick Freeman in his essay 'Impressionism in *The Soul of London*' in *Ford Madox Ford and the City*, ed. Sara Haslam, Amsterdam and New York: Rodopi, 2005, p. 28. See also Max Saunders' essay in the same volume.
4   *England and the English: An Interpretation*, New York: McClure, Phillips and Co., 1907, p. xviii.

5   Quoted by Max Saunders in *Ford Madox Ford: A Dual Life,* Oxford: Oxford
    University Press, 1996, 2 vols – henceforth 'Saunders'; vol. 1, p. 195.

6   In *Haunts of Ancient Peace* (1902), Alfred Austin writes of the city as a place of
    'ungraceful hurry and worry, perpetual postmen's knocks, an intermittent shower
    of telegrams'. The quotation comes from a book by Martin Weiner: *English
    Culture and the Decline of the Industrial Spirit,* Cambridge: Cambridge
    University Press, 1981, p. 45. Late Victorian novels, like Gissing's *New Grub
    Street* (1891), also provide examples of the widespread theory of urban
    degeneration.

7   Introduction to *1900: A Fin-de-Siècle Reader,* ed. Mike Jay and Michael Neve,
    London: Penguin, 1999 – henceforth *1900;* p. xiii.

8   Samuel Hynes, *The Edwardian Turn of Mind,* Princeton: Princeton University
    Press, 1975, p. 34.

9   See my article 'Ford's Training' in *Ford Madox Ford's Modernity,* ed. Max
    Saunders and Robert Hampson, Amsterdam: Rodopi, 2003, for a discussion of
    this subject.

10 Linda Colley, *Britons: Forging the Nation 1707-1837,* London: Pimlico, 1994, p.
    5.

11 Alun Howkins, 'The Discovery of Rural England' in Robert Colls and Philip
    Dodd (eds), *Englishness: Politics and Culture 1880-1920,* London: Croom Helm,
    1986, p. 67.

12 Hynes, *The Edwardian Turn of Mind,* p. 22, discusses the 1904 'Report of the
    Inter-Departmental Committee on Physical Deterioration'. See *The Soul of
    London,* p. 103. Ford evidently isn't convinced by the validity of this popular
    notion, turning it into a kind of joke in the text by questioning when it began to
    strike men down and making it an ancient rather than a modern problem.
    However, not surprisingly due to the subject matter, he comes closer to accepting
    some of the parameters of this debate in the later books.

13 Weiner, *English Culture and the Decline of the Industrial Spirit,* p. 5.

14 Andy Beckett in a review of *England: An Elegy, The Englishman's Handbook,* by
    Idries Shah, and *Utopian England: Community Experiments 1901-1945,* by
    Dennis Hardy, in the *Guardian,* 21 October 2000.

15 Jeremy Paxman quotes a substantial chunk of the speech in which this phrase was
    coined in chapter eight, 'There Always was an England', of his book *The English,*
    London: Penguin, 1999, p. 143.

16 Edward Garnett had been instrumental in securing Ford's first publication, the
    fairy story *The Brown Owl,* in 1891. Ford knew the Garnett family well from the
    early 1890s: see Saunders, vol. 1, pp. 43-6.

17 Letter quoted by Saunders, vol. 1, p. 165.

18 See Saunders, vol. 1, p. 220.

19 Robert Colls, 'Englishness and the Political Culture' in *Englishness: Politics and
    Culture 1880-1920,* p. 47.

20 Alma Louise Lowe, introduction to James's *English Hours,* London: Heinemann,
    1960, p. xxii.

21 Christopher Gillie calls it Hebraism versus Hellenism, or 'conscience' versus
    'consciousness' following Matthew Arnold's coinage in *Culture and Anarchy*
    (1869). Arnold identified two basic attitudes of mind, one moral, and practical,
    the other cultural and aesthetic, to which he gave these names. Gillie, *Movements*

in English Literature 1900-1940, Cambridge: Cambridge University Press, 1975, p. 4.

22 Irving Babbitt, *Masters of Modern French Criticism* (1912), Westport, CN: Greenwood Press, 1977, p. 345.

23 Michael Levenson, *A Genealogy of Modernism*, Cambridge: Cambridge University Press, 1984, p. 36.

24 Hilaire Belloc, *Paris*, London: Edward Arnold, 1900, p. vii.

25 See the extract from Ford's *Joseph Conrad: A Personal Remembrance* quoted in the Norton edition of *The Good Soldier*, New York and London: Norton, 1995, p. 276.

26 Peter Gay quotes this phrase (which dates from 1867) in *Pleasure Wars,* London: HarperCollins, 1998, p. 57.

27 Robert Colls and Philip Dodd suggest that 'society-as-organism' analogies were increasingly common in both fiction and non-fiction around 1900: *Englishness: Politics and Culture 1880-1920*, p. 7.

28 Henry James, 'London' in Alma Louise Lowe ed., *English Hours,* London: Heinemann, 1960, p. 17.

29 An extract from *The Crowd: A Study of the Popular Mind* (1896) is published in *1900*, pp. 152-3.

30 George Eliot, *Middlemarch*, Middlesex: Penguin, 1985, p. 226.

31 H. V. Morton, *In Search of England* (1927), London: Methuen, 1984, p. 2.

32 This image appears in Sturt's journals, and is quoted by David Gervais in *Literary Englands: Versions of 'Englishness' in Modern Writing,* Cambridge: Cambridge University Press, 1993, p. 112.

33 M. A. Crowther, 'The Tramp' in *Myths of the English,* ed. Roy Porter, Cambridge: Polity Press, 1992 – henceforth 'Porter'; p. 92.

34 Emsley states that a 'creeping militarization of the police' was a traditional 'English concern' in his essay 'The English Bobby: an Indulgent Tradition' in Porter, pp. 127-8.

FORD AMONG THE ALIENS

Andrzej Gasiorek

Writing of two poverty-stricken men in *The People of the Abyss*, Jack London remarks: 'And naturally, their guts a-reek with pavement offal, they talked of bloody revolution. They talked as anarchists, fanatics, and madmen would talk. And who shall blame them?'[1] His pungent imagery, mistrust of revolutionary rhetoric, and humane empathy nicely capture the conflicting sentiments aroused in turn-of-the-century observers of the metropolitan scene. Anxieties about poverty, housing, immorality, immigration, and degeneration were rife. These anxieties, in turn, were emblematic of a wider preoccupation with national identity. The three volumes of Ford's *England and the English*, although they were not published as a single volume under that title in Britain, contribute to an ongoing public debate. But the stance Ford takes, especially in *The Soul of London* (1905),[2] is a characteristically complex and ambivalent one, which not only insists on the impossibility of attaining a totalising view of the city but also suggests that the capital's fragmentary nature is to be cherished. Treating London as a symbol of modernity itself, Ford engages in a polemic with powerful contemporary voices who were trying to articulate a narrow and exclusive version of Englishness.

In this chapter I explore several related Fordian concerns: the difficulty of coming to terms with a London that is a place of personal impressions and knowledges; the contrast between the squalor in which one segment of the population lives and the comfort enjoyed by a moneyed class; the city's assimilative nature, its capacity to embrace all sorts and kinds of people, whom it remakes as modern cosmopolitan subjects; the ambivalence with which Ford responds to this assimilative process, which eradicates cultural differences and promote a standardisation of the self; the need to resist the tentacular power of bureaucracy and industry in the name of an individualism that is indispensable to a vibrant civic community; the fear of metropolitan anonymity, which may act as cover for the violent criminal or political revolutionary. I want to ask, finally, what are the implications of all this for Ford's conception of national identity at the turn of the century?

My chapter is divided into four sections. The first concentrates on the political context in which Ford was writing, especially with regard to debates about immigration. The second explores what I take to be a major tension in *The Soul of London* between two opposed views of modernity, one stressing its cosmopolitanism, the other emphasising its determinism; I look in detail at Ford's account of assimilation, which I compare with Conrad's *The Secret Agent*, focusing in particular on the shared trope of cannibalism. In the third part of my essay I challenge David Trotter's account of Ford in his book *Paranoid Modernism*, which suggests that Ford's antipathy to system may be dated from after the First World War. Contrasting *The Soul of London*'s celebration of contingency and chaos with the linguistic purism of Ezra Pound and the political purism of *The Secret Agent*'s Professor, I argue that Ford espouses a form of tolerant and humane cultural anarchism. Finally, and *contra* Matthew Arnold, I read this cultural anarchism in relation to Ford's practice of literary collage in *The Soul of London*. This text defends social and ethnic diversity as an ethical good, and the wider literary implications of this defence are visible most obviously in Ford's later memoir *Return to Yesterday*, where different rings of foreign literary conspirators hatch their plots against English insularity.

Aliens, Paupers, and Immigration

There is an important social and political context to *The Soul of London*. Begun in 1903 and published in 1905, it was written at a time of intense political debate about poverty, unemployment, housing, and immigration. Ford's subtle title hints that nothing less than the 'soul' of the nation is at stake, since so many of the immigrants who came to England settled in London, typically inhabiting the impoverished slums of the East End. According to Bernard Gainer, immigration 'into England trebled between 1899 and 1902'.[3] Anxiety about immigration led to the passing of the Aliens Act in 1905, which sought to restrict immigration by confining entry points to fourteen ports and putting into place rigorous inspections of passengers, who could be refused right of entry if they were deemed to belong to undesirable categories. Racial stereotypes abounded, and anti-Semitism was rife. The union leader Ben Tillett was hostile to Jewish immigration and was opposed to foreigners working on English ships:

'I have no objection to the alien as such, but he is always a cheap and obsequious worker, and alternates between slavish humility and too often treachery in the use of the knife'.[4] Socialists and anarchists did not officially fall into 'undesirable' categories, but there was a suspicion, as Gainer puts it, that 'London was the secret international headquarters of the [anarchist] movement, where its horrible crimes were planned'. The restriction of immigration had the double purpose of raising 'the material position of the poor', on the one hand, and fending off 'revolution', on the other, and throughout the agitation for an Aliens Act it was the scurrilous, disreputable, and politically intemperate foreigner who was associated with revolution.[5]

The poverty of new immigrants, and the consequent pressure on housing and the threat to jobs, was a major concern, which picked up on existing anxieties about the living conditions of an indigenous underclass. Titles such as C. F. G. Masterman's *From the Abyss* and Margaret Harkness' *In Darkest London* evoke the infernal regions into which the intrepid social explorer must descend if he is to learn about and possibly emancipate the benighted inhabitants.[6] The notion of a civilising mission, which informed much nineteenth-century imperialist rhetoric, was transferred to London's slum denizens who could then be troped as heathens and savages, or even as an altogether different 'race'. James Grant's *The Great Metropolis* (1837) castigates the poor for their immorality, promiscuity, intemperance, profligacy, dishonesty, and lack of religion; the task at hand is 'the moral regeneration both of the inhabitants of tropical climes and of the metropolis in which we live'.[7] Jack London and Masterman saw this *Lumpenproletariat* as an emergent species. London wrote of how he 'saw a nightmare, a fearful slime that quickened the pavement with life, a mess of unmentionable obscenity . . . a menagerie of garmented bipeds that looked something like humans and more like beasts' (*PA* 114); Masterman, in turn, described a 'new city race' that to the observer represented 'a sudden unaccountable revelation of an invasion dropped from nowhither upon his accustomed ways'.[8]

These depictions call to mind Wells's Martians from *The War of the Worlds*, whose slimy, fungoid appearance fills the narrator with 'strange horror' and overcomes him 'with disgust and dread'.[9] The Martians are the fantasised embodiment of an alien life-form that threatens to take over the human world. Like *Dracula*'s Renfield, described as 'a zoophagous (life-eating) maniac' who seeks to 'absorb as many lives as he can', the Martians are vampiric creatures who feed off the life-force of those they kill: 'They did not eat, much less digest. Instead, they took the fresh, living blood of other creatures, and *injected* it into their own veins' (*WW* 119).[10] Whether it was consciously intended or not, there is an imaginative link here to jingoist rhetoric about immigration. Arnold White, who agitated on behalf of the Aliens Bill, referred to 'foreign paupers . . . replacing English workers and driving to despair men, women and children of our blood', and in a polemic titled 'England for the English' he denounced the 'pauper foreigner' for 'successfully colonising Great Britain under the nose of H. M. Government'.[11] Neither Ford nor Conrad were paupers, although Conrad routinely experienced financial difficulties, but it is not hard to imagine how a recently domiciled Pole and an Englishman bearing a German surname might have felt in such a climate. Conrad's fury at being positioned as an exotic alien is telling in this context. As he put it in an exasperated letter to Edward Garnett: 'I've been cried up of late as a sort of freak, an amazing bloody foreigner writing in English (every blessed review of S. A. [*The Secret Agent*] had it so – and even yours) that anything I say will be discounted on that ground by the public'.[12] There is a real anxiety here about a failure to assimilate, to be accepted by the English as 'one of us', and Conrad's uneasiness about his place within English society was surely exacerbated by the kind of xenophobic rhetoric that demonised immigrants from Russia and Poland especially.

When Ford, rejecting this rhetoric, insists that London can overcome potentially threatening differences of racial outlook by assimilating the foreigner, he is playing his own small role in creating a cultural counter-myth to resist England's parochial fear of the alien other. On this view, London signifies tolerance, open-mindedness, and heterogeneity. But there is a dark underside to this humane vision. Ford insists that cultural differences are not maintained in a spirit of diversity but are *eradicated*: the cultural *work* that London performs does away with differences, creating subjects who are modern 'types'. This erosion of differences creates a problem, for individuals become anonymous, no longer stand out from the crowd, are forged as mass products. There is a twofold danger here: first, that the individual is being wiped out, with disastrous consequences for civic life, which becomes dominated by faceless bureaucracies and capitalist corporations; second, that the anonymity imposed on these mechanical subjects, which is the outward sign that they have been assimilated, provides a camouflage under the cover of which they may engage in criminal or revolutionary activity. As Dracula tells Jonathan Harker: 'I am content if I am like the rest, so that no man stops me if he see me, or pause in his speaking if he hear my words, to say "Ha, ha! A stranger!"' (*D* 31-2).

Assimilation in the Metropolis

Max Saunders has pointed out of Ford's trilogy *England and the English* that in contrast to much Edwardian writing on the 'Condition of England', these books 'don't foment hysteria about foreign invasions, the degeneration of the race, and the "Woman Question"' (Saunders, vol. 1, 195). This is, in my view, absolutely right. Consider, first, Ford's imagery. It evokes a city that is an impressionistic 'atmosphere', Ford's goal being, he writes, to 'throw a personal image on to the paper' (*SL* 3). Equally importantly, however, the ambience that Ford creates is connected to a particular argument about the social significance of the metropolis, and here he is engaged in a debate with nationalistically minded exclusionists. In strict opposition to those who agitated on behalf of an Aliens Bill, depicting the immigrant as a source of pollution and degeneration, Ford argues in favour of London's capacity to *assimilate* all incomers, and he sees the immigrant as an unthreatening addition to English culture and society. This argument is advanced as much by his fleeting imagery as by his explicit statements. Describing 'clinging veils of steam' (*SL* 3), 'the blur of lamps in fogs' (*SL* 8), 'mists, great shadows, great clouds' (*SL* 9), and 'glamorous smirched sunset[s], curling clouds . . . wisps of mist' (*SL* 23), Ford conjures a London that is all shades, tints, and vapours. The cloud is perhaps the most dominant image in *The Soul of London*, its evanescence hinting at the writer's inability ever fully to capture the essence of the metropolis. At the same time, the cloud is an image of indeterminacy and liminality; it can easily pass away, just like the nebulous visions of the city that emanate from the observer's mind. More significantly, it hints at the blurring of outlines and boundaries that signifies the city's assimilationist spirit. Thus on the opening page of *The Soul of London* Ford suggests that his 'personal image' aims to convey 'the idea that all these human beings melt, as it were, into the tide of humanity as all these vapours melt into the overcast skies' (*SL* 3).

Ford aligns himself with the pluralism of the social 'melting-pot', and London becomes the site of a possible cultural diversity. Diversity is signalled in a variety of ways: in the text's insistence on the multiple perspectives from which London needs to be observed; its emphasis on the impossibility of an all-embracing view of the city; its evocation of the capital's natural history, the forests that have been cleared to make way for it and the marshes that lie beneath it; its stress on the co-existence of the past and the present in the urban environment; its invocation of contrasts, associations, and aspects; above all, perhaps, its claim that London is 'illimitable' (*SL* 15). London, moreover, is for Ford an instance of the modern spirit because it permits the interaction of a range of ethnic and cultural groups:

> Immense without being immediately impressive, tolerant without any permanent preferences, attracting unceasingly specimens of the best of all earthly things without being susceptible of any perceptible improvement, London, perhaps because of its utter lack of unity, of plan, of the art of feeling, is the final expression of the Present Stage. It owes its being to no one race, to no two, to no three. It is, as it were, the meeting place of all Occidentals and of such of the Easterns as can come, however remotely, into touch with the Western spirit. (*SL* 13)

This admixture is able to occur because metropolitan modernity cannot control historical contingency, cannot impose system on haphazardness. As an ideal expression of modernity, London is a 'melting-pot' that belongs to no single people and is the product of multiple ethnic traditions.

But in keeping with its subject *The Soul of London* is itself constructed around various tensions and ambiguities. If the modern spirit, for example, is associated with pluralism and a seemingly benevolent turmoil, then it is also seen to be inseparable from economic forces that threaten human individuality. Ford's observation from an electric tram of 'a steam crane at work' calls forth the following reflections:

> It was impressive enough – the modern spirit expressing itself in terms not of men but of forces, we gliding by, the timbers swinging up, without any visible human action in either motion. No doubt men were at work in the engine-belly of the crane, just as others were far away among the dynamos that kept us moving. But they were sweating invisible. That, too, is the Modern Spirit: great organisations run by men as impersonal as the atoms of our own frames, noiseless, and to all appearances infallible. (*SL* 29-30)

When he considers the destruction of small, long-established trades and industries by new mechanised processes, Ford is appalled by the inarticulate suffering of the unemployed, and he sees as 'sinister' those impersonal forces that 'are working invisible, like malign and conscious fates, below the horizon' (*SL* 69). When he reflects on the monotony that is enforced on workers, he is horrified by the way mechanised work destroys individuality, since it doesn't just turn workers into machines but, more distressingly, turns them into *contented* machines who desire no other form of existence.

There is, I am suggesting, a tension in *The Soul of London* between two conflicting conceptions of modernity, one emphasising its cosmopolitanism and openness, the other stressing its determinism and insensibility. For the destruction of the individual by the industrial machine is for Ford but an instance of more profound processes of rationalisation and bureaucratisation. What is at stake here is not just the fate of the individual *qua* individual but rather that of the public sphere. For if, as Ford maintains, 'the heaviest indictment that can be brought against a city or a world' is that it 'blunts our sense of individualities' (*SL* 94) then this is in large part because this erosion undermines the very basis on which a civic community rests. Consider the following passage:

> [A]s soon as a city becomes a mass of Corporations, individualities die out and are wasted of necessity. We may consider Athens, which was a city not more vast than is Kensington High Street: probably its inhabitants were not really more cultured or more wise, but certainly they had, each one of them, better chances of influencing *all* their fellow inhabitants. And that for humanity would seem, in the Individualist's eyes, to be the best of social units. Only the most hardened of Democrats, seeing humanity not as poor individuals but as parts of a theory, as negligible cog-wheels of a passionless machine, would deny that, from a human point of view Athens was better than Kensington High Street, or than Westminster itself. . . . What prophet shall make London listen to him? Where is London's "distinguished fellow citizen?" These things are here unknown, and humanity, as the individual, suffers. Economically the city gains. Social reformers, those prophets who see humanity as the gray matter of a theory, would make our corporations more vast, our nations still more boundless, for the sake of fiscal efficiency, for the avoidance of overlapping, in order to make our electric light more cheap or our tram services more adequate. . . . But what we gain thus in the rates we must inevitably lose in our human consciousness and in our civic interests. (*SL* 95-6)

Ford's own view of what constitutes a healthy polity is crystal clear in this passage: he opposes an abstract conception of humanity that construes it as a machine-like entity to an empathic view of humanity that sees it as a congeries of feeling individuals. Thus in mocking what he calls *la justice nouvelle*, by way of which the uncompromising utopian reformer proposes to replace humans with numbers, and historic buildings with a portable aluminium architecture, Ford pins his colours to an individualism that will in his eyes never finally be eradicated and to a view of the human race as congenitally resistant to the fantasies of the political extremist.

But if this is the case, how are we to read the earlier part of *The Soul of London*, which suggests that the metropolis is principally to be thought of in terms of its assimilative powers? Does not Ford claim that London devours the very individual on whose behalf he is waging a campaign against industrial corporations and political reformers? And if the city does devour the individual in this way, then how tolerant of racial and cultural diversity is the country's capital city in actual fact? The text appears to be ambivalent with respect to these questions, for on the one hand Ford asserts that London 'tolerates all the types of mankind . . . has palaces for the great of the earth . . . crannies for all the earth's vermin [. . . and] is wonderfully open-minded' (*SL* 12), but on the other hand he suggests that if 'in its tolerance [London] finds a place for all eccentricities of physiognomy, of costume, of cult, it does so because it crushes out and floods over the significance of those eccentricities' (*SL* 12).

This image of crushing the individual calls to mind a more extreme depiction of assimilation: Conrad's emphasis on cannibalism in *The Secret Agent*. In *The War of the Worlds* the Martians ingest the blood of their victims, using this method not only to nourish themselves but also to incorporate their victims, an apt metaphor for their intended take-over of the whole world. *The Secret Agent* offers a variation on this theme. Cannibalism is an assimilative strategy that takes a tabooed form: it is not something other to the self that is ingested but something that is *of* the self, something that is related to it by contiguity. Cannibalism entails violence against the self, at one remove. In *The Secret Agent* it is associated with a violence against fellow human beings, which threatens to destroy an equitable social order. One of the novel's anarchists describes 'economic conditions' as 'cannibalistic', insisting that England's rulers 'are nourishing their greed on the quivering flesh and the warm blood of the people' (*SA* 50), a diagnosis so terrifying to Stevie that he is put 'out of his mind' by this image of 'eating people's flesh and drinking blood' (*SA* 56).[13] In one of the novel's bitterest ironies, it is the dismembered body of Stevie himself that will provide the most decisive reprimand to the anarchists' revolutionary fantasies: the dream of a utopian social existence in which economic conditions will no longer be cannibalistic is revealed to be part of the same anthropophagy to which it is opposed. Stevie's remains resemble 'an accumulation of raw material for a cannibal feast' (*SA* 77), and Chief Inspector Heat's study of them is compared to that of 'an indigent customer bending over what may be called the by-products of a butcher's shop with a view to an inexpensive Sunday dinner' (*SA 79*).

Ford in *The Soul of London* uses the trope of cannibalism differently, deploying it to depict the city, rather than the social structure, as a gigantic maw that devours all who enter its precincts before disgorging them as remade urban subjects. *The Soul of London* has something of *The Secret Agent*'s uneasiness. For inasmuch as the city has the capacity to overcome differences, it does so, as Alan Hill notes, by swallowing 'up all comers pitilessly' and by producing a 'prevailing note of loneliness and anonymity' (*SL* xxiii). Modern London creates an anonymity that destroys respect for alterity and erodes the individualism upon which a vibrant polity depends. Tolerance, it now seems, does not signify a respect for cultural differences that permits them to flourish but rather a capacity to do away with them altogether. London is characterised by its ability to absorb all its inhabitants and then to transform them into metropolitan units:

> In its innumerable passages and crannies it swallows up Mormon and Mussulman, Benedictine and Agapemonite, Jew and Malay, Russian and Neapolitan. It assimilates and slowly digests them, converting them, with the most potent of all juices, into the singular and inevitable product that is the Londoner – that is, in fact, the Modern . . . London is the world town, not because of its vastness; it is vast because of its assimilative powers, because it destroys all race characteristics, insensibly and, as it were, anaesthetically. A Polish Jew changes into an English Hebrew and then into a Londoner without any legislative enactments, without knowing anything about it . . . London will do all this imperceptibly' (*SL* 13).

There are different ways to read this. By emphasising the capital's ability to assimilate ethnic, cultural, and religious differences Ford is challenging those who saw in immigration a threat to the integrity of the nation. He is also indicating that varied social groups may cohabit peacefully and that the violent rhetoric associated with a parochial nationalism is out of place: assimilation, he declares, occurs in its own quiet way – anaesthetically and imperceptibly. But Ford also suggests that the typical modern individual is a *hybrid* subject; thus he appears to be resisting the social imperialism of a resurgent National Toryism that associated deracination with cosmopolitanism and routinely emphasised the ties of blood and the historic attachment to soil. There is no indication in *The Soul of London* that those who have come from elsewhere constitute a *threat* to the nation-state. Ford's refusal to countenance this possibility thus pits him against a long nationalist tradition. Benjamin Disraeli, for example, had already argued in 1872 that the Liberals sought to 'substitute cosmopolitanism for national principles', and he insisted that the choice facing the British people was one between *nationalist* and *cosmopolitan* values.[14] When Arthur Boutwood restated this Tory position in his 1913 book *National Revival* he echoed Disraeli's sentiments, asserting that the 'Tory is a Britisher and an Imperialist, and is never a little Englander or a cosmopolitan', although he didn't go quite as far as the jingoistic imperialist who could claim with a straight face that 'Wherever Great Britain has set her foot, two blades of grass have grown where one grew before'.[15]

In *The Soul of London* Ford suggests that the city's assimilative power does not give rise to a healthy cosmopolitanism but manufactures standardised human subjects. The capital thus stands convicted of the same disregard for differences as corporations and reformers:

> As a city, it seems . . . not only to turn Parsees into Londoners but to make us, who are Londoners, absolutely indifferent to the Parsees, the Kaffirs, the pickpockets or the men of genius we may pass in its streets. It blunts, by its vastness, their peculiarities, and our interest it dulls. So that it seems to be a City formed, not for you and me, not for single men, but for bands of Encyclopaedists, Corporations, Societies. (*SL* 94)

We may now see that if in Ford's view London has the capacity to assimilate difference because it 'crushes out and floods over' it (*SL* 12), then this assimilative power is for him no less destructive than that of a mechanised economy, which 'crushes out the individuality' of the worker (*SL* 59).

But the metropolis of London is also shown in another way to deform enlightenment aspirations. Emphasising London's 'brooding and sinister glow' (*SL* 23) and its 'gloomy and shadowy depths' (*SL* 49), Ford sees the city in terms of a conflict between rich and poor. This conflict is mapped directly onto urban space: whereas the wealthy Londoner lives in a West End of 'large, almost clean, stone buildings, broad swept streets and a comparative glare of light' (*SL*

48), the impoverished worker is surrounded by 'rigid rows of streets all of blackened bricks' and 'windows that are square openings' covered in 'begrimed enamelled iron advertisements' (*SL* 49). Conrad's London, a 'monstrous town' that is 'the cruel devourer of the world's light' (*SA* 10), is a deterministic nightmare, whereas Ford's is a place of contrasts, but the latter's text nonetheless reveals anxieties about threats to its stability, not least because its anonymity gives social misfits room to manoeuvre. Thus in *The Secret Agent* the principle of visibility on which surveillance depends is shown to fail because urban space does away with identity. When the Assistant Commissioner descends into the 'slimy aquarium' of the city, for example, we are informed that 'the genius of the locality assimilated him. He might have been but one more of the queer foreign fish that can be seen of an evening about there flitting round the dark corners' (*SA* 124).

Aligned with Verloc and Winnie, the Assistant Commissioner is no longer distinguishable from those he is hunting. Similar anxieties may be discerned in Ford's text, in which London offers visions of 'slinking, horribly suggestive . . . figures' (*SL* 17) who hover in the shadows and who quite obviously have not been assimilated. London is, moreover, the site of a class struggle between two groups who are 'very foreign' and 'very hostile the one to the other' (*SL* 49), and Ford's awareness of this conflict between two classes permeates his text. At the same time, because all one ever gets is glimpses of the numerous little events that constitute daily life, the incidents that, as Ford remarks, 'one never sees completed' (*SL* 43), an air of mystery hangs over the inner life of the capital, which remains unreadable and unknowable. Ford makes the point with his characteristic wit, when he describes a transient scene observed from a train:

> A little further on a woman ran suddenly out of a door; she had a white apron and her sleeves were tucked up. A man followed her hastily, he had red hair, and in his hand a long stick. We moved on, and I have not the least idea whether he were going to thrash her, or whether together they were going to beat a carpet. At any rate, the evening papers reported no murder in Southwark. (*SL* 42-3)

Paranoia, Purism, Contingency

David Trotter claims that '*England and the English* is a democratic book, perhaps even a liberal book'. But he argues that Ford:

> was never a good or consistent liberal in that he could not bring himself to
> advocate or to enjoy consensus. Consensus, after all, precludes paranoid
> symmetry: the adjustment of the degree of fantasized grandeur to the degree
> of fantasized persecution. So Ford cannot wholly have believed his own
> propaganda about rule-of-thumb systems and muddling through.[16]

This line of argument forces Ford into the symmetry of Trotter's own system: if consensus thwarts the structure of paranoia, then Ford, aligned here with the paranoid sensibility, cannot properly believe in consensus. But there are numerous alternative reasons why one might be sceptical about the value of consensus. Among these one might instance two of its most obviously problematic features: firstly, consensus may mask various forms of coercion; secondly, it may disclose a lack of respect for different ways of living in the world. Ford, I would suggest, was suspicious of consensus *not* because it obviated 'paranoid symmetry' but because it could modulate into tyranny. On that topic, he was peremptory, whether expressing his support for Home Rule in Ireland or his contempt for the Liberal attitude to the working man.[17] Under the terms of the schema he imposes on several modernist writers (Hulme and Lewis among them), Trotter is obliged to interpret Ford's pre-war social scepticism as the product of paranoia; this enables him to read the post-war Ford as a man who has freed himself from earlier distortions. Whereas paranoiacs 'find themselves by eliminating muddle', in *Parade's End*, Ford valorises muddle and thus declares 'his new antipathy to system'.[18]

The problem with this is that there is nothing new about Ford's antipathy to system. In *Ancient Lights* he writes of the loss of 'the sense of a whole, the feeling of a grand design, of the co-ordination of all Nature in one great architectonic system', and he greets this as a sign of freedom and honesty.[19] *The Soul of London* on every page attests Ford's hostility to fixed structures, which he thinks lead to dominative systems, and its impressionism celebrates contingency and lack of method. Ford's stress on London's illimitability calls forth a multi-perspectival narrative mode that is well suited to his subject, and his text's cloud-like porousness, which hints at its own evanescence, has a further significance. It rebukes the monologic purism that characterises the mind-set of utopian reformers. Ford *explicitly* rejects the abstract assumptions of the theorists against whom he polemicises in *The Soul of London*, but he is also, I think, *implicitly* engaged in a dialogue with fellow writers such as Pound and Conrad.

Pound's response to Ford's *Return to Yesterday* is illuminating as well as amusing: 'Fordie,' he writes in not entirely mock exasperation, 'you AVE got a rummy job lot of "idées reçues". And [*sic*] I come back to it that you HAVE bitched about 80% of yr/ work through hanging onto a set of idées reçues'.[20] Ford's impressionism was Pound's target here, and he castigated Ford for his disregard for veridical truth, reminding the unrepentant fabulator that sometimes facts are important. But what is really at stake for Pound is that impressionism depends on an agnostic and open-minded cognitive stance, which is at odds with Pound's desire to proselytise. Impressionism was for Pound *passive* (it depended on the impact made by external events on the receptive mind) and *superficial* (it failed to penetrate the surface of social phenomena in order to expose their underlying relations). Pound was willing to concede that it had been the first significant assault on a sterile academicism, but he insisted that it had not gone far enough, precisely because he was seeking a far-reaching social and cultural transformation that Ford believed was unrealistic. In contrast to Pound's missionary zeal, his desire to *purify*, which would lead him to fuse the political with the aesthetic, Ford was a sceptic who wrote that 'We stand today, in the matter of political theories, naked to the wind and blind to the sunlight'.[21]

Pound's early work had aimed at a renovation of language and a sweeping away of moribund values.[22] Imagism and Vorticism were ushering in a new age, concentrating energies and ideas so that they could have social effects. By the 1920s, the collocation of the political and the aesthetic had become yet more potent for him. The aesthetic power of the artist was now to be supplemented by the political power of the dictator, so that for Pound, as William Chace puts it, 'an imagination disengaged from politics was a derelict agency of the mind'.[23] The significance for Pound's view of avant-gardism lay in this yoking of word to act, which discloses a commitment to praxis, but his advocacy of a fusion between ideas and action had its origins in the project of linguistic cleansing, which he thought of as the prolegomenon to social change. This purist project could not have been further removed from Ford's tolerant humaneness. Of the two writers, we might well wonder in retrospect whose job lot of *idées reçues* proved to be the rummier.

A more disastrous purism even than Pound's is at work in Conrad's *The Secret Agent*. Indeed, *contra* Trotter, we should say that if there is a paranoiac in the case, it is not Ford, but Conrad's

Professor. Whereas figures like Heat and the Assistant Commissioner adopt ironic perspectives that disclose the conventional nature of the social edifice, the perfect anarchist is a Stirnerian egoist whose monologic view of the world admits of no uncertainty and no compromise. The Professor's putative struggle for justice masks a desire for social recognition and personal self-aggrandisement, which refuses the other-directed claims of intersubjectivity, the very feature of communal life that Ford seeks to protect. *The Secret Agent*'s subtle delineation of a character sometimes mistakenly taken to be a caricature suggests that the separation of the ego-driven subject from others results in a derealization of the external world, which sanctions a cannibalistic view of them that in turn sanctions the pitiless unleashing of terrorist violence. In contrast to the Professor's monomania, Ford appeals to an empathic view of human variability and its attendant shortcomings. The Professor's desire to destroy everything derives from his fear that humanity will never countenance his cleansing program; thus he is oppressed at the 'thought of a mankind as numerous as the sands of the seashore, as indestructible, as difficult to handle' (*SA* 243), and the novel ends with him 'averting his eyes from the odious multitude of mankind' (*SA* 249).

How different from Ford's reaction:

> And beneath and amongst all those clouds – thunderclouds, the cloud of buildings, the clouds of corporations – there hurries still the great swarm of tiny men and women, each one hugging desperately his own soul, his own hopes, his own passions, his own individuality. To destroy these individualities is impossible. (*SL* 102)

The jumble and muddle of London that Ford has celebrated, and which I will shortly read as a form of literary collage, does, I think, approach an anarchism of sorts, but it is one that has nothing to do with the purism of Conrad's Professor. We might say, even as we imagine Matthew Arnold turning over in his grave, that Ford advocates a *cultural* rather than a *political* anarchism. The very terms that Arnold construed as diametric opposites, seeing in 'culture' a solution to the problem of 'anarchy', are here superimposed, giving rise to a way of thinking and writing that sees a potential for liberation in the diversity that the great nineteenth-century writer could only disparage as chaos.

Collage and Cultural Anarchism

Matthew Arnold, reacting with hostility to John Stuart Mill's validation of personal freedom, opposed reason to liberty and offered the moral agency of 'culture' as a corrective to the disorder of 'anarchy'. In this schema the two terms stand as polar opposites. But Ford's depiction of London suggests that the centralisation sought by Arnold is culturally and socially problematic because it erodes a healthy individualism. Thus the city's want of harmony symbolises for Ford a heterogeneity to be cherished rather than feared. And this valorisation of heterogeneity, I want to suggest, manifests itself most clearly in the form of *The Soul of London*, which moves from an impressionist aesthetic to a practice of collage.[24]

An early review of the book praised it for offering 'the latest and truest image of London, built up out of a series of negations, that together are more hauntingly near to a composite picture of the city than anything we have seen before'.[25] A composite picture is exactly what Ford produces, but, as in collage, he foregrounds the process of creation, the constructed nature of the artefact, and the impossibility of attaining a complete view of the object of scrutiny. Consider the telling images out of which he gradually builds up his syncretic picture. London is 'a ragoût of tit-bits' (*SL* 10) and a 'hotchpotch' (*SL* 6); it is a 'chaotic crowd . . . an apparently indissoluble muddle of grey wheel traffic' (*SL* 16); or it is the 'queerest jumble of old terraces, shadowed by old trees, grimed by the soot of generations long dead, jostled by the newest of shops dwelt in by generations as new' (*SL* 36). The effect all these images of confusion and disorder produces on the observer is, Ford avers, 'one of jumble and the incongruous', for everything is 'all mixed together, it is not possible to get any zones to "synchronise"' (*SL* 38).

What better account of collage could there be? Collage not only turned the art of juxtaposition into an aesthetic principle but also emphasised incompleteness and lack of unity over totality and seamless form. As Dennis Brown has argued in a valuable essay on Hulme's 'Cinders', implicit in the collage aesthetic is 'a denial of overall order, an endorsement of the connoisseurship of relative chaos'.[26] Ford, I am arguing, presents the anarchy of the metropolis not only as the guarantor of social heterogeneity but also as the source of just such an aesthetic. This aesthetic, like impressionism, takes the unrelated fragments of everyday life and, by juxtaposing them, constructs an art that embodies the indeterminacy of the modern age.[27]

James Clifford's account of an 'ethnographic surrealist practice' indebted to the lessons of collage is pertinent in this context; the defamiliarizing strategies by which it engages in 'a permanent ironic play of similarity and difference, the familiar and the strange, the here and the elsewhere' are for him 'characteristic of global modernity'.[28] Ford puts it more simply. 'London', he remarks, 'is a thing of these "bits"' (*SL* 23).

David Weir has made the compelling argument 'that anarchism succeeded culturally where it failed politically', most notably in the field of Modernism. Weir makes the generally accepted point that 'Modernist culture . . . is characterized by nothing so much as a tendency toward fragmentation and autonomy', but he makes the further claim that the respect for cultural diversity that Modernism has promoted is to be distinguished from pluralism on the grounds that 'the various cultural languages spoken today are not inflected by a universal grammar'.[29] Political anarchism virtually disappeared after the First World War, as Weir rightly notes, but he suggests that it survived as an active force in the cultural domain. How far-fetched is it to regard Ford in this light?

Ford's own history, he repeatedly emphasised, positioned him as a member of what he called 'the governing classes of the artistic and literary worlds' (*RY* 16) and as an inheritor of Bohemian tendencies that existed outside bourgeois value systems. When he writes of his father's love of Schopenhauer and Wagner, he links these twin passions to the public fear of atheism, sexual immorality, socialism, and 'the throwing of bombs' (*MI* 63). His grandfather Madox Brown he describes as 'a hard-swearing, old-fashioned Tory' but notes that 'his reasoning . . . and circumstances made him a revolutionary of the romantic type' to such a degree that he might have 'called himself an Anarchist, and have damned your eyes if you had faintly doubted this obviously extravagant assertion' (*MI* 32). Ford's own political predilections were of course remarkably similar: his oft-repeated advocacy of a 'Toryism' with roots in the seventeenth century went hand in hand with 'revolutionary' sentiments that were certainly romantic. He was not unaware of this. Reminiscing about his early interactions with former Communards, he wrote: 'Thus I early developed a hatred for tyrants and a love for lost causes and exiles that still, I hope, distinguish me. Poland, Alsace-Lorraine, Ireland and even the Jews exiled from their own country – those were the names of romance of my childhood. They so remain for me' (*MI* 46-7).

Return to Yesterday reverts again and again to the social conditions that fostered Anarchist thought, and although, as one would expect of Ford, there is much humour in his portrait of this *milieu*, he gives us a serious account of the connection between extreme poverty and revolutionary politics. After he had earnestly lectured an aristocratic young lady 'about the conditions of the poor', her disconcerted mother took him aside in order to admonish him: 'Fordie, you are a dear boy. Sir George and I like you very much. But I must ask you not to talk to dear Beatrice . . . about Things!' (*RY* 63). The anecdote mocks ruling class blindness to profound social inequalities, a point that Ford underscores when he goes on to note that even *Punch* was 'almost suppressed' when it dared to refer to 'Things' (*RY* 63). For Ford, the 'natural corollary of these pressures was . . . Anarchism, Fabianism, dynamitings, Nihilism' (*RY* 63-4).

There is, of course, a world of difference between propaganda of the deed and the pursuit of artistic excellence. But the writer may be aligned with the anarchist in that both are unassimilable to the social order; both are outsiders, aliens, foreigners. Thus Ford insisted in his memoir of Conrad that 'in any popular assembly, anywhere, the artist must needs feel a foreigner and lonely', and he emphasised his own distance from the country in which he had been born, frequently choosing to use the telling word 'alien' when he did so.[30] This sense of his own alienation was a marked feature of Ford's cultural predicament, part of his lifelong struggle against English parochialism and philistinism; his frustration, he explained, referred not to issues of politics and governance but rather to the realm of art and culture, for it was, he wrote, 'only from the aesthetic and intellectual side of English life that [he] was growing daily more alien' (*RY* 255).

The 'Coda' to *Return to Yesterday* is revealing in this context because Ford ends this book of reminiscences on the eve of the First World War, just at the point where the 'fourfold tradition' with which he opened it (Conrad, Crane, Hudson, and James) is about to be smashed by the youthful iconoclasm of Marinetti's Futurists and Lewis's Vorticists as well as by the explosion of the war itself. The meandering narrative of *Return to Yesterday* thus completes a circle and establishes a cyclical view of literary change, for the pattern by which Victorian literature had been overthrown is now repeated. In both cases, moreover, the revolutionaries are all interlopers and aliens. Ford cites Wells's sense that he had at the turn of the century felt besieged by 'a ring of foreign conspirators plotting against British letters' (*RY* 21) with relish, going on to claim that without this 'foreign penetration' English literature would have been 'empty' and 'lacking a nucleus' (*RY* 22); but Ford's *tour-de-force* description of his super-session at the hands of an aggressively expostulating 'D. Z.' (recognizable to those familiar with the literary history of the period as Wyndham Lewis) suggests that he is no less delighted at the thought of his own demise, because once again English literature is going to be revivified by extraneous influences. He not only makes the link between these two cultural moments explicit but also relates them to his thesis about metropolitan assimilation: 'It was in a sense another foreign invasion, like the one with which this book opens. There was hardly a born Londoner in it. D. Z., Ezra, H. D. the beautiful poetess, Epstein, Fletcher, Robert Frost, Eliot were all Transatlantically born from the point of view of London. Henri Gaudier was a Marsellaise. They had all become Londoners because London was unrivalled in its powers of assimilation' (*RY* 312).

In this 'Coda' the botched assault on Greenwich Observatory in *The Secret Agent* receives an aesthetic rebuke. Ford contrasts this simplistic act of violence with what he sees as the more progressive assault mounted by foreign-led literary avant-gardes such as Futurism and Vorticism. *Return to Yesterday* thus ends with a different kind of blast, a literary explosion that is brought about by *cultural*, not *political*, anarchists. Ford contrasts the failure of physical-force anarchists to make a significant impact on the social order with the more potent intervention of those writers and artists who were trying to transform society by way of culture. Unlike Pound, Ford did not seek to yoke the aesthetic to the political; and unlike Conrad's Professor, he did not seek to remake society from a year zero. He upheld the civilising value of humane letters, never deviating from the view that the arts should be cosmopolitan and international. His use of collage functions, as Dennis Brown believes Hulme's also does, as 'the opposite of all totalitarianisms'.[31] In the early 1900s Ford felt himself to be an alien among aliens, a foreigner within a country besieged by the voices of a witless nationalism: his complex, many-sided portrayal of London shows just how committed he was to social diversity, which he saw as the sign of a beneficent cultural anarchy.

NOTES

1 Jack London, *The People of the Abyss* (1903), London: Pluto, 1998 – henceforth *PA;* p. 37.

2 All citations from *The Soul of London: A Survey of a Modern City* refer to Alan G. Hill's edition, London: Dent, 1995 – henceforth *SL.*

3 Bernard Gainer, *The Alien Invasion: The Origins of the Aliens Act of 1905*, London: Heinemann Educational, 1972, pp. 2, 3.

4 Jonathan Schneer, *London 1900: The Imperial Metropolis*, London: Yale University Press, 1999, p. 60.

5 Gainer, pp. 101, 102. For more on this point, see William J. Fishman, *East End Jewish Radicals, 1875-1914*, London: Duckworth, 1975, p. 60.

6 C. F. G. Masterman, *From the Abyss: Of its Inhabitants by One of Them* (1902), New York and London: Garland, 1980. Margaret Harkness [written under the pseudonym 'John Law'], *In Darkest London* (1889), Cambridge: Black Apollo, 2003.

7 James Grant, *The Great Metropolis,* New York and London: Garland, 1985, pp. 308-9.

8 Masterman, *From the Abyss*, p. 4.

9 H. G. Wells, *The War of the Worlds*, London: J. M. Dent, 1998 – henceforth *WW*; pp. 19, 20.

10 Bram Stoker, *Dracula*, ed., Maurice Hindle, Harmondsworth: Penguin, 1993 – henceforth *D*; p. 95.

11 Quoted in Fishman, *op. cit.,* pp. 70 and 71.

12 Joseph Conrad, *The Collected Letters of Joseph Conrad*, Vol. 3: 1903-1907, ed. Frederick R. Karl and Laurence Davies, Cambridge: Cambridge University Press, 1988, p. 488.

13 Joseph Conrad, *The Secret Agent*, Harmondsworth: Penguin, 1975 – henceforth *SA*; pp. 50, 56.

14 Benjamin Disraeli, *Selected Speeches of the Late Right Honourable the Earl of Beaconsfield*, ed. T. E. Kebbel, London: Longmans, Green, and Co, 1882, pp. 524, 534.

15 Arthur Boutwood, *National Revival: A Re-Statement of Tory Principles*, London: Herbert Jenkins, 1913, p. viii; Ernest C. Maccatta, quoted in Schneer, *op. cit.,* p. 88.

16 David Trotter, *Paranoid Modernism: Literary Experiment, Psychosis, and the Professionalization of English Society*, Oxford: Oxford University Press, 2001, p. 200.

17 See Ford Madox Ford, *Memories and Impressions*, ed., Michael Killigrew, Harmondsworth: Penguin, 1979 – henceforth *MI*; pp. 223; Ford Madox Ford, *Return to Yesterday*, ed., Bill Hutchings, Manchester: Carcanet, 1999 – henceforth *RY*; p. 64.

18 Trotter, *op. cit.*, pp. 333, 336.

19 Ford Madox Hueffer, *Ancient Lights and Certain New Reflections: Being the Memories of a Young Man*, London: Chapman and Hall, 1911, pp. 62, 65.

20 Brita Lindberg-Seyersted, ed., *Pound/Ford: The Story of a Literary Friendship*, London: Faber, 1982, p. 100.

21 Ford Madox Hueffer, *Henry James: A Critical Study*, London: Martin Secker, 1913, pp. 47, 120.

22 See, for example, Ezra Pound, *Selected Prose, 1909-1965*, ed., William Cookson, London: Faber and Faber, 1978, p. 291.

23 William M. Chace, *The Political Identities of Ezra Pound and T. S. Eliot*, Stanford, California: Stanford University Press, 1973, p. 104.

24 I am indebted to Helen Carr for suggesting this line of approach to *The Soul of London* in a talk she gave at the University of Birmingham on 'Modernist Migrants'. For more on the relation between collage and cultural heterogeneity, see Helen Carr, 'Imagism and Empire', *Modernism and Empire*, ed. Howard Booth and Nigel Rigby, Manchester: Manchester University Press, 2000, pp. 64-92.

25 Quoted in Saunders, *Ford Madox Ford: A Dual Life*, Oxford: Oxford University Press, 1996, Vol. 1, p. 195.

26 Dennis Brown, 'T. E. Hulme's "Cinders": Towards a Collage Aesthetic', *The Great London Vortex: Modernist Art and Literature*, ed. Paul Edwards, Bath: Sulis, 2003, pp, 96-102, p. 98.

27 To put it like this is not to suggest that Ford is blind to the class inequalities that are also embedded in the urban environment, as his detailed descriptions of its districts and its architecture make perfectly clear. See, for example, *SL* 62, 73, 92.

28 James Clifford, *The Predicament of Culture: Twentieth-Century Ethnography, Literature, and Art*, Cambridge, Massachusetts: Harvard University Press, 1996, p. 146.

29 David Weir, *Anarchy and Culture: The Aesthetic Politics of Modernism*, Amherst: University of Massachusetts Press, 1997, pp. 5, 6.

30 Ford Madox Ford, *Joseph Conrad: A Personal Remembrance*, London, Duckworth, 1924, p. 240. Ford also claimed that Conrad chose the title of *The English Review* because he 'felt a certain sardonic pleasure in the choosing so national a name for a periodical that promised to be singularly international in tone, that was started mainly in his not very English interest and conducted by myself who was growing every day more and more alien to the normal English trend of thought, at any rate in matters of literary technique' (*RY* 284).

31 Brown, 'T. E. Hulme's "Cinders"', p. 101. Later in his life, of course, Ford's internationalism was more overt. It went hand in hand with an ecologically responsible commitment to small-scale agricultural production: 'I live about the world with no politics at all except the belief – which I share with Lenin – that the only thing that can save the world is the abolition of all national feelings and the prevailing of the Small Producer – and the Latin Tradition of clear-sightedness as to what one means oneself'. Ford Madox Ford, *Letters of Ford Madox Ford*, ed. Richard M. Ludwig, Princeton, New Jersey: Princeton University Press, 1965, p. 238.

THE IMPRESSIONISTIC 'RENDERING' OF ENGLISHNESS IN FORD'S *FIFTH QUEEN* TRILOGY

Karen McDermott

Ford Madox Ford's three sequential novels on Katharine Howard were written at a time when he was also preoccupied with another trilogy – eventually published together as *England and the English*.[1] The publication dates of this sequence were *The Soul of London* (1905); *The Heart of the Country* (1906); *The Spirit of the People* (1907): that of the Katharine trilogy, *The Fifth Queen* (1906); *Privy Seal* (1907); *The Fifth Queen Crowned* (1908).[2] It is not surprising, then, that with this overlapping of dates comes a similarity of theme between the two projects. Both are centrally concerned with Englishness. But whereas *England and the English* is concerned with changes and continuities in the England of the turn of the twentieth century, *The Fifth Queen* invokes a Tudor England as key phase in the making of a specifically English modernity – the historical point when Henry VIII breaks ties with European Catholicism and pioneers a Protestant nationalism.[3] And just as *The Soul of London* deploys the techniques of Impressionism, which he had been discussing with Joseph Conrad since 1898,[4] so *The Fifth Queen* trilogy becomes a showpiece of impressionistic 'rendering', creating a powerful evocation of Tudor England.

In this, as has often been noted, Ford uses the relative paucity of 'facts' about Katharine's personality, in particular, to create his own idealised portrait. This was, in fact, his conscious, and theorised, choice of procedure. As he put it in his later book of reminiscences *Ancient Lights*:

> This book, in short, is full of inaccuracies as to facts, but its accuracy as to impressions is absolute [. . . .] I don't really deal in facts [. . . .] I try to give you what I see to be the spirit of an age, of a town, of a movement. (*AL* xv)

Ford originally researched the Tudor period intending to write a biography of Henry VIII but was persuaded to put his research to a fictional use instead,[5] and the result was his remarkable novelistic sequence. It may be that part of the attraction was that Henry, like Ford himself, was not temperamentally monogamous and both found themselves within historical changes they found it hard to adjust to. Both too were torn between the contrasting beliefs and cultures of Catholicism and Protestantism. Be that as it may, he adapts the history he has read to create his own mythic Tudor Englishness, employing a variety of impressionistic devices within the Walter Scott legacy of somewhat-counterfactual[6] fiction.

In this, he made some bold imaginative decisions. Against the little evidence available ('barely literate' or 'not illiterate'),[7] he created a Katharine fluent in literary Latin and well-versed in classical texts. He wanted to characterise his heroine as poised, confident and erudite – the sort of woman who might, in reality, have ordered her own execution block.[8] In this way he is able to construct an educated Catholic foil to Thomas Cromwell's pragmatic English Protestantism. He also includes references to such historical figures as Lady Salisbury and Doctor Barnes to provide historical credibility and recruits the actual Nicholas Udall ('Udal' in his version) for the same reason. The historical Udall was, of course, one-time Provost of Eton college and author of the early English play *Ralph Roister Doister*,[9] and Ford presents Katharine's encouragement of 'good learning among women' (*FQC* 464) in terms borrowed from Udall's recorded opinion of Katherine Parr.[10] If Ford is cavalier with the 'factuality' of recorded gossip, he certainly creates a striking characterisation, perhaps even (in Paul Ricoeur's words) bringing 'features to light that were concealed'.[11] Like Shakespeare in, say, *Richard III*, *Henry V* or *King Lear*, he exploits the limited historical resources to create his own fiction – in this case of a queen who is a match for the strong English king.

In such instances, Ford might be said to anticipate the much later 'post-modern' mistrust of truth-as-documentation, of the reliability of memory and, indeed, the ideal of objectivity. For instance, he alters the numbers of Cicely Elliott's dead family members and suitors each time she tells the story – ranging from five to seven, and then encompassing the number of her whole family, including her mother and sister (*FQ* 117, *FQ* 215, *PS* 279, *PS* 284). The voices of historical witnesses may themselves manifest impressionism. In the same way that in *Parade's End*, inconsistencies as to Christopher Tietjens's siblings indicate psychological pressure,[12] Cicely's dramatised muddles may seem occasioned by the shock of Henrician religious and political changes. At the same time, Ford wishes to subvert the Pre-Raphaelite idealisation of courtly love by contrasting the 'romance' of Katharine and Henry with the depiction of Cicely and Rochford, the broken down knight, whose lance falls from his hand. This ironisation of chivalric myth is reinforced by the knight's mantra of repetition-compulsion: 'I am Rochford of Bosworth Hedge' (e.g. *FQ* 215 and *PS* 281). History is composed of the confused actions and perceptions of infirm historical actors – a relativistic 'rendering' rather than a de-monstration of fact and cause-and-effect.

Such impressionistic representation is also conveyed through the select use of archaic diction, which embeds nationality within a cultural development manifesting its own hybrid origins. As in Shake-speare's plays, Ford's language exemplifies and exercises the ongoing opportunism of English as spoken and written idiom. There is, for instance, his deliberate usage of historically 'exotic' terms: 'quean' (saucy girl); 'redd up' (to tidy); 'gradely' (fine); 'cate' (delicacy); 'videlicet' (to wit); 'springald' (young man); 'cresset' (raised lamp). At the same time, the characters exchange Latin (and even Greek) quotations, and employ idioms such as 'Body of God', 'By cock!' or 'Bones of St Nairn!' Even syntax may, at times, be altered to give an archaic flavour – 'She bent above a sea coal fire on the hearth where boiled, hung from a hook, a great pot' (*PS* 355). Such linguistic de-familiarisation helps create an impression of Tudor authenticity which mere Edwardian prose could not.

In such ways the reader becomes an impressionistic participant in the unfolding drama. It permits a kind of historical 'virtual reality' which is, arguably, the best way to present a past that is, in fact, another country. Another device, which Ford uses throughout, is to convey a character's inner reactions in terms of dramatic friezes rather than interpretive commentary. For example, we experience Katharine's ultimate subjection to Henry's power through the rendering of appearance: '[h]er head fell back, her eyes closed, so that she seemed to be dead and her listless hands were open in her skirts' (*PS* 413). The open hands say it all. Similarly, when Mary's hands fall 'powerless to her sides,' the reader feels (because shown) her reaction, even without her cry '"Merciful God! … Have I such a father?"' (*FQC* 582). Ford, as author/narrator, remains largely outside the scene, in Flaubertian manner; what he supplies are signifying suggestions which enable the reader to be sensually and hermeneutically engaged with the text. We are not so much told as cajoled – as, for instance, when we are shown Cromwell standing, authoritatively, on his barge (*FQ* 24).

An important, and often noticed, aspect of Ford's fictional technique is, also, his use of pictorial suggestivity. Here he employs allusions to Hans Holbein's work, most particularly, to make it portray Henry's England as the arena for a socio-political paradigm-shift – from the Mediaeval world-picture of Pre-Raphaelite painting to the newer world of Machiavellian politics and sinister, interiorised diplomacy. In place of heraldic decoration comes the domestic, upper-class portraiture of power-brokers. Holbein's art, in fact, is almost automatically linked to the era of Henrician reform. As Ford writes, 'the power of Holbein' is that he constitutes 'a mass, or a force; he calls up a mood' (*Holbein* 81). That 'mood' corresponds to the educated reader's idea of the Tudor court – a kind of nationalised island-power presided over by a splendidly-robed, full-bearded, stolid mountain of a man. However, Ford's first 'portrait' of Henry uses Holbein's pictorial method to undermine the idealisation of hearty virility in the best-known works:

> His great brow was furrowed, his enormous bulk of scarlet, with the great double dog-rose embroidered across the broad chest, limped a little over his right knee and the foot dragged. His eyes were bloodshot and heavy, his head hung forward as though he were about to charge the world with his forehead. From time to time his eyebrows lifted painfully, and he swallowed with an effort as if he were choking. (*FQ* 39)

This impression shows the man within the king, highlighting his physical and emotional suffering as well as his ruthless drive to command. It concentrates on Henry's red-clothed bulk and psychic intensity. The vivid red, symbolic of the period's blood-shedding, subsequently becomes an heraldic icon in the Tudor roses decorating so many church roofs.

Such pictorial rendering continues in Henry's proximity to Rochford's misfortune, which, in fact, mirrors Henry's own increasing senility:

> The old knight came into view, motioning with his lance to invisible horsemen …
> Suddenly Cicely Elliott cried out:
> "Why, the old boy hath dropped his lance! …" … The old man shook his iron fist at the sky, and his face was full of rage and shame in the watery

sunlight that penetrated into his open helmet. . . . the knight sat, his head
hanging on his chest, like one mortally stricken riding from a battlefield. (*FQ*
160)

The old knight and the 'invisible horsemen' symbolise the Mediaeval
world, and the dropped lance indicates its ending, as well as senile
impotence. Thus whereas the interest Ford had had since boyhood in
pre-Tudor history (*SP* 272) focused on feudal fighting for land and
honour, in *The Fifth Queen* trilogy he is interested in an emergent
Englishness, as the nation jostles for global position. Ford underlines
this change with Henry's increasing inability to take part himself in
chivalric jousting. Rochford's fist shaken at the sky, and therefore at
God, is also a clear indication that the old order is changing, and
knighthood ('to succour the Church of God'; *PS* 283) is giving way to
bureaucratic manoeuvre. The world portrayed by the Pre-Raphaelites
is being superseded by Holbein's realm of interiorised power through
authoritarian delegation. The stricken knight contrasts strongly with
Sir John Everett Millais's 'Sir Isumbras at the Ford'. Millais's knight,
also old, is still able to carry the children safely through that water,
whereas Ford's 'Fall of Rochford' has 'watery sunlight' penetrate the
incompetent knight's armour. Mediaevalism is over.

However, Ford's use of pictorialism is not confined to individualised portraiture and focus. His construction of suggestive 'tableaux' of outdoor, inter-active dramas is equally effective in rendering
an Englishness in turbulent times. And here he draws on a wide range
of iconography, from, say, Uccello to Breughel:

> All in among the winter trees the City men in their white and silver were
> fighting with the Lutherans in their grey frieze. The citizens' hearts were
> enraged . . . .
>
> Men struck out at all and sundry. A woman, covered to the face in a fur
> hood and riding a grey mule, was hit on the arm . . . . A man in green at the
> mule's head . . . sprang like a wild cat . . . .
>
> Hands were already pulling the woman from her saddle, but the guards
> held their pikes transversely against the faces of the nearest, crushing in noses
> and sending sudden streaks of blood from jaws. . . .
>
> The mob raged round them . . . . The soldiers put down the points of their
> pikes and cleared more ground. Men lay wallowing there when they retreated.
> . . .
>
> The red jerkins of the King's own guards came in a heavy mass round the
> end of the wall amid shrieks and curses. Their pike-staves rose rhythmically
> and fell with dull thuds; with their clumsy gloved hands they caught at
> throats, and they threw dazed men and women into the space that they had
> cleared before the wall. (*FQ* 36-38)

This is a 'rendering' of historical Englishness in terms of mob turb-
ulence, clash and authoritarian discipline which has characterised
street protest ever since. Ford stresses primary colours, metonymic details and contrastive group dramas to make such scenes as vivid and
symbolically resonant as possible. In contrast to the somewhat idealised and generalising tendency of *The Spirit of the People*, Englishness is here portrayed as dynamic and embodied challenge and
response.

One aspect of Ford's project is, in fact, to involve, even startle,
the reader and keep response keenly awake. From the beginning, he
builds up an ongoing relationship with readers' expectations, acting as
a kind of impresario to the ongoing historical drama. He frequently
uses surprise. For instance, in *The Fifth Queen*, he teases us by setting
up expectation of a noble wedding, but *Privy Seal* begins with the
substitute comic bathos of the marriage of Nicholas Udal (the scrawny
scholar) and the 'widow' (who is of 'a comfortable ... girth'; *PS* 243).
The Widow is a political animal, like Henry: she knows that a
marriage performed by a friar, far from being a meaningless ritual as
the naïve Udal believes, will be valid if Catholicism is reinstated. A
further irony is that, despite this, Udal is lazily contented in his
marriage, 'with a bellyful of carp' (*PS* 247), whereas Henry is left
disappointed and bitter. Such ironic 'rendering' gives the impression
of an England itself threaded through by contrasts and reversals rather
than an arena in which there is a 'gradual growth of liberty'[13] in an
orderly fashion.

Ford stressed that 'the first business of Impressionism is to
produce an impression, and the only way in literature to produce an
impression is to awaken interest' (*CW* 47-48). One way in which he
does this is to work in terms of strong contrasts which emphasise the
important historical issues at stake in terms of the growth of modern
Englishness. Religious and political forces are here represented by
bold contrasts in personality. Katharine represents committed, Latin-
ate Catholicism: Cromwell, the modernising Protestant, is intent on
extirpating all Papal influence. Englishness is here placed at the crossroads: and the road taken will affect not only the coming 'Elizabethan
Settlement' but English attitudes to European identity afterwards,
even beyond the second world war to the present day. In Tudor times
religion was a major factor. Henry's Reformation occasioned a paradigm-shift in relation to a hierarchical Christianity centred on the

Roman pontiff and opened the way for later liberalising tendencies within Anglicanism. At the same time, despite Henry's personal ambivalences, English Christianity was stripping itself of superstitious accretions, such as Lady Rochford's conviction that her physical ailments can be automatically healed by the 'Sacred Blood of Hailes' (*FQ* 119). Seamus Duffy has recently queried the asserted popularity of the changes afoot;[14] however, their intellectual appeal to many is clear, and Printer Badge's press indicates the future direction of a slowly-emergent democracy – public dispute rather than ecclesiastical *diktat*, and the rise of a vigorous 'gutter press'. To an extent, Ford relies in the trilogy on precisely the techniques of awakening 'interest' that dominate our tabloid culture.

The King's fond ideal is 'to let his eyes rest upon a great view of this realm that was his, and to think nothing' (*FQC* 427) – the dream of contented 'green' Englishness where even class differences, such as Poins's outrage at being beaten '"by a ploughman's son from Lincolnshire!"' (*PS* 356), can be united in a single polity – as Culpepper and Hogben are united by their county inheritance. However, the nature of the changes which Henry allows Cromwell to implement makes for the opposite of such a peaceful vision. Henry is possessed by an impossible vision of a 'blessed Utopia of the lost islands' (*FQ* 163) and, in Protestant terms at least, his ecclesiastical revolution remains incomplete, and he himself stranded indecisively between the old and new worlds. Katharine, by contrast, is preoccupied with an England as lost 'Golden Age' (*PS* 405) and her stoical Romanism is wholly at odds with the emergent Englishness, where London is pitted against country ways, the Bible against priest-craft, public debate (and riots) against absolutism and the living English tongue against dead classical literature. The impression that Ford creates of a land in exciting development is much like his vision of contemporary modernity in *The Soul of London* – a collage and metamorphosis.[15]

Such a model of Englishness-in-the-making is subtly reinforced by the trilogy's Shakespearean allusions. Shakespeare's history plays, in particular, represent an authoritative Englishness as battle-pageant and ongoing dialogical struggle, anchored in varieties of national character. There are some obvious minor references, such as the use of the name 'Hal' or Henry's habit (like Henry V) of 'wandering about among his faithful lieges unbeknown' (*FQC* 474), or the similarity of the Poins-Culpepper-Hogben comic triangle to that of

Dogberry, Verges and the Watch in *Much Ado About Nothing*. But the more generalised similarities are impressionistically more telling. Henry's character and role is a kind of colourful amalgam of the problem-beset monarchs in virtually all the history plays, and Katharine an extended study of such plays' harried and bereaved queens (as in *Richard II*). The atmosphere of court intrigue, the graphic contrast between 'high' and 'low' characters and customs and the sense of a world caught between traditional and new moralities and mores is reminiscent of the world of *Hamlet*. The blend of blood-soaked chivalry and coarse farce (e.g. at Greenwich where the 'beef-bones lay on the road before the door, and . . . the widow, black, begrimed and very drunk, lay inverted on the clay of the floor . . . too fuddled to do more than wave her legs'; *PS* 363) is typical of Elizabethan theatre in general, and of Shakespeare's mixed-mode work in particular. And, altogether, the Tudor world of town and court life is filtered through a 'hybrid' Shakespearean lens where 'all human life' is experienced as theatricality-in-action. Ford is astute here. For the Shakespearean 'touch' guarantees an aura of Englishness to modern readers – and, in this sense, Ford's text is, at times, highly intertextual. In *The Spirit of the People*, Ford characterises the English as knowledgeable about poetry, with a mind 'compact of quotations' (*SP* 242).

However, as might be expected from a writer who grew up among painters, Ford's impressionism remains predominantly visual. Irrespective of particular artistic styles (as compared above), he frequently uses colour, in particular, to create vividness and make representational scenes symbolically significant. Besides his emphasis on Cicely's black dress, for example, there is considerable use of this colour (contrasted with whiteness) throughout the novels. Katharine chides Henry for dressing himself and Edward in black (*PS* 335), and Cicely's general magpie appearance help convey a world of stark opposition (e.g. Protestant versus Catholic). Throckmorton laments that Katharine's eyes '"see the black and the white of a man. The grey they miss"' (*FQ* 173). In fact, the grey also has a symbolic resonance – when, for instance, Cicely and Rochford watch the Queen in the falling dusk and seem to withdraw themselves from her world, becoming merely spectators (*FQ* 213). Arguably, grey is, as it were, the colour of the future in terms of eventual Anglican compromise between purist Catholicism and Calvinist Protestantism. Throughout the sequence, colour-suggestion – whether black, red, white, green or grey – constitutes a powerful mode of 'rendering' aspects of the changing English world.

There is also a frequent 'filmic' quality to Ford's impressionism – appropriate to the era of writing, when cinematic 'vocabulary' was being pioneered. The following passage, for instance, presents a montage of simultaneous scenes (later replicated in Joyce's Vice-Regal procession through Dublin in *Ulysses* or Woolf's use of the backfiring car and sign-writing aeroplane in *Mrs Dalloway*):

> It was noon of that day when Katharine Howard set out again from Richmond . . . and at noon of that day Throckmorton's barge shot dangerously beneath London Bridge, hastening to Hampton Court. At noon Thomas Culpepper passed over London Bridge . . . at noon, too, or five minutes later, the young Poins galloped furiously past the end of the bridge and did not cross over . . . . And at noon or thereabouts the King, dressed in green as a husbandman, sat on a log to await a gun-fire, in the forest . . . . (*PS* 372)

This passage provides a double *progression d'effet*.[16] It conveys a sense of speed and urgency via the images of Throckmorton and Poins, and yet this is contained within and contrasted by the slower-moving actions of Katharine and Henry. Elsewhere, Ford anticipates film-Gothic as Throckmorton's eyes watch Poins (*PS* 313) and the shadow of the King keeping 'hands from throats in the palace' (*FQ* 34) foreshadows techniques in German Expressionistic cinema. There are also, oddly (deliberate?) mistakes in 'continuity' – Henry rising from his stool and then remaining on it (*FQ* 226-7), or Udal dropping his cap and book twice over (*FQC* 440, 443). And there is also the instance where Lascelles no longer knows Culpepper, and Throckmorton seems not to recognise Lascelles, despite all three having been in the same room together (*PS* 396, *FQC* 510, 517).

Ford makes use of 'flashback' (which he called the 'time-shift') too.[17] For instance, on pages 185-6 of *The Fifth Queen*, Poins tells Margot that Katharine has been arrested by Cromwell and he, himself, has just escaped. Then from page 207 onwards, we are taken back to the time of Poins's capture, and then from page 213, we are shown what happened just before Katharine is supposedly taken. In the middle of this, from page 186, Ford creates even more suspense with further flashbacks, this time concerning the general movement of the Court and an intense discussion on English politics and espionage, which moves on to the trivial details of how Katharine loves a certain sweet cake. The effect of such scenes is to create, in the reader, a sense of surprise and shock which eventually gives way to relief (*CW* 48).

Ford wrote that 'one is an Impressionist because one tries to produce an illusion of reality – or rather the business of Impressionism is to produce that illusion' (*CW* 43). This may be produced by bold friezes but also by small and subtle touches. For example, when Cromwell brings 'one white soft hand from behind his back to play with the furs upon his chest' (*PS* 296), while listening to Katharine, his involuntary gesture betrays the fact that he has just reassessed his opinion of her. Other details of this kind are more theatrical – as when Throckmorton 'scratched with his finger nail a tiny speck of mud from his shoe-point, balancing himself back against the chimney piece and crossing his red legs above the knees' (*PS* 345). This is a small incident, but, coming where it does towards the end of *Privy Seal*, it greatly enhances *progression d'effet* by revealing his developing intimacy with Katharine. His casual attitude in her presence is a tacit indication that he feels comfortable, and that there now exists between them an ease that was previously not possible.

The intensity that *progression d'effet* can create is evident in *The Fifth Queen Crowned*. Closely linked, mainly interior scenes – in the basement of Pontefract Castle, the Lady Mary's room, Hampton Court – lead to Katharine's denunciation of Henry, and so to her death. The first book had introduced her as an idealist; the second set up the marriage, leading to the ironic 'romance' of the last. Here is revealed the impossible situation that Katharine's ideals have placed her in. She cannot reconcile them with her romantic love for Henry: hence the need for her tragic sacrifice to ensure the new English future. A sense of diffused claustrophobia – room after castle room – becomes exacerbated by the diffused net of lies being woven around her. The impressionistically-constructed atmosphere of confining walls, heavy tapestries, secret panels, echoing corridors and dire dungeons beneath state rooms gives expression to a dangerous new world where castles no longer harbour queens and ladies, as knights ride out to repulse threatening enemies, but have evolved into grandiose stately houses where intrigue and sudden violence make women as much at risk as their erstwhile defenders.

However, even in the third novel of the sequence, Ford continues to create (deceptively?) idyllic scenarios:

> [T]he grass . . . had been scythed, and nearly the whole space was covered with many carpets of blue and red and other very bright colours. . . . there was a great pavilion of black cloth, embroidered very closely with gold and held up by ropes of red and white. Though forty people could sit in it round the table, it appeared very small, the walls of the castle towered up so high. They towered up so high, so square, and so straight that from the terrace below you could hardly hear the flutter of the huge banner of St George, all red and white against the blue sky, though sometimes in a gust it cracked like a huge whip, and its shadow, where it fell upon the terrace, was sufficient to cover four men.
>
> To take away from the grimness of the flat walls many little banners had been suspended . . . . These were all painted green . . . being the emblem of Hope. (*FQC 427*)

As elsewhere, the 'rendering' builds up a vivid and evocative overall impression – scythed grass and grim walls, gold, blue sky and shadow, bright-coloured carpets and fluttering heraldic banners. In one sense, the scene exists purely for itself – a 'Tudor' set piece – but the inherent symbolism, especially in terms of colour-coding (red and white – Lancaster and York) are open to varieties of interpretation by the reader. In this way, impressionism may, in fact, tease its readership – enforcing involvement, since the final meaning of the scenarios will be in terms of the trilogy as a whole. In *Joseph Conrad: A Personal Remembrance*, Ford records Conrad's observation that English words are 'instruments for exciting blurred emotions' (*JC* 214). Whether generally true or not, Ford's style can certainly have that affect. Tudor Englishness, here, is a matter of interpretation: what Ford gives us is a dramatic evocation, inciting readers to feel empathetically connected to their ancestors in their own way, in terms of both tragedy and idyll.

Overall, as in the trilogy *England and the English*, Ford creates in *The Fifth Queen* sequence an impression of Englishness in change. But it remains a 'rendering' rather than accurate chronicle. It is significant that (as in classical Greek drama) key elements – most particularly the execution of Katharine at the end – occur 'offstage'. Thus while an ongoing plot is important from book to book, the connections between events are not the main point. Like his friend and one-time collaborator Conrad, Ford focused rather on perception and sensation ('to make you hear, to make you feel ... before all, to make you *see*').[18] The techniques of 'rendering' considered here are all attempts to represent Englishness in these terms. As Ford himself wrote in his 'Appendix' to *England and the English*: '[t]his author's treatment of historic matters must ... be "presentations"' (*SP* 335). In short, what characterises the trilogy's version of Tudor history is the felt sense of a finally indefinable entity presented in terms of vigorous, bustling, poignant and picturesque scenes. In his idealising study of the English, Ford believed that, whatever the historical situation, the people have a genius for reconciling differences and living together. The English, he writes, are 'humane beyond belief' (*SP* 237): hence this nation has 'shown to all the world how great and teeming populations may inhabit a small island with a minimum of discomfort, a minimum of friction' (*SP* 247). It is Katharine's misfortune that her absolute idealism is at odds with this and she becomes, rather paradoxically, the scapegoat for this vision of an increasingly tolerant Englishness. In *The Fifth Queen* sequence, the atmosphere of intrigue and repressed anarchy makes us feel more the vigour and political cunning of Englishness than its beneficent inclusiveness. However, Ford is evoking an emergent nationality at a key moment of historical development. This is what gives the trilogy its novelistic intensity and power. It is a triumph of Impressionism as a way of engaging with national identity. And the suppression of Katharine's scene of execution ensures that possibilities remain open for a more specifically English future – one where tragedy is comparatively marginal.

NOTES

1   Ford, *England and the English,* ed. Sara Haslam, Manchester: Carcanet Press Limited, 2003 comprising *The Soul of London (SL); The Heart of the Country (HC)* and *The Spirit of the People (SP).*
2   Ford, *The Fifth Queen;* London: Penguin Books Ltd, 1999 comprising: *The Fifth Queen: And How She Came to Court* (1906 – *FQ); Privy Seal* (1907 – *PS)* and *The Fifth Queen Crowned* (1908 – *FQC).*
3   Arthur Mizener quotes from Ford writing in his original synopsis that Henry 'represents the modern world being born out of the medieval': *The Saddest Story: A Biography of Ford Madox Ford,* London, The Bodley Head, 1972, p. 470.
4   Ford, *Joseph Conrad: A Personal Remembrance,* London: Duckworth, 1924 – henceforth *JC*; pp. 167-215.
5   Ford, *Return to Yesterday,* Manchester: Carcanet Press Limited, 1999 – henceforth *RY;* p. 133.
6   John Sutherland, *Victorian Fiction – Writers, Publishers, Readers,* Basingstoke: Macmillan Press Ltd, 1995, p. 1.

7   Alison Weir, *The Six Wives of Henry VIII,* London: Pimlico, 1992, p. 424. Antonia Fraser, *The Six Wives of Henry VIII,* London: George Weidenfeld and Nicolson Ltd, 1992, p. 317.

8   Weir, p. 607.

9   Fictionalised here as the play Udal writes in the 'vulgar tongue' for Cromwell (*FQ* 237).

10 Weir, pp. 549-50.

11 Paul Ricoeur, *Time and Narrative Volume 3,* trans. Blamey, K., Pellauer, D., London & Chicago: University of Chicago Press, 1988, p. 158.

12 Ford, *Parade's End,* London: Penguin Books, 1982, pp. 171, 177, 737.

13 A point Ford disputes *contra* 'a very liberal relative' in *SP* 275-6.

14 Eamon Duffy, *The Stripping of the Altars – Traditional Religion in England 1400 – 1580,* New Haven & London: Yale University Press, 1992, Part II, pp. 377-477.

15 This point is particularly brought out with respect to *The Soul of London,* in Andrzej Gasiorek's contribution to the present volume: see Chapter 4.

16 In *JC* 210-11 Ford defines this term ('for which there is no English equivalent') as indicating that 'every word set on paper [. . .] must carry the story forward and, that as the story progressed, the story must be carried forward faster and faster and with more and more intensity'.

17 See for example Ford, *It Was the Nightingale,* London: Heinemann, 1934, pp. 143, 147, 193.

18 Joseph Conrad, *The Nigger of the 'Narcissus',* London: Penguin Books Ltd, 1989, p. xlix.

A ROAD NOT TAKEN: ROMANCE, HISTORY AND MYTH IN FORD'S *FIFTH QUEEN* NOVELS

Donald Mackenzie

'Ford's last Fifth Queen novel is amazing. The whole cycle is a noble conception – the Swan Song of Historical Romance – and frankly I am glad to have heard it.'[1] So Conrad, writing to Galsworthy on 20th February, 1908, saluted the *Fifth Queen* trilogy – with whatever degree of ambivalence we may wish to invest that salute[2]. Romance and swan-song we shall come back to. But I want to open by considering the *Fifth Queen* novels not in relation to historical romance at large but as a late, sophisticated fining-down of a specific kind of historical romance first bodied forth by Scott in *Kenilworth*. Ford in *The English Novel* of 1929 and in the 1938 *March of Literature* dismisses Scott with a high Flaubertian hauteur that is – it must be said – uncomprehending if not ignorant.[3] So in drawing on *Kenilworth* to help define *The Fifth Queen* I am advancing a paradigm, not claiming an influence. But in bringing the Scott to bear I have found – unless I delude myself – that paradigm sufficiently illuminating.

I

Kenilworth belongs to the phase of Scott's work initiated by *Ivanhoe*, the first Waverley novel to be subtitled 'A Romance' and rightly seen as marking a decisive break in his career as a novelist. It is the first of his novels to step outside a Scottish setting and outside the period that can be spanned by oral history. Beyond that, Jane Milgate has suggestively characterized the break in terms of its 'relinquishment of psychological and historical realism in favour of the elegant deployment of a stylised and simplified narrative design, reminiscent of the mode, mythological rather than historical, of Scott's early verse narratives'.[4] The relation of romance to the mythological will be touched on later. But within this large-scale shift in Scott's oeuvre, what kind of romance is *Kenilworth*? Its predecessors, *The Monastery* and *The Abbot*, had been what we might call Telemachus romances – stories of a young man's initiation into an adulthood achieved through the testing of his integrity and resource as he adventures through a world characteristically perplexing, deceptive, mysterious. With the mysterious we come upon one core element in all romance: the encounter – whether in the central books of the *Odyssey*, in protagonists like Bercilak and Heathcliff, or on a science-fiction planet of such alien beauty as C. S. Lewis's Malacandra – with the other as radically strange. *Kenilworth* might be characterized as transposing into a Renaissance drama of pageant and intrigue the distinctive mystery of medieval romance whose world has been luminously characterized by Lewis as:

> a world where everything may, and most things do, have a deeper meaning and a longer history than the errant knight would have expected; a world of endless forest, quest, hint, prophecy. Almost every male stranger wears armour; not only that there may be jousts but because visors hide faces. Any lady may prove a fay or devil; every castle conceal a holy or unholy mystery. The hero is a sort of intruder or trespasser, always, unawares, stumbling on to forbidden ground.... The hard, gay colours make this world very unlike that of Kafka, but it has some of the same qualities. You might call it inverted (or converted) Kafka: a Kafka who enjoyed the labyrinth.[5]

Kenilworth's transposing of this world is neatly captured in the reflections of the harassed Wayland Smith in Chapter 29:

> 'Here have I offended, for aught I know, to the death, the lord of this immense Castle, whose word were as powerful to take away my life, as the breath which speaks it to blow out a farthing candle. And all this for a mad lady, and a melancholy gallant; who, on the loss of a four-nooked bit of paper, has his hand on his poignardo, and swears death and fury! – then there is the Doctor and Varney – I will save myself from the whole mess of them – life is dearer than gold – I will fly this instant, though I leave my reward behind me.'
> These reflections naturally enough occurred to a mind like Wayland's, who found himself engaged far deeper than he had expected in a train of mysterious and unintelligible intrigues, in which the actors seemed hardly to know their own course.[6]

The baffling, labyrinthine world of medieval romance has been refigured in a plot of misunderstanding, deception and the equivocations and cross-purposes these generate. The plot hinges on the secret marriage of Amy Rosbart to the Earl of Leicester who cannot acknowledge her as his wife without destroying his own position as Elizabeth's favourite. Elizabeth's role in the plot points up a second defining feature of this kind of romance: its centring of known and major historical figures. (On this score we have travelled a long way from

Waverley where Charles Edward has only two scenes – admittedly striking – and the battle of Culloden takes place off-stage.) In Scott, such centring can be of two kinds. It can evoke the historical protagonist as a figure iconic from tradition or legend in the reader's imagination: this is what happens with the initial positioning of Mary Queen of Scots in Chapter 21 of *The Abbot*. Or the centring of the historical protagonist can be carried through in a sustained analytic dramatizing, as with Louis XI and Charles the Bold in *Quentin Durward*. (Ford's Henry VIII can be claimed to combine both kinds of centring.)

Lastly, *Kenilworth* deploys the defining strangeness of romance in its evoking of a past made exotic by distance and surface colouring. The latter is created by the lavish detail of dress and furnishings ('We had no idea before that upholstery could be made so engaging' the *Edinburgh* reviewer dryly observed[7]). This, too, can claim a kinship with the world of medieval romance, with 'the hard gay colours' Lewis notes and its often rich or resplendent décor. Scott's sources for *Kenilworth* document[8] the deployment of such decoration in that political pageantry which is a notable feature of later medieval and Renaissance culture, on into the Jacobean masque. And in the novel itself such décor fashions history into pageant, and pageant, in turn, configures itself in tableaux which can be galvanized into suddenly dramatic or melodramatic encounter as in Elizabeth's coming (Chapter 34), in the grounds of Kenilworth Castle, on the hapless Amy whom she initially perceives as a sculpted figure and then takes as a stage-frightened masquer. (The whole encounter might be read as a sad revision of that classic romance climax, the statue scene of *The Winter's Tale*.)

Such is the kind of historical romance which Ford orchestrates – each time one revisits the trilogy one is struck by further matchings and echoings — and fines down. The orchestrating is done with an insistent art that can risk the artful; and the fining down is not without loss, if we compare the Shakespearean largesse of Scott's drunken ruffler, Michael Lambourne, with Ford's Jonsonian obsessives: Culpepper, Nicholas Hogben, the Magister Udal, perhaps Hal Poins and even the Princess Mary. The labyrinthine world, now a world of fully Kafkaesque melodrama, is the world of spies and fatal court intrigue. Its drama can topple into the ludicrous, as in the scene (*The Fifth Queen Crowned*, Part Four, III) of Henry coming masked to the master-printer's house to hear the denunciation of his wife. It can be drawn taut, almost operatically stylised, in such scenes as the climax of *Privy Seal* (Part Three, I) where Throckmorton holds Lascelles at dagger point, beside the uncomprehending Culpepper, while he strives to win Viridius for the intrigue-against-time that will bring Cromwell down; or the bedroom scene of *Fifth Queen Crowned* (Part Two, V; Part Three, I) where Katharine's enemies have sent Culpepper, drunk and half-demented, into her room for her to be found with him and fatally compromised. It is worth pausing on this last for a moment to illustrate how Ford stretches his conventions. The scene initially plays itself out in terms of the historical swashbuckler – an episode from, as it might be, Dumas, but played in an aesthetic slow motion:

> She set both her hands upon his neck and pressed down the whole weight of her frame, till the voice died in his throat. His body stirred beneath her knee, convulsively, so that it was as if she rode a horse. His eyes, as slowly he strangled, glared hideously at the ceiling, from which the carven face of a Queen looked down into them. At last he lay still, and Katharine Howard rose up. (*FQC* 536)

With the entry of the King, this modulates into the rather different drama of his consciously relished manoeuvring to protect Katharine and its touch-on-touch revelation of Henry's personality ('in spite of his scarlet and his bulk he had the air of a heavy but very cunning peasant'). And it finally settles into the domestic poising of his uxorious content, when the episode is closed, against Katharine's sadness at his announced delay, once again, in the submission to Rome and at the world in which he manoeuvres: 'if she admired and wondered at her lord's power skilfully to have his way, it made her sad to think – as she must think – that so devious was man's work' (*FQC* 546). The whole sequence has a genuine melodramatic verve. At the same time it is deftly touched with memories of Jacobean tragedy: Katharine undressing before her mirror may recall the Duchess of Malfi in her bedroom scene; Culpepper enters like the tranced Macbeth on his way to the murder of Duncan, with perhaps a hint of the mad Hamlet of Ophelia's description: 'The man in green, his bonnet off, his red hair sticking all up, his face pallid, and his eyes staring like those of a sleep-walker, entered the room. In his right hand he had a dagger' (*FQC* 541). More particularly we may recall the willow-song scene in *Othello* and the whole episode has an *Othello*-like lacing of dramatic menace with farce – its resolution turning on what can or cannot be seen through the opened bedroom door.

The centring of historical figures, again, is carried to the point where Graham Greene can claim that:

> in *The Fifth Queen* we have virtually no fictional characters – the King, Thomas Cromwell, Katharine Howard, they are the principals; we are nearer to the historical plays of Shakespeare than to the fiction of such historical writers as Miss Irwin or Miss Heyer.[9]

This opens up large questions (for exploring on another occasion) about Ford's casting of his historical protagonists, and especially his Katharine Howard (from the spelling of her Christian name – to accentuate its etymological root in Greek *katharos,* pure, as the historically accurate "Catherine" does not – onwards). But taking up Greene's citation of Shakespeare's Histories, we could say that the primary affinity of Ford's cycle is with the First Tetralogy, not the Second. The former, as Emrys Jones has well demonstrated, is a deeply Tudor rather than Elizabethan work, not least in its politics of Fortune and tragedies of fall from high estate.[10] In Shakespeare these can find choric expression in Henry VI's lament from the sidelines at the Battle of Towton, or the lamenting queens of *Richard III* or the processional ghosts of Richard's victims that come to him on Bosworth Eve. Ford's trilogy comes nearest such choric effects in its roll-calling of Henry VIII's queens who have preceded Katharine, the fifth. This is a leitmotiv first sounded by Cromwell early in *The Fifth Queen:* "'Why, I have outlived three queens'", he said to himself, and his round face resignedly despised his world and his times' (*FQ* 29). It is taken up at the end of Part Two of *Privy Seal* where Cromwell stands on the cusp of his power and his impending fall:

> And pondering upon the wonderful destiny that had brought him up from a trooper in Italy to these high places, he saluted the moon with his crooked forefinger – for the moon was the president at his birth.
> 'Why,' he uttered aloud, 'I have survived four queens' days.'
> For Katharine of Aragon he had seen die; and Anne Boleyn had died on the scaffold; and Jane Seymour was dead in childbed; and now with the news from Cleves, Anne's reign was over and done with.
> 'Four queens,' he repeated. (*PS* 386-7)

And it has a last sounding from the Princess Mary at the end of her scene of proud and stylized surrender to Katharine's purposes in *The Fifth Queen Crowned*:

And, Queen, again I bid you beware of calling any day fortunate till its close.
For before midnight you may be ruined utterly. I have known more Queens
than thou. Thou art the fifth I have known. (*FQC* 520)

Finally, surface colouring, and the detail of clothes and furnishings
and buildings in which Ford has soaked himself,[11] are variously
deployed – not least in that orchestrating of light and shadow on
which accounts of *The Fifth Queen* habitually remark. This controls
our experience of the labyrinthine world and it belongs principally to
that first novel where it climaxes in Throckmorton's pursuit of Katharine through the darkness of the corridors until: 'As she ran a red
patch before her eyes, distant and clear beneath the torch, took the
form of the King' (*FQ* 221). With this we reach the anti-climactic
climax of the whole novel: we find that Throckmorton, in seeming to
trap Katharine, has been playing a double game against his master
Cromwell, that it is Cromwell who is in danger and Katharine safe.
This section (Part Three, IV) of the novel has opened with the tableau,
passing into epiphany, when Hal Poins (whose name, incidentally,
combines that of Shakespeare's master-politician prince with that of
his less-than-brilliant sidekick) has been detected in his carrying of
letters for Katharine:

They had the form of the boy, wet, grey and mud-draggled, lying on the
ground between them. Cicely Elliott rose in her chair; it was not any part of
her nature to succour fainting knaves, and she let him stay where he was. Old
Rochford raised his hands and cried out to Katharine;
  'You have been sending letters again!'
Katharine stood absolutely still. They had taken her letters!
She neither spoke nor stirred. Slowly, as she remembered that this was
indeed a treason, that here without doubt was death, that she was outwitted,
that she was now the chattel of whosoever held her letters – as point after point
came into her mind, the blood fled from her face. Cicely Elliott sat down in her
chair again, and whilst the two sat watching her in the failing dusk they
seemed to withdraw themselves from her world of friendship and to become
spectators. (*FQ* 213)

That epiphany of Katharine's isolation and entrapment is not
cancelled out by the reversals and revelation – Kafkaesque melodrama
indeed – which end this section. Rather they precipitate her vulnerability into a recoil against the world she inhabits ('Her first feeling of
horror at this endless plot hardly gave way to relief'; *FQ* 224) – and
then into her final, exhausted half-yielding to the King in the closing

sentence of the book ('She got upon her legs wearily, and, for a moment, took his hand to steady herself'; *FQ* 232).

Henry's own role in this climactic episode – burdened, benevolent, dangerously powerful and dangerously volatile – both counters, and expands from, our first sight of him at the novel's beginning:

> 'Let me not be elbowed by cripples,' and then: 'A' God's name let them come,' changing his mind , as was his custom after a bad night, before his first words had left his thick heavy lips. His great brow was furrowed, his enormous bulk of scarlet, with the great double dog-rose embroidered across the broad chest, limped a little over his right knee and the foot dragged. His eyes were bloodshot and heavy, his head hung forward as though he were about to charge the world with his forehead. From time to time his eyebrows lifted painfully, and he swallowed with an effort as if he were choking.
>
> Behind him the three hundred windows of the palace Placentia seemed to peer at him like eyes, curious, hostile, lugubrious or amazed. He tore violently at his collar and muttered: 'I stifle.' His great hand was swollen by its glove, sewn with pearls, to an immense size. (*FQ* 39)

This too is tableau passing into epiphany, in this case an epiphany of power baffled in its brocaded display, and moving in a baffling, spectatorial world. And what both epiphanies reveal are the enclosing structures of the novel's mundane, historical, political world, invested with no hint of the mythic or the transcendent.

II

> When Romance mates with History to fertilize fairy tales with the seed of the real world, they beget Myth. We are given young Abe Lincoln, on the one hand, reading by log-light, and Robin Hood on the other, splitting infinity with an arrow as neatly as Abe's rails. The form of the swashbuckler, the border tale, the costume romance, seems essentially unserious, and in our day it has become just another popular genre, not more significant than the thriller or the sitcom, the western or the soap.[12]

So William Gass in the best account of the Fifth Queen novels I have come across. Its formulation of historical myth is – deliberately? – overblown and reductive. But it signals a real crux. Myth and history – serious myth, at least, and serious history – may well seem *prima facie* not only distinct but antithetical, not only antithetical but mutually exclusive. I cannot argue here for their compatibility, only claim that historical myths share with other kinds of myth an archetypal simplicity of story and archetype's power to configure. Like other myths they root the human and the contingent in a realm of sacred and transcendent powers. And, like other myths, their configuring power can discharge itself in, and is under-girded by, the re-enactments of ritual: Passover celebration, Orange parades, Henry V's projection on the morning of Agincourt of the surviving veteran 'who will yearly on the vigil feast his neighbours/And say, "Tomorrow is Saint Crispian"'.

An elementary taxonomy of historical myths would group them as foundation myths; passion myths of fall, suffering, redemption; and myths of the iconic figure in whom a people find their ideal identity or a concentration of defining features of their history. Such iconic figures can be historical (Nelson – never to be separated from his brotherhood of captains, Lincoln, Parnell), or legendary (King Arthur), or fictional (Cooper's Natty Bumpo), or modulated out of history into fiction like Tolstoy's Kutuzov in *War and Peace*, or out of history into legend like El Cid. Nor need the basic groupings be themselves exclusive. The two canonical foundation myths of our culture are the Old Testament Exodus and Virgil's *Aeneid*: in both, foundation myth overlaps or is intertwined with passion myth. The founding of Rome begins with the sack of Troy; the Exodus is a deliverance from the house of bondage in Egypt; and, in turn, its refiguring and transfiguring in the second section of the Book of Isaiah colligates it with the seminal passion myth of the Suffering Servant of the Lord. A few years before Ford's trilogy, Yeats had made the iconic folk-lore figure of Cathleen ni Houlihan the vehicle for a potently nationalist passion myth:

> *Old Woman* It is a hard service they take that help me. Many that are red-cheeked now will be pale-cheeked; many that have been free to walk the hills and the bogs and the rushes will be sent to walk hard streets in far countries; many a good plan will be broken; many that have gathered money will not stay to spend it; many a child will be born and there will be no father at its christening to give it a name. They that have red cheeks will have pale cheeks for my sake, and for all that, they will think they are well-paid. [*She goes out; her voice is heard outside singing.*
> They shall be remembered for ever,
> They shall be alive for ever,
> They shall be speaking for ever,
> The people shall hear them for ever...
> *Peter* [*to Patrick, laying a hand on his arm*]. Did you see an old woman going down the path?
> *Patrick*. I did not, but I saw a young girl, and she had the walk of a queen.[13]

And a few years later Patrick Pearse was to forge a nationalist reading of Irish history into the sinister, hypnotic passion myth of the pamphlets which he wrote as an incantation for that 1916 rising which was, not accidentally, timed for Easter:

> Let no man be mistaken as to who will be lord in Ireland when Ireland is free. The people will be lord and master. The people who wept in Gethsemane, who trod the sorrowful way, who died naked on a cross, who went down into hell, will rise again glorious and immortal, will sit on the right hand of God, and will come in the end to give judgment, a judge just and terrible.[14]

For nineteenth century England the Whig Interpretation of modern English history as a history of the battle for freedom provides a classic foundation myth. Macaulay in his early essay on Milton casts the mid-seventeenth century conflict of King and Parliament as a clangorous cosmic and Manichean drama:

> the very crisis of the great conflict between Oromasdes and Arimanes, liberty and despotism, reason and prejudice. That great battle was fought for no single generation, no single land. The destinies of the human race were staked on the same cast with the freedom of the English people.[15]

In the secularized Protestantism of Froude's *History of England* the axial period has shifted from the seventeenth century to the sixteenth; the cardinal event is no longer the Civil War or the Revolution of 1688 but the defeat of the Armada :

> If the enormous resources of the [Armada] fleet had been made available ... to the Church's cause, it is likely that sooner or later the Catholic despotism would have been re-established everywhere, and that the first great effort for the emancipation of Europe would have failed.[16]

Earlier, in his seminal 1852 essay on 'England's Forgotten Worthies', Froude, celebrating Hakluyt's *Voyages* as 'the Prose Epic of the modern English nation', declared:

> The Catholic faith was no longer able to furnish standing ground on which the English or any other nation could live a manly and a godly life. Feudalism, as a social organisation, was not any more a system under which their energies could have scope to move. Thenceforward, not the Catholic Church, but any man to whom God had given a heart to feel and a voice to speak, was to be the teacher to whom men were to listen; and great actions were not to remain the privileges of the families of the Norman nobles, but were to be laid within the reach of the poorest plebeian who had the stuff in him to perform them. Alone,

of all the sovereigns in Europe, Elizabeth saw the change which had passed over the world. She saw it, and saw it in faith, and accepted it. The England of the Catholic Hierarchy and the Norman Baron, was to cast its shell and to become the England of free thought and commerce and manufacture, which was to plough the ocean with its navies, and sow its colonies over the globe; and the first appearance of these enormous forces and the light of the earliest achievements of the new era shines through the forty years of the reign of Elizabeth with a grandeur which, when once its history is written, will be seen to be among the most sublime phenomena which the earth as yet has witnessed.[17]

(One should immediately add that J. W. Burrow in his admirably nuanced account of Froude and the sixteenth century brings out how much less the exploits of the English seamen figure in his central work, the *History*, 'the creation of a far more complex, haunted and lugubrious mind' than this rhetoric would suggest;[18] but the testament to a secularised Protestant myth remains.)

A countering Catholic myth configures the Reformation as a passion myth of fall and awaited redemption. Disraeli in *Sybil* grafts this, secularisingly, into a radical Tory myth of the two nations. Waugh, Ford's successor, as Naipaul is Conrad's and Eliot James's, offers a credally infused version in the opening of his Campion biography: the Tudor dynasty

left a new aristocracy, a new religion, a new system of government; the generation was already in its childhood that was to send King Charles to the scaffold; the new, rich families who were to introduce the House of Hanover, were already in the second stage of their metamorphosis from the freebooters of Edward VI's reign to the conspirators of 1688 and the sceptical cultured oligarchs of the eighteenth century. The vast exuberance of the Renaissance had been canalised. England was secure, independent, insular; the course of her history lay plain ahead; competitive nationalism, competitive industrialism, competitive imperialism, the looms and coal mines and counting houses, the joint-stock companies and cantonments; the power and weakness of great possessions.[19]

The pivotal formulation there comes in 'The vast exuberance of the Renaissance had been canalised. England was secure, independent, insular'. With that Waugh deftly turns the flank of the secularised Protestant myth – so resoundingly proclaimed in 'England's Forgotten Worthies' – which colligates the break from Rome, Protestantism and freedom with England's entry into its destiny of ocean and island empire. Against it he implicitly evokes that radical critique of industrialism, grounded in a romantic medievalism, which runs from

Cobbett through Disraeli to Morris and on to Chesterton and Belloc. And at the same time he evokes the other component of this passion myth: a European Catholic culture by which English insularity is judged. In Waugh's own fiction, this myth stands rampant in the elegiac opulence (and sentimentalising) of *Brideshead Revisited*; it provides a chastened undertext for the *Sword of Honour* trilogy. English history has been deflected into an insularity of the industrial modern; its true continuity is carried by the Catholic tradition, hidden, displaced, awaiting (though not in Waugh[20]) its parousia.

III

However we estimate Ford's Catholicism, he equally saw the sixteenth century as the founding period of modern England. In *The Spirit of the People* he focuses that founding in terms countering suggestively both Froude's Protestant myth and the Catholic myth I have cited from Waugh:

> Roughly speaking, the ideals of the chivalric age were altruistic; roughly speaking the ideals of the age that succeeded it were individualist-opportunist. It was not, of course, England that was first in the field, since Italy produced Machiavelli. But Italy, which produced Machiavelli, failed utterly to profit by him. England, on the other hand, had to wait many years before falling into line with the spirit of its age. It had, as it were, to wait until most of the vested interests of the middle ages were got rid of – until practically the last of the great barons were brought to the ground. It had to wait until a man could climb from the very lowest stage of the body politic into the very highest chair that the republic could offer. But then it profited exceedingly, so that England which, at the opening of Henry VIII's reign, had been the laughing stock, became, towards the close of that reign, the arbiter of Europe.
>
> But it *did* produce from its depths, from amidst its bewildering cross currents of mingled races, *the* great man of its age; and, along with him, it produced a number of men similar in type and strong enough to found a tradition. The man, of course, was Thomas Cromwell, who welded England into one formidable whole, and his followers in the tradition were the tenacious, pettifogging, cunning, utterly unscrupulous and very wonderful statesmen who supported the devious policy of Queen Elizabeth – the Cecils, the Wootons, the Bacons and all the others of England's golden age. [21]

That centres sixteenth-century English history on Cromwell and his achievement in welding England 'into one formidable whole'. Cromwell's statement of his credo in the great confrontation with Katharine at the climax of *Privy Seal*, Part One (*PS* 297-304) soaringly expands this claim, as a later passage on Throckmorton gives a sombre gloss on the tradition Cromwell has founded:

it had always been part of the devious and great bearded man's policy – it had
been part of his very nature – to play upon people's fears, to trouble them with
apprehensions. It was part of the tradition that Cromwell had given all his men.
He ruled England by such fears. (*PS* 313)

All this opens up again the question of Ford's rendering of his
historical protagonists. The role he gives Cromwell puts him,
interestingly, much closer to the dominant modern historian of the
period, G. R. Elton, than it does to the major Tudor historian of his
own day, A. F. Pollard. The latter's 1902 biography, *Henry VIII*, in its
exaltation of Henry decidedly plays down Cromwell's significance.[22]
Conversely the complex Henry presented by Ford – troubled, massive,
dangerous, cunning, fluctuating, finally weak – is as removed from
Froude's sane, masculine, national leader and Romance hero[23] or
Pollard's admired ruthless master of *realpolitik*, as he is from the pre-
Froude version of Henry as tyrant, a version most pungently phrased
by Dickens: 'a most intolerable ruffian, a disgrace to human nature,
and a blot of blood and grease on the History of England'.[24]

In the passage from *The Spirit of the People* quoted above, not
only the detail ('the tenacious, pettifogging, cunning, utterly unscrup-
ulous and very wonderful statesmen who supported the devious policy
of Queen Elizabeth') of the tradition Cromwell founds but the very
concept of a tradition of political practice, cuts firmly against the
mythic. *The Spirit of the People* (1907) is the third volume of the
trilogy on England that twines, chronologically and more than
chronologically, about Ford's Tudor trilogy. In it his mapping of
English history takes its bearings from the continental as consciously
as in Belloc or Waugh: but the continents in question are not only
Europe but also North America. It opens with the anecdote of the
German Professor commenting on the violence of English history
from a standpoint in that once-Anabaptist Münster which is, or should
be, drenched in the memory of sixteenth-century violence. Its second
chapter takes off from another mythic image of England as the island
empire, not, this time, world-mastering but robustly or idyllically
secure. This is the image articulated by Shakespeare in the closing
lines of *King John* which Ford quotes. He goes on to meditate
playfully on a myth of English history as a history of assimilation (*SP*
248-56) before coming down on his own key image of England as:

a goodly inn, a harbourage upon a western road.... Upon it the hordes of European mankind have rested during their secular flight westwards in search of the Islands of the Blest. If they have succeeded only in founding a 'race' more mingled, more ungraspable, a race that is a sort of pluperfect English race, a race to whom no doubt the future belongs; if, instead of finding a classical ideal, they have only founded a very modern and very inscrutable problem, that fact must be regarded rather as a comment upon the proneness of humanity to fall short of its ideals than as a refutation of the convenient image that England is a road, a means to an end, not an end in itself. (*SP* 257-8)

That image of England returns at the end of Chapter II, bringing together both the touchstone lines from Shakespeare and the Münster Anabaptists; it resounds in the close of the *Envoi*: 'For if this people be not the chosen people, this land will always be the one that every race would choose for its birthings and its buryings until the last Aaron shall lead the last of the conquering legions across the world' (*SP* 326).

This close is very much of its period in its apocalyptic sweep. It is also characteristically Fordian in its inflecting of that sweep with irony, not least in its recalling the lines from Plautus, spoken by a slave, which provide the whole book with its teasing epigraph:

Omnes ordines sub signis ducam, legiones meas,
Avi sinistra, auspicio liquido, atque ex sententia.
Confidentia est inimicos meas me posse perdere.
('On I'll lead my legions all, in line beneath their standards, a bird on my left, my auspices clear and quite to my liking. I'm confident that I can finish off my foemen.')[25]

In the Tudor novels a movement westwards is articulated as the quest for the Islands of the Blest or the Fortunate Isles which becomes another of the trilogy's leitmotivs. *The Fifth Queen* sounds it in the exchange where Cicely Elliott sardonically advises Katharine to rid herself of the dangerous Culpepper by sending him in quest of them (*FQ* 116). Katharine herself evokes 'the Islands of the Blest that hide amid the Bermoothean tempest' when she performs in the Bishop of Winchester's masque before the King (*FQ* 139); and he takes up the myth in his subsequent conversation with her in that stable scene which brings together his own burdened middle age and the out-datedness of the chivalric order embodied in the old knight Rochford:

The blessed Utopia of the lost islands had stirred in the King all sorts of griefs that he would shake off, and all sorts of remembrances of youth, of open fields, and a wide world that shall be conquered – all the hopes and instincts of

happiness, ineffable and indestructible, that never die in passionate men. He
said dully, his thoughts far away:
'What errand have they sent him upon? Who is your goodly cousin?' (*FQ*
163-4)

That opens a window into that world of renewal which seems to
pervade the opening stretch of *The Fifth Queen Crowned*. But in this
novel it is flanked by Katharine's two conversations with the masterspy Throckmorton, just before and just after this scene. The first has
come in the darkness of the cellar into which he has had her rapt on
her way back from the masque and where he initiates her lessoning in
the ways of the world in which she has to act – 'If you will fight in a
fight you must have tools,' (*FQ* 148). In the second he inflects the
leitmotif of the Fortunate Isles another way in his incisive analysis of
Henry ('It is by his doubts you may take him') – an analysis that the
rest of the trilogy will elaborate:

> It is when you call this realm the Fortunate Land that you make his Highness
> incline towards you – and doubt. "Island of the Blest," say you. Then his
> Highness rejoices, saying to himself: "My governing appeareth Fortunate to
> the World." But his Highness knoweth full well the flaws that be in his
> Fortunate Island. And specially will he set himself to redress wrongs, assuage
> tears, set up chantries, and make his peace with God. (*FQ* 177)

The court masque has carried a myth of England as the Fortunate
Isles: Throckmorton's glinting political intelligence points up how the
tension between myth and reality opens up a space, and can generate
an energy, for political action. And in a later conversation, midway
through *Privy Seal*, that goes on to define the ideological opposition
between his Renaissance Machiavellianism and her no less Renaissance idealism of an ancient Plutarchan virtue, Katharine brings together again Culpepper and the mythic western islands:

> 'He shall have the seeking for the Hesperides or the city of Atalanta, where
> still the golden age remains to be a model and ensample for us.' Her eyes
> looked past Throckmorton. 'My cousin hath a steadfast nature to be gone on
> such pilgrimages...'
> 'Madam Howard,' Throckmorton grinned at her, 'if men of our day and
> kin do come upon any city where remaineth the golden age, very soon shall be
> shewn the miracle of the corruptibility of gold.' (*PS* 348-9)

Those duelling conversations with Throckmorton run up into
Katharine's confrontation with Cromwell (*PS* 297-304) where his

creed and hers come into full clash and balanced statement, with the diminuendo of Cromwell's clear-eyed worldly wisdom tilting the balance towards the trilogy's bleak denouement:

> 'Ye speak no word of God,' she said pitifully.
> 'God is very far away,' he answered. [26]

That exchange has its counterpoint in Katharine's interview with Anne of Cleves (*PS* 365ff) with its epiphanic moment:

> 'You have more courage than I,' the Queen said.
> Suddenly she made a single gesture with her hands, as if she swept something from her lap: some invisible dust – and that was all. Still Katharine did not move or speak; she had prepared speeches – speeches against the Queen's being disdainful, enraged, or dissolved in tears. She had read in books all night from Aulus Gellius to Cicero to get wisdom. But here there were no speeches called for; no speeches could be made. The significance of the Queen's gesture of sweeping dust from her lap slowly overwhelmed her. (*PS* 367)

This witnesses to a key moment in the downward trajectory of emptying out which intersects the trajectory of Katharine's rise to the power, as queen, which will enable her carry out her ideal of a Catholic restoration. After *The Fifth Queen's* world of shadow-dominated interiors, *Privy Seal*, in the sub-titles of its successive parts ('The Rising Sun', 'The Distant Cloud', 'The Sunburst') has directed us to an outdoor world of changing weather, albeit weather seen primarily from indoors. The openings of those three parts are organized in an advancing sequence of the outdoors: the inn at Paris where the Magister Udal spies and is trapped into marriage; the gateway into Calais, the frontier town of French and English territory where Poins waits for the manic Culpepper; and, finally, the harsh-crowd scene at Smithfield where a heretic is to burn, and Culpepper is sucked into Throckmorton's decisive move against Privy Seal. With Anne's surrender of her queen-ship to Katharine comes a carefully crafted vignette of an outdoors, greenwood Englishness as Henry celebrates his renewed youth:

> and, taking from his yeoman-companion, that was the Earl of Surrey, his great bow, he shot a mighty shaft along the glade, to shew how far away he would have the deer to pass like swift ghosts between the aisles of the trees. (*PS* 373)

This, with its significant, climactic touch of the ghostly, points us forward into the first Part of *The Fifth Queen Crowned* where Katharine's marital happiness, and the impending reconciliation with Rome to which she has dedicated herself, move in an outdoor world of pavilions and hunting and the North country: what Byatt calls its 'archaic outdoor scenes'.[27] And it is not only the scenes which are archaic. *The Fifth Queen Crowned* shifts from the dramatic encounters which dominate the first novel, and, to some extent, the second, to a presentation primarily narrative, in a style which can recall a William Morris prose-romance. A crassly imperceptive contemporary review dismissed it as 'Wardour Street English'[28]; but the style out of Morris is new in the trilogy, is there for a purpose and is deftly controlled. It creates from the start an effect of the distanced, tinged with the elegiac. It wells into a lucent evoking of the idyllic, organic pre-Reformation society – now seemingly restored – of the Catholic myth:

> It was reported, too, that a cider press in Herefordshire had let down a dozen firkins of cider without any apples being set in it, and this was accounted an omen of great plenty, whilst many sheep had died, so that men who had set their fields down in grass talked of giving them to the plough again, and upon St. Swithin's Day no rain had fallen. All these things gave a great contentment, and many that in the hard days had thought to become Lutheran in search of betterment, now looked in byres and hidden valleys to find priests of the old faith. For if a man could plough he might eat, and if he might eat he could praise God after his father's manner as well as in a new way. (*FQC* 452)

This style gathers to a head in the opening of Part Two where it is suddenly shadowed with the political and the savage in Norfolk's hanging of the forty Scots borderers and cattle thieves whom Henry had intended to hand, pardoned, to the Scottish King at the meeting the latter has prudently eschewed:

> And, laughing over their shoulders at this fine harvest of fruit, gibbering and dangling against the heavens on high, the King and his host rode back into the Border country. It was pleasant to ride in the summer weather, and they hunted and rendered justice by the way, and heard tales of battles that had been there before in the north country. (*FQC* 494)

At the beginning of the next section of Part Two this modulates into the flatland narrative of a saga opening in order to introduce Mary Lascelles whose testimony will help destroy Katharine. Her brother, the spy, has seemed only a survivor from the shadow-world of Cromwell's police state that has rolled away (*FQC* 451). (The masterspy Throckmorton is now retired as a country gentleman, who writes to warn Katharine as the plotting against her gathers: *FQC* 513ff.) As that last citation indicates, the world of Cromwell has not been – and cannot be – left behind. *The Fifth Queen Crowned* opens in the underground room where the letter that will bring reconciliation with Rome is to be drafted, a scene that gives us a notably Conradian evocation of Henry:

> When he was in that mood he spoke with a singular distinctness that came up from his husky and ordinary joviality like something dire and terrible – like that something that upon a clear smooth day will suggest to you suddenly the cruelty that lies always hidden in the limpid sea. (*FQC* 420)

The Cromwellian shadow-world blazes up in the epiphany (tinctured from the Matthean Passion narrative) of his fall that haunts Cranmer – ('the chamber had seemed to fill with an awful gloom and darkness; men showed only like shadows against the window lights; the constable of the Tower had gone in with the warrants, and in that gloom the earth had appeared to tremble and quake beneath the Archbishop's feet'; *FQC* 477). And that world returns, finally, climactically, chastened to the elegiac, in the arraignment of Katharine and in her self-committing to death:

> She went slowly down over the great stone flags of the great hall. It was very gloomy now, and her figure in black velvet was like a small shadow, dark and liquid, amongst the shadows that fell softly and like draperies from the roof. Up there it was all dark already, for the light came downwards from the windows. She went slowly, walking as she had been schooled to walk.... Near the doorway it was all shadow, and soundlessly she faded away among them. (*FQC* 591-2)

The elegiac is one of the major modes into which romance, in its long story as a genre, has often and fruitfully married. It is the mode in which it has most readily and potently engaged with history – as it does, classically, in Scott's *Redgauntlet*; as it does on a smaller scale in Buchan's post-war historical novels of defeat, the Jacobite *Midwinter*, the novel of the Montrose campaign *Witch Wood*, and the Tudor *Blanket of the Dark*. The second of these deploys the same image from romance-as-elegy with which Buchan, in his Montrose biography, concludes the account of his hero's 1644 campaign:

> The little party galloped up the Yarrow vale, and at Broadmeadows took the drove-road across Minchmoor to Tweeddale. As they disappeared into the

green hills with them disappeared the dream of a new and happier Scotland.
Montrose's cycle of victories had proved like the fairy gold which vanishes in
a man's hand. The year of miracles was ended.[29]

Ford's refusal, in the trilogy, of any mythic reading of the
founding of modern England includes the refusal of a romance-elegiac
myth, Catholic or Catholic-tinctured, of what might have been. The
refusal is a deliberate choice, issuing out of a deliberated vision. A
passage in the 1905 *Holbein* monograph voices some of what will be
the trilogy's burden when it observes that:

> The eyes in Holbein's portraits of queens are half closed, sceptical, challeng-
> ing, and disbelieving. They look at you as if to say: "I do not know exactly
> what manner of man you are, but I am very sure that being a man you are no
> hero." This, however, is not a condemnation but an acceptance of the fact that,
> from Pope to peasant, poor humanity can never be more than poor humanity.[30]

But the refusal of historical myth – the road not taken by Ford in this
work – can also issue from the internal dynamics of romance as a
genre, a genre less naturally apt to serve as a carrier for myth than
either lyric or epic – epic whose narrative successors in nineteenth
century English are not the novelists but the historians. Romance side-
steps, even in the *Odyssey*, the *gravitas* of epic.[31] Conversely it can
foreground, from the *Odyssey* on, a lambent play of fictivity[32] – a play
that may flicker with intimations of the transcendent. The dialectic of
fictivity and transcendence finds a natural medium in dream with its
polarity of otherness and the waking return to a mundane world now
experienced as bleak or emptied. Such an awakening can be seen as
transposing, or countering, that primary ending of romance, the
homecoming (with or without an Odyssean purging of the
commandeered and overrun homestead). Against both homecoming
and awakening as romance endings we may set a third paradigm,
which also can be read as a transposing of the Odyssean return. This is
the formal exercise of judgment, whether massed as at the climax of
Sidney's *Arcadia* or incisive as at the climax of *The Tempest* or
melodramatic as at the climax of Dumas's *Three Musketeers* and
Count of Monte Cristo. It is this third form Ford deploys for the
sealing of his trilogy. Katherine comes to judgment – in the full
doubleness of that phrase. Her long final speech is shaped to suggest
her humanist education, maybe also to stir memories of the final
speeches of Tudor martyrs like More, though given a defiance of
rejection and renunciation quite alien to theirs. Renunciation passes

into that rejection of all shaping which takes up the anti-heroism of the
passage I quoted above from the *Holbein*:

> I was of the opinion that in the end right must win through. I think now that it
> never shall – or not for many ages – till our Saviour come again upon this earth
> with a great glory. But all this is a mystery of the great goodness of God and
> the temptations that do beset us poor mortality. (*FQC* 590)

Prune the liturgical phrasing and we are near the wholly agnostic
tragedy of *The Good Soldier*:

> Here were two noble people – for I am convinced that both Edward and
> Leonora had noble natures – here, then, were two noble natures, drifting down
> life, like fireships afloat on a lagoon and causing miseries, heartaches, agony
> of the mind, and death. And they themselves steadily deteriorated. And why?
> For what purpose? To point what lesson? It is all a darkness.[33]

But the *Fifth Queen* cycle is already agnostic of any shaping myth that
could redeem history from within history. Here, in a sense beyond
what Conrad may have intended, Ford's historical romance has a
quality of swan-song.

In the longer perspective of his work the trilogy presents a
massive bridge out of his early writing, including the collaborations
with Conrad, into his fictional masterpieces of the next two decades.
(The movement could be marked in the dedications of the first volume
to Conrad and the last to Arthur Marwood, traditionally seen as one
model for Tietjens.) Its renunciation of a mythic reading of the
founding history of modern England, with the vacancy this brings, can
be seen as a clearing of the ground for an iconic myth (to be evoked in
texts which belong with the major Edwardian novels of mapped
Englishness and apocalypse: *Tono-Bungay, Howards End, Women in
Love*) of the English gentleman. It is that myth Ford essays in the
Tietjens novels.

NOTES

1   *The Collected Letters of Joseph Conrad, Volume 4 1908-1911,* ed. Frederick R.
    Karl and Laurence Davies, Cambridge: Cambridge University Press, 1990, p. 48.
2   Cf. the editors' footnote *ad loc.*

3   *The English Novel*, London: Constable & Co: 1930, pp. 102-4; *The March of Literature*, London: Allen & Unwin, 1947, pp. 646-9.
4   *Scott in Carnival*, eds. J. H. Alexander and David Hewitt, Aberdeen: Association for Scottish Literary Studies, 1993, p. 274.
5   C. S. Lewis, 'The Anthropological Imagination' in *Selected Literary Ess*ays, Cambridge: Cambridge University Press, 1969, pp. 309-10.
6   Sir Walter Scott, *Kenilworth* ed. J. H. Alexander, Edinburgh: Edinburgh University Press, 1993, p. 276. For a useful survey of medieval romance elements in *Kenilworth*, see Jerome Mitchell, *Scott, Chaucer and Medieval Romance*, Lexington: University Press of Kentucky, 1987, pp. 148-50.
7   Quoted in Andrew Lang's Editor's Introduction to the Border Edition (1893) of *Kenilworth*, p. xxv.
8   See *Kenilworth*, ed. Alexander, pp. 473f.
9   Introduction to *The Bodley Head Ford Madox Ford*, vol. 1, London: The Bodley Head, 1962, p. 10.
10 Emrys Jones, *The Origins of Shakespeare*, Oxford: The Clarendon Press, 1977; see e.g. p 193: 'Although in the obvious historical sense "Elizabethan" literature is no more than a part of "Tudor" literature, for the purposes of literary history the two terms are usually and justifiably distinguished. "Elizabethan" refers to what is unique to the second half of Elizabeth's reign: a glisteningly fresh post-Pleiade world of lyrical poetry whose high points include *The Faerie Queene, A Midsummer Night's Dream*, and the best songs scattered through the miscellanies of the eighties and nineties…. If "Elizabethan" literature celebrates Nature, the favourite "Tudor" theme is Fortune, whose grim realm – in literature at any rate – is defined by the court, the prison and the scaffold'.
11 As commented on in the perceptive contemporary review of *The Fifth Queen Crowned* by R. A. Scott-James, reprinted in *Ford Madox Ford: The Critical Heritage,* ed. Frank MacShane, London: Routledge & Kegan Paul, 1962, pp. 28-31.
12 William Gass, "The Neglect of *The Fifth Queen*" in Sondra J. Stang ed. *The Presence of Ford Madox Ford*, Philadelphia: University of Pennsylvania Press, 1981, p. 29.
13 W. B. Yeats, *Collected Plays*, London: Macmillan, 1982. The passage quoted, the final lines of the play, comes on pp. 86-8.
14 Patrick Pearse, *Political Writings and Speeches*, Dublin: Talbot Press Limited, 1952, p. 345.
15 Thomas Babington Macaulay, 'Milton' [1825] in *Critical and Historical Essays,* J. M. Dent: 1963, vol. 1, p.171.
16 James Anthony Froude, *History of England from the Fall of Wolsey to the Defeat of the Spanish Armada*, London: Longmans, Green and Co.: 1910, vol. XII, p. 479. Hereafter cited as *History*.
17 James Anthony Froude, reprinted in the first series of *Short Studies on great Subjects* London: Longmans, Green and Co., 3rd edition, 1868; the passage quoted is on p. 302.
18 See J. W. Burrow, *A Liberal Descent*, Cambridge: Cambridge University Press, 1981, pp. 233f.
19 Evelyn Waugh, *Edmund Campion*, London: The Catholic Book Club, 1952, pp. 3-4.

20 Contrast e.g. Hopkins's baroque caroling at the end of *The Wreck of the Deutschland*, the plangent rhetoric of Newman's 1852 sermon, 'Second Spring' and the crossbench summoning up of such a rhetoric at the end of David Knowles's *The Monastic Order in England*, Cambridge: Cambridge University Press, 2nd edition, 1963, pp. 692-3.

21 Ford, *England and the English,* ed. Sara Haslam, Manchester: Carcanet, 2003, comprising *The Soul of London* (*SL* – 1905); *The Heart of the Country* (*HC* – 1906) and *The Spirit of the People* (*SP* – 1907). *SP* 270-71.

22 A. F. Pollard, *Henry VIII*, London: Jonathan Cape, 1970; see e.g. pp. 211, 281, 312. For Froude's much more appreciative assessment of Cromwell, see *History*, vol. III, pp. 339-41.

23 See e.g. Froude's final judgment on Henry in *History*, vol. IV, pp. 235-43. For Froude's Henry as Romance hero, see Burrow, *A Liberal Descent*, pp. 259-61.

24 Charles Dickens, *The Old Curiosity Shop* [and] *A Child's History of England*, London: Hazell, Watson and Viney, Ltd, n.d., p. 648.

25 From *Plautus* vol. IV, trans. Paul Nixon, Loeb Classical Library, London: Heinemann, 1932, p. 229.

26 One might perhaps compare the end of *Nostromo* Part Second, Chapter 5.

27 In her Introduction to the Penguin edition of *The Fifth Queen*, London: Penguin Books, 1984, p. xv.

28 *Ford Madox Ford: The Critical Heritage*, p. 32.

29 John Buchan, *Montrose,* London: Thomas Nelson and Sons, 1931, p. 290. *Witch Wood* uses the image of fairy gold for the same historical situation in Chapter XIII.

30 Ford, *Hans Holbein the Younger*, London: Duckworth & Co, 1905, p. 17.

31 A matter for criticism by what Frye dubs Iliad-critics (in *A Natural Perspective*, New York: Columbia University Press, 1965, p. 1), from Longinus, in *On the Sublime*, onwards.

32 See e.g. the splendid opening of Lucian's *True History*; and, within the *Odyssey* itself, such passages as Alcinous to Odysseus in XI, 362f and Pallas Athene to Odysseus in XIII, 291f.

33 Ford, *The Good Soldier*, London: John Lane, The Bodley Head, 1915, p. 192.

'WHAT I AM ALWAYS WANTING TO SAY':
FORD MADOX FORD
AND THE ENGLISH 'LITERARY MYTH'

Peter Easingwood

… the writer is forced by his writing into a cleft stick: either the object of the work is naively attuned to the conventions of its form, Literature remaining deaf to our present History, and not going beyond the literary myth; or else the writer acknowledges the vast novelty of the present world, but finds that in order to express it he has at his disposal only a language which is splendid but lifeless.

Every writer born opens within himself the trial of literature, but if he condemns it, he always grants it a reprieve which literature turns to use in order to reconquer him.

Roland Barthes, *Writing Degree Zero*[1]

The remarks quoted above characterise the recurrent effort by which contemporary writing tries to redefine itself against existing literary conventions. In characterising such a process, Barthes refers to 'the search for a non-style or an oral style, for a zero level or a spoken level of writing….'. According to this formulation, 'writing' wishes to escape from a 'literature' which paradoxically is always ready to reclaim it as its own. *Writing Degree Zero* was first published in 1953. If Barthes continues to attract readers, presumably this is because of his widely-discussed distinction between 'readerly' and 'writerly' texts, his concentration on the act of writing, and his creative interest in the circumstances and even the materials of writing. The reason for introducing Barthes as a mediating figure between readers of the present time and Ford is that Ford's texts required a change in reading habits, involving questions of the relationship between writing and reading, which the British public at the time never quite seemed to catch onto. Ford's writing about writing is still too much taken for granted and perhaps needs a touch of defamiliarisation. Ford had completely internalised 'the trial of literature' well before 1914. Above all, he is the figure through whom the precepts and practices of modernism first make contact with English culture. Ford achieved effects of change in the perception of writing in relation to literature that predate *The Good Soldier* (1915) and are not confined to a critique of the novel as a literary form. Indeed much of the story of Ford's early modernism extends over a wider field of discursive writing which may be called 'novelistic', in the sense that it reconfigures conventional boundaries between fiction and non-fiction. Ford's poetry is also often discursive and novelistic in its attempt to address contemporary experience in contemporary language. Ford explains his view of this process in the Preface to *Collected Poems* (1913).

The essay title uses a quotation from one of Ford's most remarkable letters. This was written to Lucy Masterman on 23 January 1913.[2] The letter belongs to a period of literary activity and personal distress of peculiar intensity even for Ford.[3] In the form of advice to a friend, the letter is evidence of Ford's last testimony concerning the trial of literature in England before the Great War. Looking forward to what Ford describes as a decisive moment in his life with the publication of *The Good Soldier*, the reader of Ford today anticipates the beginning of the Great War and, as a consequence for Ford himself, a break in his contribution to the history of English modernism. There are of course other well known instances of a wartime crisis and recovery. Wyndham Lewis and D. H. Lawrence offer further different examples of this. The case of Ford is especially significant for the way in which he then continually revisits and rewrites the past. The foundations of a series of modernist narratives which would actually incorporate the travail of the author were laid down by Ford before the War. To borrow a phrase from Malcolm Lowry, a Ford narrative usually comprehends 'the bloody agony of the writer writing'.[4]

The letter to Lucy Masterman conveys a sense of the living moment. It assumes a conversational style but the trial of literature is in session. Ford insists that issues of literary style and language cannot be separated from perceptions of social change. This awareness is evidently missing from the poems by Lucy Masterman, on which Ford wishes to offer some friendly advice:

> To jump quickly to what I want to say – to what I am always wanting to say – the note is too refined, too remote, too LITERARY.... Forget about Piers Plowman, forget about Shakespeare, Keats, Yeats, Morris, the English Bible and remember only that you live in our terrific, untidy, empirical age, where

not one single problem is solved and not one single Accepted Idea from the past has any more magic. (*LF* 54)

There are strong signs of an established performance in the letter. Ezra Pound recalls Ford at Giessen in that same year, rolling wordlessly on the floor, head in hands, in an effort to mime his critique of Pound's third volume of poems. Pound's acknowledgement that 'that roll saved me at least two years' is linked to his conclusion that 'none of us has found a more natural language than Ford did....'[5] Issues of technique in Ford's writing stem from his wide-awake opposition to the clichés, mannerisms and diehard conventions of English poetic and narrative expression in his time. There is much in the letter to suggest that the present time appears highly inauspicious: '... for the moment a medium becomes literary it is remote from the life of the people, it is dulled, languishing, moribund and at last dead' (*LF* 54). Literary performance invites a judgement on the writer's sense of his or her relationship to the existing repertoire of style and technique. Ford's distinctive achievement as an English writer of the period was to sustain within his own sphere of influence an extended trial of literature in the country which he called the home of Accepted Ideas. As editor of *The English Review*, he remarked that the title chosen by himself and Conrad for the journal was really an oxymoron.

Looking back across the years that divide him from pre-war England, the opening of Ford's *Return to Yesterday* (1931) promises a narrative performance based on the refinement of memories and impressions: 'Thinking of Henry James the other day I was led to wonder when I first went to the Antient Town of Rye'.[6] As usual, what Ford is wanting to say involves both a critique of English culture and a close meditation on the act of writing. He positions himself as the *jeune homme modeste* whose own ambitions to write are scarcely even acknowledged by the Master. The narrative reflects on English culture by introducing scenes from the author's life in Kent and in London: the division of experience between the country and the city is a concern to which Ford's imagination turns and returns throughout his writing.

Both of these settings may alternate between utopian and dystopian perspectives. The utopianism which had been so heavily represented among the modes and conventions of writing in English in the pre-war years had become a complex issue within modern memory. From a later point of view, only a transatlantic perspective redeems the English scene for Ford. He is uncompromising in his judgement that, if it were not for James and other 'strangers and foreign settlers', specifically Stephen Crane, W. H. Hudson and Joseph Conrad, the English literary scene would have reached a point where it had to be considered 'empty' and 'lacking a nucleus' (*RY* 29). *Return to Yesterday*, composed by then from a New York perspective and addressed to an American as well as a British audience, fluently recalls the scenes of his first contact with each of these writers, who are collectively described as a transforming influence on English letters. Admirers of Ford's literary reminiscences are likely to consider *Return to Yesterday* as one of his best performances. Hostile critics are equally likely to find it marred by the same faults attributed to his other memoirs: impressionistic writing; reliance on anecdote; repetition of stories already published; and the display of an egotism that sometimes tends towards self-pity. Indeed the dedication to *Return to Yesterday* does seem to be rehearsing a story that has already been told before:

> I don't know how much of my writing you have read. It is probably little enough; you have better things to do and be. But it is certainly more than I shall ever read of my own. I am one with the struggling millions who cannot read me. So, if you have read me at all, you may here find things I have written before. Please don't mind that. Often enough it is unconscious: at my age one does repeat oneself and, since I possess practically none of my own books I cannot refer to them to see what I have written before and I should not have the patience to read them if I had them. But in a number of cases I have done it advisedly to keep the thread of the novel together. (*RY* vii)

The passage which appears most obviously to play into the hands of unsympathetic critics demonstrates conversely the qualities that keep Ford's narrative alive. To have published and to have seen go out of print more books than the author himself will ever reread, or than any reader can be expected to know, may at first look like an admission of defeat; but the story that Ford has to tell depends on the irony of this situation. The writer certainly flirts with the idea of oblivion, since he himself cares so passionately about writing in an environment that appears to value good letters so little. Crane, Conrad and even the magisterial James, are all chosen as examples of the way in which the trial of literature exacts extreme discipline but offers uncertain reward. This is the true source of pathos in Ford's writing. The very idea that so few people really care becomes for Ford the occasion and indeed the obligation to write. His desire 'to keep the thread of the novel together' (*RY* vii) is a characteristic emphasis on the choice of a novelistic form. Ford's non-fiction overrides conventional distinctions between 'literary criticism,' 'sociological impressionism,' 'autobio-graphy,' and 'fiction.' *Return to Yesterday* is a late example of a novelistic commitment that can be traced back to the years before the Great War. This consists in the employment of a mode of discourse which has elements of a story, though the story is not ultimately plot-driven as in a novel.[7] Instead, impressions are gathered in a form of notation that allows the narrator to reflect on progressions of effect and on other investments in literary style. The 'story' is one that Ford has been telling for a long time but the 'discourse' provides an indication of the writer's self-renewal, of the nature of his contract with the reader, and of the survival of his idea of culture.

The text of *Return to Yesterday* introduces into the big picture that it presents of English life before 1914 a modernist reflection of the process of writing and of the figure of the disappearing author:

> I have tried to keep myself out of this work as much as I can – but try as hard as one may after self-effacement the great 'I,' like cheerfulness, will come creeping in. Renan says that as soon as one writes about oneself one poetises a little. I don't think I do. On the other hand, being a novelist, it is possible that I romance. [For a long time] I have gone about the world looking for the person of the Sacred Emperor in low tea shops.... I have seen some Emperors – and not a few pretenders. These and the tea-shops of the Chinese proverb I have tried to make you see. If you sometimes see my coat-tails whisking round the corners you must pardon it.... So this is a novel: a story mirroring such pursuits. (*RY* vi)

The trope involving the Emperor and the tea shop is far-reaching. Official culture explains that the proverb signifies a form of hypocrisy, since it is obvious that the Sacred Emperor is not to be found in low tea shops. Ford, however, becomes the representative of a hybrid un-official culture that brings high and low together. In *No Enemy: A Tale of Reconstruction* (1929), which is both fictional and highly autobio-graphical, the proverb is quoted with special reference to the discovery of a great modern artist in the person of Henri Gaudier-Brzeska, killed on the front line early in the war: a tragically brief glimpse of the celestial radiance for Ford. The narrative constructions that Ford refers to as his memories and impressions are specially designed to focus on such rare moments of recognition. The performative aspect of Ford's writing has been generally underestimated: the sense in which it en-acts as well as describes the preoccupations of the writer. *Return to*

Yesterday recalls Ford's collaboration with Conrad not simply in the manner of a character sketch of Conrad. It takes the reader through a roundup of some of the current clichés of popular literature and journalism. It characterises the agonising search for *le mot juste* but understands that writing, as an escape from the merely literary, has wider implications than that. Writing degree zero can be a harder model to follow than eloquence itself. 'The trouble, however, with Conrad and myself was this: we could not get our own prose keyed down enough' (*RY* 216). Over the length of the book as a whole, the demonstration of writing goes well beyond a concern with *le mot juste*. Discussion of earlier narratives will show how the novelistic or writerly text had made an appearance in England before 1914.

The story that Ford has to tell about the origins of modern writing does not depend entirely on minimalist detail. There is always the big picture. Ford's conviction that the novelist is the historian of contemporary life led to his project from 1929 onwards of writing *A History of Our Own Times*, eventually left uncompleted. The context is transatlantic in scope. There is a chapter on 'Anglo-Saxondom 1870-1880'. Ford introduces a topic which he regards as a key to the main cultural changes leading into the modern period: the transformation in the relationship between the country and the city.

> The main characteristic of the histories of both sides of the Atlantic has been the growth of great towns…. Thus it is convenient, if not to the letter exact, to regard our main topic when dealing with Anglo-Saxondom as being the struggle between what used to be called the Town and Country Parties. The generalisation is a little dangerous because its employment is apt to lead us into party politics but the image is so attractive that it is difficult to be avoided. If we regard – as we have every warrant for regarding – the American Civil War as mainly a contest between industrial and agricultural interests, the image becomes almost irresistible. It is Town versus Country.[8]

The level of generalisation required is clearly a problem for the writer. As usual in Ford's texts, there is a certain tension between the idea of grand narrative and the anecdotal tone. The function of the anecdote as Ford uses it is to suggest that the narrative must always be kept open to allow for other contingencies and to invite the reader's provisional assent. To Ford the argument is an attractive proposition but it is not intended to be taken too literally. Within his writings as a whole, impressions of the country and the city lead a long way back in time from this passage. That some vital connection had been lost between Town and Country is a commonplace of late Victorian and

Edwardian literature. Ford had turned to the simple life in Kent in the 1890s but his itinerary was to lead him to London, Paris and New York, and eventually onwards in the direction of Provence and The Great Trade Route. The prospects of finding the good place and living the good life are entertained at the most intimate level of communication throughout his writing. Both his fiction and non-fiction reproduce the impression that, in turning to landscape as a physical environment, the wholeness or otherwise of the human subject is displayed. The Great War, according to the narrative of Gringoire in *No Enemy*, is quite specifically an outrage on the land itself as well as on the people. Gringoire imagines a population of many millions mobilising to sustain the conflict on a strip of ground about a mile wide stretching the length of France, showing the results of a rupture between industrialisation and culture. For Ford, the context in which 'writing' first makes its challenge to 'literature' arises from his critique of town and country as components of Edwardian literary myth. *Return to Yesterday*, beginning with a section entitled 'Landscapes and Letters', correlates associations of place with literary referenccs throughout. The design of the book is to re-enact the early scenes in which landscapes and letters both appeared to need redefinition.

 Return to Yesterday is an ambitious design in several respects. There are various significant temporal and topographical shifts from New York at the present time of writing to Kent in the early years. The climax of the narrative comes on the day war is declared, at a country house in Berwickshire, in a scene which has special resonance within the history of modernism, since it has been recorded both by Ford and by Wyndham Lewis. The beginning of the narrative is equally resonant. Ford introduces himself as a young man who, rather against his own inclination at first, gradually makes the acquaintance of a circle of writers in exile who had made themselves at home in England: Henry James, Stephen Crane, Joseph Conrad and W. H. Hudson. The origins of modern writing in English are traced to a series of encounters around Rye and other locations in Kent between the *jeune homme modeste* and the exiles who in their distinctive ways were to become exemplary figures for him. W. H. Hudson had the gift of being able to merge completely with the countryside, when observing colonies of rooks, for example. However Hudson 'had before him the problem of whether or no he himself was a writer' (*RY* 28). This author's style seems to Ford as perfectly natural as the grass growing. He takes his place at one end of a literary spectrum that extends to include the highly elaborate mannerisms of Conrad and James.

> [Hudson] had always considered himself a naturalist. Now he was conscious that he was regarded as a great writer by a great many writers. He had therefore – just as in the case of the rooks – set out to observe writers, visiting James, Conrad, Crane, round Rye and, I believe, Mr H. G. Wells, Mr Kipling and the Poet Laureate – then Sir Alfred Austin, who lived as it were in a patriotically protective ring round that settlement of aliens. (*RY* 28)

The narrator's style in *Return to Yesterday* is one of comic self-effacement in the company of genius but the encounters with Conrad, James and the other 'aliens' are noted with mimetic and novelistic flair. The long chronological perspective, from the scenes described as yesterday to Ford's present time of writing and the publication of the book in 1931, introduces a wide range of cultural and geographical references deriving from Ford's subsequent experiences in Europe and the United States. This range of reference constitutes an international theme which makes it appropriate that Henry James should be invoked in the opening words of the narrative as the key representative figure and presiding influence. The 'Englishness' of the scenes which are to be described is by now unthinkable without its cross-channel and transatlantic connections and correspondences.

To return to yesterday in the form of Ford Madox Hueffer's text, *Ancient Lights and Certain New Reflections: Being the Memories of a Young Man* (1911), is to engage with Ford's story in its Edwardian context, without the post-war time-shifts and the consequent progressions of effect. Comparisons between the two memoirs bring out continuities and discontinuities in the telling of the story. The more pronounced anti-Victorian emphasis is consistent with an immediately contemporary sense of impending cultural change. Even so, Ford's Victorians are not figures of straw. The discussion of work by the Pre-Raphaelite Brotherhood is organised and discriminating. Years later, in *Return to Yesterday*, Ford would recall Henry James's expression of dislike for Ford's Pre-Raphaelite connections. For Ford himself, the position is complicated. Recent criticism has argued that he achieved 'a rapprochement with his Pre-Raphaelite childhood' that 'combines an openly antagonistic engagement with a deeply-informed exploitation of his inheritance'.[9] One can certainly agree that to come to terms with such an inheritance is no easy critical task. The opening of the narrative is dominated by Ford's grandfather Madox Brown, whose image provides a memorable pathway into the text:

> As I remember him, with a square, white beard, with a ruddy complexion, and with thick white hair parted in the middle and falling to above the tops of his ears, Madox Brown exactly resembled the king of hearts in a pack of cards. In passion and in emotions – more particularly during one of his fits of gout – he was a hard-swearing, old-fashioned Tory: his reasoning, however, and circumstances made him a revolutionary of the romantic type. I am not sure, even, that towards his later years he would not have called himself an anarchist, and have damned your eyes if you had faintly doubted this obviously extravagant assertion. But he loved the picturesque, as nearly all his friends loved it.[10]

The image is emphatically individual but the cards metaphor and the political references suggest that there is also a collective dimension to the discussion of Madox Brown and his influence. Ford himself is haunted throughout his life by the ambition to gather together a circle of artists and writers. The Pre-Raphaelites provide him with an example of this. On the other hand, the choice of the word 'picturesque' introduces a limiting term into his appreciation of their artistic and intellectual achievements. His literary reminiscences are novelistic in the way they desire to imagine such a community. In *Ancient Lights*, James is mentioned only once and Conrad twice but they are already acknowledged as the only fitting successors of Flaubert and Turgenev to write in English. Ford's conviction is that the future of English letters may turn on a single text or even on a single sentence. Crane appears only once but to strong effect:

> I remember hearing him, with his wonderful eye flashing and his extreme vigour and intonation, comment upon a sentence of Robert Louis Stevenson that he was reading. The sentence was: 'With interjected finger he delayed the motion of the timepiece.' 'By God, poor dear!' Crane exclaimed. 'That man put back the clock of English fiction fifty years.'

Ford continues:

> I do not know that this is exactly what Stevenson did do. I should say myself that the art of writing in English received the numbing blow of a sandbag when Rossetti wrote, at the age of eighteen, *The Blessed Damozel*. From that time forward and until to-day – and for how many years to come! – the idea has been inherent in the mind of the English writer that writing was a matter of digging for obsolete words with which to express ideas dead and gone. (*AL* 52-53)

Underlying the whole argument is the modernist conceit that, according to Flaubert, France could have saved itself from the defeat of 1870 by reading *L'Education Sentimentale* (*AL* 183). Ford is already the enemy of the 'literary' and the literal-minded.

The discursive strategy of *Ancient Lights* includes the figure of the small boy. This precedes by two years Henry James's autobiographical volume *A Small Boy and Others* (1913). One of the frontispieces to *Ancient Lights* reproduces a detail from Madox Brown's picture 'Tell's Son', described as being in the author's possession. A fair-haired male child gazes towards the viewer with considerable self-confidence, holding the two halves of an apple. The illustration has the caption: 'I seem to be looking at myself from the outside'. The image of the small boy lends itself to scenes of fantasy through which the great figures of the Victorian drawing room can be deconstructed: '...when I was not being severely disciplined I moved amongst somewhat distinguished people who all appeared to me to be morally and physically twenty-five feet high' (*AL* viii). This novelistic task of demythologising the past brings into focus a narrator who describes himself as approaching forty and a little mad about good writing. The passing of the Victorian great figure is accompanied by an increasing interest in issues of gender. Ford identifies himself as a wholehearted supporter of the suffragette cause. He offers the opinion that the best nineteenth-century poetry in English was written by Christina Rossetti on the corner of the washstand in her own room, with the door firmly closed against the sound of masculine voices from the drawing room.

Ford's investment in novelistic and anecdotal forms of notation is already quite explicit at this stage. The author anticipates the objections of his critics: 'This book, in short, is full of inaccuracies as to facts, but its accuracy as to impressions is absolute' (*AL* xv). The completion of *The Good Soldier* is usually considered as marking his most significant achievement at this time, following Ford's own opinion. Yet the phrase 'a little mad about good letters' (*AL* 296) resonates across a wider field of writing than just fiction. *Ancient Lights* indicates an alternative conception of writing for the future in the novelistic, anecdotal text that crosses genres between autobiography and the novel. In *Ancient Lights*, the contemporary state of the English book trade is itself considered as a topic of material interest, though Ford considers at this stage that neither Conrad nor James would be familiar with the vulgar expression 'price per thou' which he is too often forced to use (*AL* 239). Among the English modernists, Ford has the widest conception of the imaginative possibilities and the sharpest appreciation of the commercial constraints of writing.

Ancient Lights ends with a turning away from the Country and a return to Town. The turn and return are to be highly characteristic of Ford's future writing but this time the author's sense of an ending is that the place to be is in Town. The simple life appeared to be over.[11] Time in the country is recalled merely as an interlude. The atmospheric effects of the book as a whole arise overwhelmingly from Victorian London as a source and most especially from the household of Madox Brown. The house at 120 Fitzroy Square, with a giant funeral urn over the front door, described by Thackeray in *The Newcomes*, provides one of various points of reference in and around central London. The preponderant note is that of 'gloom' but Ford satirises the literal-minded in a discursive aside on average weather conditions in Bloomsbury and the electoral district of East Saint Pancras. This had been a larger than life setting for the giants of the Victorian age. Towards the end of the narrative, the author describes himself as one among crowds of Edwardian little people, strolling the night streets of London with a friend, in search of entertainment around Leicester Square and Piccadilly Circus. The crowds of the metropolis produce the most typical scenes of modern life. For the narrator who has reached this stage of his story, the years he has spent in the country seem like lost time. The blame for this is laid on the literary influence of W. E. Henley:

> I fled – into the country. Looking at the matter now, I perceive that Henley was responsible for this – Henley and his piratical gang. These people had struck me as rough and unduly boisterous when I went to them out of a Pre-Raphaelite household. But, my grandfather being dead, I suddenly reacted. I did not know then, but I know now that my brain was singing to me:
>
> > Under the bright and starry sky
> > Dig my grave and let me lie.
>
> Only I wanted to have some tussles with the 'good brown earth' before that hill-top should receive me. Well, we have most of us found the 'good brown earth' part of a silly pose – but I am not sorry . . . . the intolerable boredom of country life without sport or pursuit taught me better in time. (*AL* 241-2)

This is part of the story that will change when revisited from the future. Two other texts from the period before 1914 are windows on that future.

The Soul of London (1905) and *The Heart of the Country* (1906) are titles that may suggest that Ford was sometimes as vulnerable as the next man to Edwardian cliché.[12] The titles are somewhat ironic (like the title of *The English Review*) and they each serve as a decoy to lure unsuspecting readers into a text that is quite consciously an experiment in modern writing. Despite Ford's later recriminations in connection with Henley and the good brown earth, *The Heart of the Country* not only is incisive in its critique of Edwardian pastoral idealism but is extremely sensitive to deeper layers of fantasy and myth activated by landscape and memory. The author starts from the position that unmediated access to the country is scarcely possible. The country can only be interpreted across a variety of experience that represents the literal at one extreme and the literary at another. Negotiations between those extremes are introduced in scenes that range from lunchtime conversation in a Soho restaurant to Ford's first meeting with Meary Walker, who reappears in later texts as well, including *Return to Yesterday;* the subject of one of the 'peasant biographies' admired by Pound.[13] The narrator of 1906 is fully alert to the play of illusion that is bound to dog his footsteps in the country.

> These metaphors, this ideal of an island smoothness in Hyperborean seas, are not the less true because they are not part of our present vernacular. Our necessities, our modes of travel, our very speech, have changed; the necessity for that ideal remains. Whilst, indeed, our speech was forming itself, they wrote books with titles like 'Joyful News from the West Over Seas,' and still in the tangible unknown West, they could hope to find Happy Valleys. Now with a mapped-out world we can no longer have that hope. We travel still with that ideal, but the hope has grown intangible. (*HC* 113)

The resistance to the threat of a mapped-out world anticipates later work as far ahead as *It Was the Nightingale* (1933), *Provence* (1935) and *Great Trade Route* (1937). Meanwhile Kent, to which Ford would return after the War, hardly provided a sufficient refuge from the voices of the 'clamant charlatans' (*HC* 114) writing for the journals. The genius of the countryside, as both naturalist and writer, is W. H. Hudson, who is identified in the narrative not by name but by a choice of words that would be recalled again after twenty-five years in *Return to Yesterday*: 'He was all in grey, so that against an old stone wall you would hardly have seen him, or on a downside no bird would startle at passing him' (*HC* 112-13). The figure of speech suggests the quiet authority of Hudson's presence and of his style of writing. Even so, Ford recognises that 'this "Country" in inverted commas' is not available for any other than 'a more or less lettered, more or less educated, more or less easily circumstanced town class' (*HC* 122). Ford's interest in the recovery of a natural language acknowledges the constraints of the dominant culture on the people of the countryside. 'The shepherd's advice to his friends to keep a shut head to people wearing black coats is very generally followed in the cottages' (*HC* 184). Ford knows that his friendship with Meary needs to be described with tact. Another kind of tact appears in the description of old tools and furniture that are to be disposed of by auction as cottages are sold off. The writer's own strong investment in the pathos of these descriptions is offset by the ironic reflection that: 'Countrymen rise and fall; the auctioneer is always at the flood of his eloquence' (*HC* 223). Most readers would be able to accept that the language of Ford's observations represents a certain intimacy with cottage life. At a higher discursive level though, his argument refuses to settle for facile distinctions between observations made from inside or from outside. The modern way of life now requires a complete review of such terms:

> All this is no doubt about 'the country,' in inverted commas – about the land from the outside. It is one of the anomalies of our present civilisation that the majority of self-conscious humanity – the majority, at least, of those who read books – should regard unbuilt-upon land from that outside. It is a fact physically more remarkable in its way than the earliest systems of cosmogonies. That the earth should contain the universe was thinkable enough. That the cities should contain 'the country' is one of those unthinkable things that have passed into the subconsciousness of a great section of mankind. (*HC* 120)

The plan of notation as a whole demonstrates that Ford was under no illusion whatever regarding fantasies of the good brown earth or the open road. The whole book seems alive to the realisation that of all places where an Edwardian vocabulary of literary terms is hard to escape, the heart of the country is likely to be the hardest. The strong idealisation of W. H. Hudson's plain naturalism seems to place Hudson oddly in company with Crane, Conrad and James, until one accepts that, for Ford, Hudson is indeed one of the foremost examples of a natural language in the form of a text to which the reader can turn with pleasure. On the other hand, one must remember Ford's insistence in *Return to Yesterday* that the later Henry James is no less concerned with the pleasures of the text and with the imperative of successful communication but it is 'as if his audiences had tired him out' (*RY* 209).

The countryside produces no more fatal trap for the unwary writer than the topic of change. The changing face of the countryside as a literary cliché offers every invitation towards an acceptance of the status quo. However Ford's perception that the population of the countryside is made up by absences as well as by presences shows the writer's tact in revealing a process of social transformation that neither the locals themselves nor new arrivals are necessarily so fully aware of. V. S. Naipaul's autobiographical novel *The Enigma of Arrival* (1987) shows the full potential of such a procedure. Ford's narrative sustains this point of comparison with Naipaul's in that it is about the writer himself and the way that he learns to see into and see beyond the moment of arrival in the country.

> And 'change, change, change', is the note of all countrysides. Yet it is astonishing how little the change is in evidence once the changes are made. You put a corrugated iron roof in place of the thatch on the great barn, and in two years' time you have forgotten that the covering was ever dun-coloured and soft. You put James Harper into Penny Farthing in place of old Hooker, and, if you do not forget old Hooker, you wonder a little, when you think how well James Harper, who started as a weazened and niggardly innovator, has been bronzed, beaten and worried by weather till he fits into his place for all the world as well as old Hooker ever did. And one forgets, somehow, that Hooker died before the telegraph office was opened at the corner. One forgets even that he was there before the new tenants came to the Hall, and it startles one to hear them say that they do not even remember old Hooker's mother, who trotted about on two sticks for a year-and-a-half after old Hooker died. (*HC* 223-4)

In this book, 'the country' is quite often placed in inverted commas. That is because the subject is not only the country but also the process of writing itself. In his later work, following the Great War, Ford's style develops a new level of self-consciousness, an additional layer of irony that communicates itself to the initiated reader. This arises from the fact that so much of the author's work is already out of print, unavailable, or simply unread.

There are, however, two recent editions of *The Soul of London*.[14] Many regard it as a definitive text for the early years of English modernism. The book is not only about London but about the Modern and about Writing. *The Soul of London* sees London as an imagined community that has outgrown the conventional means of communication which used to inform its social and political structure. The former hierarchy of publications has collapsed:

> But, with the coming of the modern newspaper, the book has been deposed from its intimate position in the hearts of men. You cannot in London read a book from day to day, because you must know the news, in order to be a fit companion for your fellow Londoner. Connected thinking has become nearly impossible, because it is nearly impossible to find any general idea that will connect into one train of thought: 'Home Rule for Egypt,' 'A Batch of Stabbing Cases', and 'Infant Motorists'. It is hardly worth while to trace the evolution of this process. In the 'seventies and 'eighties the Londoner was still said to get his General Ideas from the leader writers of his favourite paper. Nowadays even the leader is dying out.
>
> So that, in general, the Londoner has lost all power of connected conversation, and nearly all power of connected thought. (*SL* 82)

The comment about 'the Book' is of acute interest because for Ford print is the main connection between the personal and political worlds. However, changes in reading habits on the scale suggested do not necessarily signify the end of literature even though, from 1911 onwards, Ford seems increasingly concerned for the future of good letters. His point rather is that former reading practices can no longer apply. London must now be imagined in terms of difference rather than community. Ford acknowledges that a literary approach to the subject of London is likely to introduce considerations of class and cultural expectation that privilege a particular set of views over other possible perspectives:

> Speaking broadly, the man who expresses himself with a pen on paper sees his London from the west. At the worst he hopes to end with that view. His London of breathing space, his West End, extends from say Chiswick to say Portland Place. His dense London is the City as far as Fenchurch Street, his East End ends with what he calls 'Whitechapel.'
>
> The other sees his London of elbow room extend from say Purfleet to say Blackwall. He is conscious of having, as it were at his back, the very green and very black stretches of the Essex marshes dotted with large solitary factories and small solitary farms. His dense London, *his* City, lies along the line from Blackwall to Fenchurch Street. (*SL* 45)

Ford's remarks recall the history of the novel in English from its beginnings: 'People read *Clarissa* by the year, and debated, at dinner tables, as to the abstract proprieties of the case of Pamela. The

Generalisation flourished, Conversation in consequence was possible'
(*SL* 82). Since the reality of London no longer corresponds to cultural
definitions from the past, *The Soul of London* explores how narrative
design, observation and description can take account of the changes.
Ford's introductory chapter dissociates itself from statistical accounts
and guidebooks. He insists that the scope of living experience in
London must now overwhelm any single point of view. This is not
entirely bad news since 'the world town' with such vast powers of
assimilation may be said to represent 'the Modern Spirit' (*SL* 12-13).
The use of the catchphrase 'the Modern Spirit,' like the dissatisfaction
that Ford expresses with the title of the book (*SL* 5-6), is a reminder of
the strain that such pre-modern elements of vocabulary now have to
bear. But Ford recognises that his subject requires a newly designed
approach. Starting with observations of London 'from a distance,' he
rehearses present and former lines of approach in a style that makes
these lines extracted from the Contents page for Chapter II look like a
parody of conventional guides to the city or even like a poem:

> Entering on a motor car
>
> Entering on an electric tram
>
> Entering London on a bicycle – Its tiresomeness
>
> Entering London on foot
>
> In a gipsy caravan
>
> Entering London on a market wagon
>
> Entering London by barge – No longer a common method
>
> Entering London by railway

This whole prospectus is actually written up in the text in novelistic
style with anecdotal details. One feels that all literary approaches to
the problem of getting into London have been covered up to 1905. The
railway still at this date represents rapid transit and indeed 'the
product of the quality of rapid transit is London itself' (*SL* 32). Ford
points out how brief glimpses of other people's lives from the railway
leave an uncompleted narrative. But he suggests that the same effect is
now to be felt on all roads into London. This runs counter to 'the
sentiment ingrained in humanity of liking a story to have an end' (*SL*
41). The opening of Ford's poem 'Finchley Road' in *Collected Poems*
(1914) celebrates the complex new patterns of interconnection:

As we come up from Baker Street
Where tubes and trains and 'buses meet...

The same poem helps to put into perspective Ford's advice to Lucy Masterman in the letter already cited: 'That is what is the matter with all the verse of to-day; it is too much practised in temples and too little in motorbuses – LITERARY! LITERARY!' (*LF* 54).

The 'literary' is to Ford a domain of established myth and ritual observances that has declined into the cultivation of empty signs. Ford's own special gift was to be able to communicate instead the excitement of writing that is capable of renewing itself. With hindsight he was fully able to appreciate the irony that his own most severe tests of self-renewal were still to come. In *Return to Yesterday*, Ford relishes the sense of an ending in which he describes how he faces Wyndham Lewis's prediction of his extinction as a writer exactly at the moment of his greatest success. Just as war is about to be declared, he reads the proofs of the novel to which he refers as 'my Great Auk's Egg': 'The Great Auk lays one egg and bursts' (*RY* 401). This is in the journal prophetically called *Blast*. Ford continued to think of the publication of *The Good Soldier* as a unique event. But that publication can also be seen as part of a longer story that crosses genres and continues between texts to narrate Ford's experiences of Englishness, modernity, and writing. This longer narrative secures Ford's place among the modernists writing in English who transformed the relationship between the reader and the literary text.

NOTES

1   Roland Barthes, *Writing Degree Zero and Elements of Semiology*, tr. Annette Lavers and Colin Smith, London: Jonathan Cape, 1967, pp.71-72. A statement by Barthes on 'An Almost Obsessive Relation to Writing Instruments' can be found in Roland Barthes, *The Grain of the Voice: Interviews 1962-1980*, tr. Linda Coverdale, New York: Hill and Wang, 1985, pp. 177-182.

2   *Letters of Ford Madox Ford,* ed. Richard M. Ludwig, Princeton: Princeton University Press, 1965 – henceforth *LF*; pp. 53-6.

3   See Max Saunders, *Ford Madox Ford: A Dual Life*, Vol. 1, Oxford: Oxford University Press, 1996, for a full critical and biographical account of the period.

4   *The Collected Letters of Malcolm Lowry*, ed. Sherrill E. Grace, Vol. 2, London: Jonathan Cape, 1996, p. 664. (Letter to Albert Erskine early June 1953.)

5   From Pound's obituary on Ford. Cited by Alan Judd, *Ford Madox Ford*, London: Collins, 1990, p. 447.

6   Ford Madox Ford, *Return to Yesterday*, New York: Horace Liveright, 1932 – henceforth *RY*; p. 13.

7   'Story' here is used to indicate in general terms the extent of the raw material, as it were, that the writer has at his disposal. 'Discourse' however implies special recognition of the unique effects of style which bring into shape any particular narrative. This distinction arises in the work of European Formalist critics unknown to Ford but roughly contemporary with the period of his writing under discussion. On Formalism, see Raman Selden, *A Reader's Guide to Contemporary Literary Theory*, Brighton, Sussex: The Harvester Press, 1985, pp. 6-12. The idea of the uniqueness of literary form, and the perception of style and language as being integral to all literary effects, are basic assumptions throughout Ford's critical writings.

8   Ford Madox Ford, *A History of Our Own Times*, ed. Solon Beinfeld and Sondra J. Stang, Manchester: Carcanet Press, pp. 45-46.

9   Pamela Bickley, 'Ford and Pre-Raphaelitism' in *Ford Madox Ford: A Reappraisal*, ed. Robert Hampson and Tony Davenport, Amsterdam and New York: Rodopi Press, 2002, p. 76.

10   Ford Madox Hueffer, *Ancient Lights,* London: Chapman and Hall, 1911 – henceforth *AL;* pp. 2-3.

11   See Saunders. See also Robin Peel, 'Ford and the Simple Life,' in *Ford Madox Ford's Modernity*, ed. Robert Hampson and Max Saunders, Amsterdam and New York: Rodopi Press, 2003, pp. 59-70.

12   All references to Ford's England Trilogy in this chapter come from *England and the English*, ed. Sara Haslam, Manchester: Carcanet, 2003; comprising *The Soul of London* (*SL* – 1905); *The Heart of the Country* (*HC* – 1906) and *The Spirit of the People* (*SP* – 1907).

13   Saunders, *Ford Madox Ford: A Dual Life*, Vol. 1, p. 95.

14   See note 12 above. Another edition is Ford Madox Ford, *The Soul of London: A Survey of a Modern City*, ed. Alan G. Hill, London: Everyman, 1995.

THE ENGLISHNESS OF *THE ENGLISH REVIEW*

Jason Harding

'[A]n *English Review* is a contradiction in terms' – *The Critical Attitude*, 1911[1]

Ford's reminiscences should be treated with caution. There is, however, a symbolic if not necessarily a literal truth in Ford's account, in *Return to Yesterday*,[2] of the naming of the *English Review*:

> It was Conrad who chose the title. He felt a certain sardonic pleasure in the choosing so national a name for a periodical that promised to be singularly international in tone, that was started mainly in his not very English interest and conducted by myself who was growing every day more and more alien to the normal English trend of thought, at any rate in matters of literary technique. And it was matters of literary technique that almost exclusively interested both him and myself. That was very un-English. (*RY* 379)

It would appear, then, that when E. V. Lucas complained to Conrad that Ford's *English Review* was 'generally too foreign for its title' he was missing a subtle irony intended by the choice of name.[3] This chapter proposes that an examination of the collaboration between Ford and Conrad during 1908 and 1909 helps us both to understand and interpret contemporary perceptions of the 'un-English' nature of the *English Review*. The chapter closes with some reflections on Ford's engagement with C. F. G. Masterman's *The Condition of England* (1909) and H. G. Wells' *Tono-Bungay* (1909), two works that made a significant contribution to the *English Review*'s construction of literary and political 'Englishness'. It will be seen that Ford's editorial vision of Englishness was altogether less confident and more controversial than a simple-minded patriotic celebration of national identity.

Krishan Kumar's recent study of English national identity[4] has identified the Edwardian decade, during which Ford launched the *English Review*, as a 'moment of Englishness': that is, an era when blows to Britain's imperial prestige, inflicted during the Boer War, led to a resurgence of *English* nationalism conceived upon narrower ethnic and cultural lines. Although Kumar's thesis has a tendency to underestimate the extent to which the terms British and English were interchangeable throughout this period and to overestimate the extent to which the British were 'steeped' in an imperial culture, his observations have an undeniable relevance to the author of the *England and the English* trilogy.[5] In *The Soul of London* (1905), Ford's vision of Englishness was remarkably unlike the pastoral nostalgia of many of his contemporaries who celebrated the gentle countryside of the Home Counties as, in some way, an epitome of English national identity. On the contrary, Ford Hermann Hueffer, the son of a 'musical Hun' (to quote Gore Vidal's tart formulation)[6] evoked in a series of impressions what he called the English 'melting-pot':[7] 'London is the world town, not because of its vastness; it is vast because of its assimilative powers, because it destroys all race characteristics, insensibly and, as it were, anaesthetically' (*SL* 12). It may seem surprising that Ford, a self-styled agrarian, should cherish the 'kaleidoscopic' modernity of London rather than the idyllic 'organic communities' threatened by Britain's relentless industrial-ization and urbanization. In Ford's eyes, the English 'melting-pot' was representative not of a nation nor a race, but a microcosm of 'the whole world, attracted to a fertile island by the hope of great gain, or by the faith that there a man may find freedom' (*SL* 278).

There was certainly nothing insular or parochial about Ford's conception of the *English Review*: a forum expressly designed to jolt John Bull from his intractable artistic philistinism. And yet, Ford would later bemoan the failure of his editorship of the *English Review* 'to enjoin upon the Englishman a critical attitude' (*CA* 4). He also suggested that the journal, like those glittering but ephemeral 'little magazines' of the fin-de-siècle, was doomed to an early death. But this belies the confident tone of Ford's editorials on the major social, political and intellectual issues of the day, positioning this 'review' as a clear successor to the great Victorian reviews of general culture. Unlike, say, *The Yellow Book*, the *English Review* cultivated the patrician tone of the 'higher journalism' hinting at connections with influential political élites. Perhaps the demise of Ford's control of the *English Review* can be ascribed to delusions of editorial grandeur, together with a wilful, albeit painful, misconception of the economic realities of Edwardian journalism. The unquestionable success of the journal, however, was its literary side: namely, Ford's achievement in publishing work from the very best international writers – the

American-born Henry James, the Russians Tolstoy and Dostoevsky, the Irishman Yeats – all in his *English* monthly review. The reminiscences of his friend and collaborator, the Ukrainian-born Pole, Konrad Korzienowski, are highly instructive in this regard and serve to highlight some of the tensions between the cosmopolitan modernists Ford championed in the *English Review* and those public-school educated Englishmen who appeared to be the 'implied readers' of his editorials.

It was in his roles as editor and amanuensis – some have even argued as 'secret sharer' – that Ford persuaded his friend to attempt (as Conrad explained to his literary agent, J. B. Pinker) 'to make Polish life enter English literature'.[8] Conrad acknowledged that without Ford's support and encouragement he would not have chosen to revisit, in print, his fraught, unhappy childhood. That this undertaking ended acrimoniously is further testimony to the profound emotions Conrad uncovered brooding upon his Polish heritage before English readers. The published memoirs of his sober guardian and uncle, Tadeusz Bobrowski, provided Conrad with the major written source for his autobiographical reflections: the lens, or prism, through which he examined his Polish ancestry. Bobrowski's memoirs furnished some of the anecdotes that spiced up this foreign dish for an English audience; e.g., the dramatic account of Conrad's grand-uncle Mickołaj, decorated for conspicuous bravery while serving in Napoleon's Polish Legions, but who suffered the hardships of the 1812 retreat from Moscow, symbolized (if Conrad is to be believed) by a diet of Lithuanian dog. Further humiliations followed the failed Polish uprisings of 1830 and 1863: during the latter the old man was stripped of his possessions, with the exception of his war medals (which fortunately found their way to his grand-nephew). Conrad's playful tone in his reminiscences was an exercise of considerable restraint given his implacable hatred of Russian autocracy and his despair at the romantic martial heroism of the Polish landowning *szlachta*. His good humour was clearly an act of politeness towards an English audience not particularly fond of emotional displays of nationalism, at least *foreign* nationalism. On the sad fate of two no less ardent family patriots, his father Apollo and his mother Ewa, Conrad's reminiscences (in spite of his original intentions as outlined in a letter to Pinker) offer few intimate disclosures – barely more than a couple of pages are allocated to the memory of his parents, even these pieties are heavily coloured by Bobrowski's memoirs. Jocelyn Baines, with a biographer's irritable reaching after fact and reason, has complained that Conrad's reminiscences contain 'no analysis, no probing below the surface'.[9] In point of fact, several significant life crises are glossed, obscured, or repressed in these sketches, including: Conrad's serious illness on his family's journey into enforced exile; his mother's gradual deterioration and early death from tuberculosis in Russian exile; his father's morbid depression during their last months together in Cracow. Tadeusz Bobrowski acknowledged the awful truth of his nephew's predicament when he told him it was a harsh fate to be orphaned at the age of eleven under such bitter circumstances. 'I felt my head was now bare to the universe, that the roof of childhood had been removed' to quote Seamus Heaney's aptly Wordsworthian contemplation of parental loss, his 'Unroofed scope' leaving the orphan exposed to the 'Knowledge-freshening wind.'[10] Bearing such shocks in mind, it was little wonder Conrad told H. G. Wells, during the anxious composition of his memoirs, that 'the stirring up of all these dead' was a nightmarish experience.[11]

It was arguably the very 'Englishness' of the *English Review* that exacerbated Conrad's autobiographical restraint. True, the journal's readership probably expected less in the manner of an English 'stiff upper lip' emotional reserve than the staple fare of Edwardian journalism. Even Ford's editorial advocacy of French literature was no catalyst. Conrad's distaste for the exhibitionism of Rousseau's *Confessions* was a gesture of solidarity with those very English men of letters who had often remarked upon the 'un-English' accent and mannerisms of this non-native speaker. Conrad was certainly sensitive to accusations of vulgar emotionalism in dealing with his Polish background, not to mention the difficulty of communicating to English readers what he perceived to be the tragic hopelessness of Poland's political situation. He was acutely aware that several Polish writers and intellectuals had accused him of disloyalty (even betrayal) – a grave charge in his moral universe. A need to justify his exile shaped the two-part liberation narrative underpinning his reminiscences: the first crux revolved around his decision to go to sea, the second recounted his ambition to become a professional writer. It was as an author of 'exotic tales' of the Malay archipelago and adventurous sea stories that Joseph Conrad was known to the English public (on whom he depended for his livelihood) and *not* as the orphaned son of persecuted Polish radicals. Never a fluent writer, Conrad underestimated the sheer difficulty of negotiating a path, in the pages of the *English Review,* through this quagmire of troubling memories.

The creative and chronological displacements in his episodic impressionistic narrative bear witness to the painful feelings he uncovered and
suppressed in this apparently genial portrait of the artist. The contingent, existential twists and turns by which Konrad Korzeniowski
became a Master in the British merchant marine and a successful
English novelist were by no means the smooth unfolding of an inex-
orable fate. On the contrary, Conrad's reminiscences are a record of
the creative sublimation of his most obsessive fears – a personal
mythology that salvaged continuity and meaning from the bleakest
moments of his past. When he recalled his decision to leave Poland as
a 'standing jump out of … racial surroundings and associations' even
the most sympathetic English reader could hardly have appreciated the
full emotional force of this declaration.[12] Zdzisław Najder, the great
Polish Conradian, blames Ford's 'irresponsibility' and 'arrogance' for
the abrupt termination of Conrad's reminiscences in the *English
Review*:[13] the question of 'Polishness' can touch a raw nerve in Polish
and foreign critics alike. But it is a moot point to what extent Conrad's
angry refusal to continue serializing his memoirs was due to the
flawed character of the editor of the *English Review* and not the
traumatic prospect of addressing Polish shades 'under English eyes'.

   This regrettable episode in the relationship of Ford and Conrad
does not make for pleasant reading and one would not wish to
rehearse the details of this quarrel were it not for the light it sheds on
cultural constructions of 'Englishness' in the *English Review*.
Conrad's 1912 'Author's Note' to *A Personal Record*, the renamed
but virtually unaltered book version of his reminiscences, characterized the memoirs as a fragment of autobiography suggesting Conrad
had planned to write a complete 'record' with Ford's assistance. Max
Saunders is surely correct to stress the fruitful reciprocity of their
literary collaborations.[14] Conrad was undoubtedly indebted to the
younger writer as a prose stylist, part of his efforts to polish his occasionally unidiomatic phraseology and syntax – those tell-tale marks of
foreignness. But Conrad's public identity as an English writer was a
problematic role and was difficult to sustain over extended periods.
Perhaps Conrad feared his autobiographical revelations might alienate
some readers of the *English Review* and consequently retreated into a
self-protective irritability, illness and eventually silence. It was
doubtless a relief not to have to meet the monthly deadlines for his
instalments, even though he must have realized that Ford, struggling

with the burden of the review's crippling financial debts (not to mention the break-up of his marriage) would have felt badly let down.

Conrad, too, felt let down by Ford's editorial note in the *English Review* in July 1909 citing serious illness as the cause of his non-appearance. Whatever the precise reasons, Conrad's autobiographical self-censorship may have betokened a fear of openly voicing to English readers the bitterness, pathos and rage that accompanied his reflections on his formative Polish background. An unhappy child-hood, compounded by an orphan's fear of rejection, help to explain why Conrad's reminiscences highlight his 'adoption' by the British merchant marine and, less plausibly, the English language. Seen in this light, Conrad's symbolism tells us that his career as an English novelist was dependent upon his escape from Polish history. Edward Said's comments on Conrad in *Culture and Imperialism* might be usefully extended to the 'marginal' character of Ford's *English Review*. Said remarks that as a Polish expatriate Conrad could scarcely have addressed the natives of imperial Britain without a degree of 'self-consciousness as an outsider' enabling him 'to comprehend how the machine works, given that you and it are fundamentally not in perfect synchrony or correspondence'.[15] As aliens in literary England, Ford (né Hueffer) and Conrad (né Korzeniowski) self-consciously fashioned their authorial personas in the pages of the *English Review*; both politely observed the decorum of Edwardian journalism while simultaneously preserving a degree of ironic distance from their implied audience. 'He is always a stranger among us' observed Virginia Woolf of Conrad. Yet her delicate sense of social discrimin-ations led her to characterize him as a stranger who 'treats us and our belongings with a courtesy which is the perfection of breeding'.[16] Compare Woolf's willingness to accommodate the 'alien' with the cultural anarchism fuelling Ford's lurid description of his inner circle of friends and novelists as 'a ring of foreign conspirators plotting against British letters'.[17]

Though not exactly a foreign conspirator, H. G. Wells was intimately involved with the founding of the *English Review* and even considered taking a sub-editorial role (Saunders, vol. 1 256). His novel *Tono-Bungay* was serialized in the first four numbers of the *English Review*. Written in dialogue with Charles Masterman's study *The Condition of England* (1909), which sought to lay bare the social conflicts and ills of Edwardian England, *Tono-Bungay* satirized the economic and political corruptions indicative of a new spirit of amoral commercialism. The novel closes with a journey down the Thames in which the ancient river is contrasted with the ugliness and vulgarity of modern London. Wells's lyrical description of this oily, polluted river-front anticipates the 'sandwich papers' and 'cigarette ends' drifting towards Greenwich in T. S. Eliot's *The Waste Land* (1922), as well as evoking Conradian allusions. 'The realities are greedy trade, base profit-seeking, bold advertisement – and kingship and chivalry', mused Wells's first-person narrator, are 'dead among it all'.[18] In a review, Arnold Bennett commented on *Tono-Bungay*: 'I do not think that any novelist ever more audaciously tried, or failed with more honour, to render in the limits of one book the enormous and confusing complexity of a nation's racial existence'.[19] In effect, *Tono-Bungay*'s sociological analysis made it an Edwardian successor to the mid-Victorian 'Condition of England' novels. It was an analogy Ford pointed out in his *English Review* article on Masterman's *The Condition of England*. Commenting upon the considerable ambitions of Masterman's study, Ford remarked: 'to write about a people mixed in race, united by no common emotions, upheld by no common faith – this is a task calling for impossible qualities if the writer is at all to dogmatise with justness'.[20] These qualities, he added, were possessed neither by Masterman nor by the author of *Tono-Bungay*. A few months later, Ford spelt out in the *English Review* his Jamesian aesthetic differences with Wells, claiming that the writer of imaginative literature must be a conscious artist and never a merely Wellsian 'man of intellect'. Ford claimed in his editorial commentary that in *Tono-Bungay* Wells had written 'a British novel along the lines of his national temperament',[21] a remark that was surely intended to be ironic given his generally low opinion of the provincialism of British novelists and their blindness to cross-cultural encounters. It appears as if the 'hybridity' of Edwardian England might be better viewed in Ford's editorial conception of the *English Review* than in Wells's anatomy of modern Britain's 'degeneration' and decline.

When E. V. Lucas complained that Ford's *English Review* was 'too foreign for its title', he was not just expressing his distaste for the journal's alarmingly 'foreign' opinions, but also suggesting that the review could never be very popular among the English reading public. Perhaps Ford's editorial control of the *English Review* confirms the gloomy portrait in George Gissing's *New Grub Street* of the worldly triumph of literary opportunism over artistic conscience: the pre-eminence of a new breed of professional writers and journalists who had emerged from the populist New Journalism at the end of the nineteenth century. When Sir Alfred Mond bought the insolvent *English Review* in 1910 he immediately sacked Ford and replaced him with Austin Harrison, then drama critic for Alfred Harmsworth's mass-circulation *Daily Mail*. Conrad professed to despise the more commercial character of the *English Review* under Mond – sentiments echoed by Ford's protégés D. H. Lawrence and Ezra Pound.

Ford's review of Conrad's *Under Western Eyes* for the *English Review* in December 1911 championed the novel as the work of a romantic Polish aristocrat who transcended 'this age of limited companies'.[22] Though *Under Western Eyes* was first serialized in the *English Review,* Ford saw it as an exemplary work of artistic integrity untainted by the commercialism associated with popular Edwardian novelists and journalists, such as the resourceful Arnold Bennett and other doyens of Mond's *English Review*. Ford's emphasis on the artist and on the technique of art showed that he was indifferent to market principles of success. Max Saunders does justice to Ford's high-minded editorial principles when he writes: 'He paid good prices, did not make a profit on his writers, and displayed a rare magnanimity as an editor, not requiring particular political, aesthetic, or moral positions from his authors; merely that their work should be well written' (Saunders, vol. 1 243). Even at the height of their quarrel in mid-1909, Conrad told Ford: 'my contributions were for a *person* not for an *editor*' – something that could never be said of his contributions to the review under Harrison.[23] Thanking Ford for his review of *Under Western Eyes*, Conrad praised the 'accent' in which he couched his appreciation:

> I am infinitely touched by what you say and by the accent you have found to express what may be critically just and true but to a certainty is the speech of a friend. What touches me most is to see that you not discard our common past. These old days may not have been such very 'good old days' as they should have been – but to me my dear Ford they are a very precious possession. In fact I have nothing else that I can call my own. And had you put them aside in your fortunate present I should have felt distinctly poorer for it.[24]

Doubtless, the accents of both Ford and Conrad sounded 'too foreign' at times to many readers of *The English Review*.

NOTES

1 *The Critical Attitude* – henceforth *CA* – London: Duckworth, 1911, p. 4.
2 *Return to Yesterday* – henceforth *RY;* London: Victor Gollancz, 1931.
3 *The Collected Letters of Joseph Conrad: Volume 4, 1908-1911*, ed. Frederick R. Karl and Laurence Davies, Cambridge: Cambridge University Press, 1990, p. 246.
4 See Krishan Kumar, *The Making of English National Identity*, Cambridge: Cambridge University Press, 2003, pp. 176-221. See also Bernard Porter, *The Absent-Minded Imperialists*, Oxford: Oxford University Press, 2004.
5 All references to Ford's England Trilogy in this paper come from *England and the English,* ed. Sara Haslam, Manchester: Carcanet, 2003; comprising *The Soul of London* (*SL* – 1905); *The Heart of the Country* (*HC* – 1906) and *The Spirit of the People* (*SP* – 1907).
6 *Times Literary Supplement,* 22 June 1990, p. 659.
7 Harriet Cooper, 'The Duality of Ford's Historical Imagination', *History and Representation in Ford Madox Ford's Writings*, ed. Joseph Wiesenfarth, Amsterdam and New York: Rodopi, 2004, pp. 189-99, discusses how Ford's use of this metaphor predates Zangwill's play of 1909 usually credited with introducing it in discussions of American culture: see pp. 192-3.
8 *The Collected Letters of Joseph Conrad: Volume 4*, p.138.
9 Jocelyn Baines, *Joseph Conrad*, London: Weidenfeld & Nicolson, 1960, p. 354.
10 See Seamus Heaney, 'Sixth sense, seventh heaven,' *The Dublin Review,* Autumn 2002, p. 119.
11 *The Collected Letters of Joseph Conrad: Volume 4*, p. 149.
12 Joseph Conrad, *The Mirror of the Sea* and *A Personal Record*, ed. Zdzisław Najder, Oxford: Oxford University Press, 1988, p. 121.
13 Najder, *The Mirror of the Sea* and *A Personal Record,* Oxford: Oxford University Press, 1988, p. xvii.
14 Max Saunders, *Ford Madox Ford: A Dual Life,* volume 1, Oxford: Oxford University Press, 1996, pp. 109-161.
15 Edward Said, *Culture and Imperialism*, New York: Vintage, 1993, p. 25.
16 *Times Literary Supplement* (3 March 1912), p. 141.
17 Cited by Max Saunders in 'Ford Madox Ford,' *Encyclopedia of Literary Modernism*, ed. Paul Poplawski, Westport: Greenwood Press, 2003, p. 125.
18 H. G. Wells, *Tono-Bungay*, London: Collins, 1969, p. 341.
19 *The New Age,* 4 March 1909; p. 384-5.
20 Ford, 'C. F. G. Masterman, *The Condition of England'*, in *Critical Essays*, ed. Max Saunders and Richard Stang, Manchester: Carcanet, 2002, p. 73.
21 See 'The Critical Attitude', *The English Review*, 3, November 1909, pp. 666-8.
22 Ford, 'Joseph Conrad', in *Critical Essays*, p. 80.
23 *The Collected Letters of Joseph Conrad: Volume 4,* p. 264.
24 *The Collected Letters of Joseph Conrad: Volume 4,* p. 224-5.

BEYOND MIMETIC ENGLISHNESS: FORD'S ENGLISH TRILOGY AND *THE GOOD SOLDIER*

Nick Hubble

There is an extraordinary passage in the first chapter of *The Soul of London* in which Ford describes how the successful internalisation of the city's ceaseless routine completes the process by which a typical young provincial is transformed into a Londoner: 'Daily details will have merged as it were into his bodily functions, and will have ceased to distract his attention'.[1] London, Ford argues, is experienced unconsciously by its inhabitants: 'a matter so much more of masses than of individuals' that 'it can only be treated as a ground bass, a drone, on top of which one pipes one's own small individual melody' (*SL* 11). Here, he repeats a metaphor from the book's 'Introductory', in which historic London is described as 'like a constant ground bass beneath the higher notes of the Present' (*SL* 4). These two themes are linked throughout Ford's trilogy, *England and the English*, as a fragile individualism, forever threatened with complete submersion in a dehumanised mass society, struggles to realise the promise of the 'Future'. It is for this reason that Ford equates the Londoner with the Modern and describes that embodiment of mass society, the suburbanite, in terms hitherto reserved for the romantic artist: 'in each of these houses dwells a strongly individualised human being with romantic hopes, romantic fears, and at the end, an always tragic death' (*SL* 5).

Ford's characterisation of modern existence was anticipated by Georg Simmel's 1903 essay 'The Metropolis and Mental Life', which begins: 'The deepest problems of modern life flow from the attempt of the individual to maintain the independence and individualism of his existence against the sovereign powers of society, against the weight of his historical heritage and the external culture and technique of life'.[2] While, as Simmel notes, these problems have existed since civilization began – with the conflict in Athens between individualised personalities and a de-individualising small town creating 'an atmosphere of tension in which the weaker were held down and the stronger were impelled to the most passionate type of self-protection' (Simmel 333) – the modern combination of money economy and industrial production exacerbated the tension between collective and individual by enabling the rise of a romantic form of individualism in competition with the classical model. Here, significance is attached not to the human quality of the unified subject, but to the existence of 'qualitative uniqueness and irreplaceability' – primarily expressed in commodified areas such as taste, style and fashion – which appealed to the masses recently 'liberated from their historical bonds'. As Simmel argues, the developing relationship between these two forms of individualism charts 'the external as well as the internal history of our time' and culminates in a peculiarly poised historical conjuncture in which both forces not only 'find themselves with equal legitimacy' but also in a condition of mutual interdependence (Simmel 339).

Ford describes a similar situation in chapter four of *The Soul of London*, concerning the relationship between the leisured upper classes and London's emergent mass society. He relates an anecdote of how he offered to find a job on a farm for a recently unemployed man, who had come to London from the country as a boy, only to be rebuffed:

> 'London's the place,' he repeated. I objected that he could not see much of London inside a soap factory. He considered for a moment and said: 'No, but it's the Saturday afternoons and the Sundays.' He paused. 'It's when ye have your leisure.' (*SL* 67)

Ford concludes: 'Thus what London attracts with the mirage of its work shining across the counties and the countries, London holds with the glamour of its leisure'. In no other observable phenomenon was this as self-evident as in the groups of shop girls and clerks parading up and down before the reflections of their fantasy-selves in shop windows; offering a vision of the future, as he somewhat playfully observes, to warm the heart of all good democrats (*SL* 85-6). In an earlier passage he has already suggested that it is precisely this weekend emulation of the Leisured Class which keeps London working and, therefore, which paradoxically enables the very existence of the Leisured Class – all are one part of a unified social system in which the function of 'the leisured class remains as a lure, as a sort of Islands of the Blest, glamorous in the haze above Park

Lane and Mayfair, an incentive to health because wealth means leisure, wealth means work, and work health' (*SL* 73).

However, despite the similarities in sociological insight, Ford differs from Simmel in that he adopts an ironic stance to the metropolitan life he describes, dryly concluding of this lower class motivation to work that 'a nobler incentive would of course be nobler …'. Furthermore, a temperamental disinclination is detectable in his references to modern democracy: 'Only the most hardened of democrats, seeing humanity not as poor individuals but as parts of a theory, as negligible cog-wheels of a passionless machine, would deny that, from a human point of view Athens was better than Kensington High Street …' (*SL* 89). Yet for all that, Ford's analysis is ultimately more penetrating than Simmel's because he demonstrates how modernity had already bypassed the crossroads in 'the world history of the spirit' that Simmel identified as having been created by the equipoise of the two competing forms of classical and romantic individualism. As Ford observes, 'poor humanity' – the mass – had already voted unconsciously against classical individualism (*SL* 94). While the defeated faction's cautionary warnings still echo a century later – 'what will your Corporations of the future be like … when you have swept away the love of place with your improvement schemes, when you have swept away all fear of public opinion by weakening our every individual tie?' (*SL* 93) – the condition of England in 2005 bears witness to the unique penetration of Ford's insight in 1905.

Ford identifies the same fundamental changes that Jürgen Habermas was later to diagnose in *The Structural Transformation of the Public Sphere* as stemming from the reversal of the separation between state and civil society and the consequent rise in state intervention and marking the depoliticisation and 'downfall' of the public sphere 'from the time of the great depression that began in 1873'.[3] According to Habermas, the bourgeois public sphere had first come into being with the amalgamation between 'court' and 'town', which brought together a public display of authority descended from feudal society with a civil society separated from the state because based on the economics of private property. Thus, the term public no longer simply designated all those who were subject to public authority as in the early Middle Ages but came to indicate an increasingly autonomous sphere. The development of print culture facilitated the exchange of ideas and enabled the existence and enlargement of this public sphere composed of 'private people engaged in rational-critical debate' (Habermas 106-7, 117). In particular, the widespread expression and discussion of private opinions was collectively manifested in the new historical phenomenon of public opinion: the high point of classical individualism and Liberalism. However, the public sphere began to break down under the pressures of industrial expansion in the second half of the nineteenth century, as its political function declined from that of a critically debating public into that of a mass electorate. Increasingly, public authority came to be inextricably linked with emergent state institutions and legislation (health, education, employment etc.), creating a universal social sphere in which the formerly distinct concepts of 'public' and 'private' were merged. A new form of social experience came into being that was shared between those who would formerly have been described as workers and those who could formerly be said to have exercised control over the means of production. That is to say that a management process, largely separate from the exercise of property rights, emerged as commercial success became increasingly dependent on the internal functioning of the social sphere and correspondingly independent of the capital market.

This change in society is very clearly described by Ford in his account of the origin and rise of the 'Modern Type': the entrepreneur who like Napoleon combines an aim to replicate others' past successes with the cultivation of popularity by attempting to fulfil social and functional needs he knows to exist from his own experience, such as the provision of a cheap reliable collar stud (*SL* 49-50). Mass success becomes dependent precisely on the extent to which social experience is shared across classes and the emulation characteristic of leisure activities is extended into the world of business, where clerks imitate millionaires 'gesture for gesture' (*SL* 51). This imitative tendency of mass democracy had been, and would be, identified by commentators from John Stuart Mill to Wyndham Lewis as a force for the suppression of differences.[4] In *Paranoid Modernism*, David Trotter argues that the desire to resist this 'social mimesis' eventually drove writers such as Ford, Lewis and Lawrence to a paranoid imposition of distinct values and meanings by which 'they deluded themselves into modernity' (p. 5). However, he concedes that *England and the English* precedes this cultural shift and is 'a democratic book, perhaps even a liberal book' (p. 200). Indeed, in his earlier book, *The English Novel in History 1895-1920*, Trotter praises the trilogy precisely for the reason that at the height of Edwardian patriotism, when Englishness was being reasserted as a defence against the rise of modern mass society, Ford calmly avoids apocalyptic prophecy by insisting that the English way has always been to rub along together. Instead, Ford's disinclination towards modern society is expressed through an 'ironic measuring of "personal deterioration" [which] establishes a critical attitude impervious both to sentimentality and to paranoia'.[5]

However, Ford's trilogy is more than just a literary curiosity: not only does it display a sociological understanding that is normally considered alien to the British empirical outlook but also it can be seen in historical context as the inauguration of a particularly English social and political discourse which still holds force to this day. In particular, Ford's achievement was to show how the spiritual homelessness or alienation inherent to modern mass society could be resisted by identification with a fantasy – almost parodic – vision of the 'Country': 'For if each man have (and each of us has) his own Heart of the Country, to each assuredly that typical nook, that green mirage that now and then shines between him and his workaday world, will be his particular Island of the Blest, his island of perpetual youth, his closed garden, which as the years go on will more and more appear to contain the Fountain of Youth' (*HC* 113). For Ford, it is precisely the pursuit of such utopia which complements the metropolitan pursuit of leisure and by maintaining individualism in mass society holds alive the possibility of the 'Future'. There are two main ways in which this strategy of Ford's can be seen as a measured response to the political demands of modernity: theoretically and in the light of subsequent history.

Giovanni Arrighi's *The Long Twentieth Century* describes long centuries as overlapping systemic cycles of capitalist accumulation, which are distinguished by a fixed commodity form. For example, the 'Fordist-Keynesian regime of accumulation' was the dominant commodity form of the twentieth century.[6] Periods of finance capitalism, when capital is released from the fixed commodity form, constitute the overlapping transitional phases between the cycles. Thus, the financial expansion of the period 1870-1914, which began with an economic depression as capital moved out of the fixed commodity form of nineteenth century industrial production, marked both the final phase of the long nineteenth century and the initial phase of the long twentieth century: a dual perspective which Ford captures adroitly in the trilogy. Of course, as we have seen, this period also saw the onset of the structural transformation of the public sphere.[7]

In response to these changes, the early German sociologists, such as Simmel, realised that social life could only be understood interpretatively from within by means of a developed version of the everyday understanding that all individuals need to function in the social sphere. However, their analyses were not merely attempts to understand society but also generated potential vehicles for social transformation, as acknowledged by Simmel's analysis of socialism in aesthetic terms 'that society as a whole should become a work of art in which every single element attains its meaning by virtue of its contribution to the whole'.[8] This model of everyday life as a site of transformation was later developed by Marxist theorists like Walter Benjamin and Henri Lefebvre, who, recognising that modern everyday life was characteristically experienced as a contradiction between the everyday – the irreducible remnant of historical consciousness – and everydayness – the reproducibility and interchangeability of money, time and human labour – sought the combination of the two in a historically conscious mass society.[9] Likewise, in *The Spirit of the People*, Ford describes the romantic 'divorce of principle from life' that characterises Englishness at the beginning of the twentieth century as originating in Puritanism (*SP* 276). Poetry, which was formerly 'the sublime of common sense' and hence the basis of classical individualism, had been marginalised by principle: 'wrong-headedness wrought up to the sublime pitch – and that, in essentials, is romance' (*SP* 272). Ford's construction of the country as the city dweller's utopia allowed the residual poetic common sense of the country to be recuperated for modern urban experience, in which principle had become so separated from life as to have passed through hypocrisy and a sense of muddling through to tolerance (see *SP* 283-4). In this, his aim was similar to the later Marxist theorists of everyday life, seeking a return to that poised historical conjuncture identified by Simmel in which the competing classical and romantic models of experience were linked in a state of mutual interdependence which provided the necessary condition for genuine human agency.

As well as this theoretical basis, a version of Ford's strategy can also be seen to have been successfully implemented in interwar England by the Conservative politician, Stanley Baldwin. Responding to the prospect of Labour majorities – the logical threat posed by the introduction of universal suffrage in 1918 – Baldwin created a mass following for the Conservative Party from the rising new middle class of salaried white-collar workers living a commuter lifestyle in rapidly expanding belts of suburban housing. He cemented support with a series of speeches promoting a pastoral ideology that cast suburbia in the mould of a timeless rural Englishness: 'To me, England is the country, and the country is England – England comes to me through my various senses – the sounds of England, the tinkle of the hammer on the anvil in the country smithy, the corncrake on a dewy morning, the sound of the scythe against the whetstone, and the sight of a plough team coming over the brow of a hill, the sight that has been England since England was a land'.[10] The result, as the historian Ross McKibbin describes, was that the Conservative Party created a huge heterogeneous stable coalition, in which 'the ruling definition of democracy was individualist and its proponents chiefly a modernised middle class'.[11] While this configuration was ruptured by the Second World War and the 1945 political settlement, the same strategy has been revived since 1990, at first tentatively by the Conservative Prime Minister, John Major and then, more successfully, by New Labour's Tony Blair.

In particular, Major's speech of 22 April 1993 can be seen as perfectly recapitulating, albeit unconsciously, Ford's parodic construction of the 'Heart of the Country': 'Fifty years from now, Britain will still be the country of long shadows on county grounds, warm beer, invincible green suburbs, dog lovers and pools fillers and – as George Orwell said – "old maids cycling to holy communion through the morning mist"'.[12] The reference is to Orwell's *The Lion and the Unicorn* (1941), in which Orwell consciously parodied Baldwin in order, like Ford, to invoke an 'Englishness' which would temper and provide a future for the restless, cultureless life evolving 'in labour-saving flats or Council houses, along the concrete roads and in the naked democracy of the swimming pools'.[13] The success of this can be seen negatively reflected in David Goodhart's now-notorious essay 'Discomfort of Strangers', first published in the February 2004 issue of *Prospect* and then reprinted in the *Guardian*.

Goodhart highlights the so-called 'progressive dilemma' that sharing and solidarity can conflict with diversity. The thinking behind this is that collective sharing – as embodied in a universal welfare system based on compulsory contributions for instance – only functions with a limited set of common values and assumptions and so is undermined by the kind of diversity resulting from equal rights being awarded to a wide range of peoples, values and ways of life. Goodhart suggests both that our current historical conjuncture – typified by 'the erosion of collective norms and identities, in particular of class and nation, and the recent surge of immigration into Europe' – is one in which the respective logics of solidarity and diversity are set to pull apart and that the residual tolerance in British society is only an accidental by-product of suburban Englishness:

> Relative to the other big European nations, the British sense of national culture and solidarity has arguably been rather weak – diluted by class, empire, the four different nations within the state, the north-south divide and even the long shadow of American culture. That weakness of national solidarity, exemplified by the 'stand-offishness' of suburban England, may have created a bulwark against extreme nationalism. We are more tolerant than, say, France because we don't care enough about each other to resent the arrival of the other.[14]

Unpacked from prejudice, this 'stand-offishness' can be seen as not accidental but as a consequence of what Ford describes as the English evolution of a 'rule of thumb system' for mass living:

> You may set down the formula as this: i. I do not enquire into my neighbour's psychology; ii. I do not know my neighbour's opinions; iii. I give him credit for having much such opinions as my own; iv. I tolerate myself; v. I tolerate him. And so, in these fortunate islands, we all live very comfortably together. (*SP* 248)

While it might be true that the parodic element discernible in this construction of Englishness serves to uphold Ford's individuality, it also emphasises how Englishness is comprised of a set of practices and, therefore, promotes the potential for social mimesis in mass society. For this reason, Ford cannot be constructed as a 'paranoid modernist' in the way that Trotter presents him. Unlike Virginia Woolf, whose opposition to the forces of social mimesis is clearly reflected in her attacks on Wells, Bennett and Galsworthy, Ford seems always to have been aware that a modernist identity could not be constructed in opposition to modern mass society, but only in conjunction with it. Ford's personal desire was not to oppose social mimesis but to go beyond it: an outcome he achieved with *The Good Soldier*.

As Sara Haslam points out, the 'germ of the story' of *The Good Soldier* is revealed in *The Spirit of the People* as part of a discussion of English emotional and sexual repression.[15] The anecdote has Ford playing Dowell to a friend's Ashburnham by accompanying him on a ride to the station to dispatch his young ward, with whom he had fallen in love, on a round-the-world trip. At the parting neither friend nor ward spoke a word. She subsequently died at Brindisi on the voyage out and he spent the next three years having nerve cures on the continent. Ford concludes that the utter silence of the parting 'seems to me to be a manifestation of a national characteristic that is almost appalling' (*SP* 315). However, he then proceeds unconvincingly to dismiss the tale as an exception that proves the rule:

> Nevertheless, to quote another of the English sayings, hard cases make bad law, and the especial province of the English nation is the evolution of a standard of manners. For that is what it comes to when one says that the province of the Englishman is to solve the problem of how men may live together. (*SP* 315)

Knowledge of this passage alerts the reader to the fact that *The Good Soldier* is concerned not only with emotional and sexual repression – the poetic sublime which had been historically marginalised by principle – but also with manners – the practice of rubbing along together evolved from the experience of urban everyday life – and, most importantly, with how the two can be reintegrated into a full consciousness.

As Dowell's narrative reveals, if the relationship between manners and emotions exists purely as a relationship between external and internal mechanisms, then it becomes possible to know everything about another person's outward behaviour without knowing anything about their inner self. The resultant false assumption, that one can know a person through his or her everyday behaviour is labelled by Dowell as 'the modern English habit of taking everyone for granted':

> You meet a man or a woman and, from tiny and intimate sounds, from the slightest of movements, you know at once whether you are concerned with good people or with those who won't do. You know, this is to say, whether they will go rigidly through with the whole programme from the underdone beef to the Anglicanism.[16]

Classical individualism, as embodied in Ashburnham and manifested in such actions as his treatment of his tenants, remains invisible to the modern way of seeing the world. Yet at the same time, Ashburnham's passionate nature is rendered equally invisible and thus he is encouraged to become complicit with the modern values that he despises in order to gratify his desires. It is this dishonest accommodation between emotion and manners that is the cause of his downfall and which illustrates the nature of the particularly English form of hypocrisy laid bare by Ford in the novel.

The other side of this act of complicity is mapped out in relation to Florence. Trotter argues that she is 'the pure product of social mimesis' (*Paranoid Modernism* 215), and cites Dowell's observation: 'she wasn't real; she was just a mass of talk out of guide-books, of drawings out of fashion-plates' (*GS* 114). However, it would be more accurate to say that, mirroring Ashburnham's classical in-dividualism, Florence embodies the modern form of romantic individ-ualism in which qualitative uniqueness is expressed through the commodified forms of taste and fashion. While it is true that she is baldly represented in these terms in the novel, this does not mean that we should necessarily follow Trotter's inference that her depiction reveals Ford's modernist disgust at the imitative tendencies of mass society. Purely at the level of narrative construction, Florence has to be identified with these forces in order to expose Ashburnham's complicity with them. Yet Florence is more than a simple cipher even in the most oft-quoted description of her: 'She represented a real human being with a heart, with feelings, with sympathies and with emotions only as a banknote represents a certain quantity of gold' (*GS* 114). Trotter contrasts this with Ashburnham's '"solid, sound, golden English sovereign": about the only thing in his life which *is* unequivocally solid and sound' before going on to suggest that Florence's issuing of paper currency against this limited gold causes the Ashburnhams to lose their 'high reserve'.[17] However, gold and paper currency represent the two poles of a unified money system which only functions by allowing units of value to be interchangeable with units of exchange. The relationship is similar to that between potential and kinetic energy: for all its solidity, the value of gold lies in its potential to be exchanged rather as a stone resting at the top of a hill stores the potential kinetic energy that will be released when it rolls down. In the same way as the stone can be described as 'wanting' to roll down the hill so gold 'wants' to be exchanged as currency. Equally, much as the stone at the bottom of the hill 'wants' to gain the potential energy of a stone at the top, paper currency 'wants' to gain the potential of gold. The aptness of these symbolic terms for representing the mutual relationship of Florence and Ashburnham is reinforced by our understanding of the period as constituting a transitional phase between cycles of capitalist accumulation in which the financial fluidity marked a particularly poised balance of exchange between gold and paper currency. Viewed from the perspective of the waning long nineteenth century, the changes of the period appear as a loss of stability. Viewed from the perspective of the emergent long twentieth century, the changes of the period appear as the origin of the present. Ford's achievement, however, in a novel he commenced to write on 17 December 1913 (*GS* 5) just before the period of financial capitalism which had run for forty years was about to come to its apocalyptic end, was to seize a moment of mutual interdependence between the two forms of individualism and hold it open in the face of its imminent historical closure.

The poised possibilities he wished to preserve were not, of course, those of Florence and Ashburnham caught in a web of hypocrisy and deception, but those presented by his narrator, Dowell. This might seem a strange claim because at one level Dowell is as much a product of social mimesis as Florence. On this point, Peter Nicholls comments:

> ... the regular association of Dowell with figures of weakness prepares us for that final moment of emotional identification which registers the full absurdity of imitative desire: thinking of Ashburnham, Dowell concludes that 'I love him because he was just myself. ... I am just as much a sentimentalist as he'.[18]

Nicholls goes on to suggest that from the modernist perspective of Wyndham Lewis: 'Dowell's passivity signals modernity's collapse into passive imitation'.[19] Yet this judgement seems to ignore the narrative framework of *The Good Soldier* which does not describe events as they happen but as Dowell chooses to retell them. The final moment of emotional identification might register the absurdity of imitative desire at one level but it also moves beyond that imitative desire in the very act of retelling it. Dowell's narration is very much a Freudian process of 'remembering, repeating and working-through' in which what was repressed – his imitative desire – is 'acted' out as a 'piece of real life'.[20] Therefore, passive imitation is transformed into active imitation and Dowell must consequently be seen as a modernist figure by Nicholls's own criteria – or, at least, Nicholls's criteria as summarised by Trotter: 'According to Nicholls, the Modernist self is a self saved from modernity's passive imitation by an active imitation of the cultural past' (*Paranoid Modernism* 9).

This, of course, is exactly the version of modernism that Trotter attempts to label 'paranoid': 'Edward Ashburnham may or may not have been a "pathological case". Dowell probably is. And Dowell's paranoia, his will-to-abstraction, is Ford's experiment' (*Paranoid Modernism* 219). According to Trotter, Dowell is driven by a disgust with social mimesis in general and a disgust with Florence in particular for being no more than an empty representation of a human being. Trotter argues that Dowell does not follow Florence upstairs on the night of her suicide 'because she has ceased to exist for him' (*Paranoid Modernism* 216). Yet an alternative interpretation exists. With Florence's uncle now having been dead for five days (*GS* 25), Dowell no longer needs to play the 'trained poodle' (*GS* 114) or to nursemaid Florence's health because he is finally in position to inherit.[21] He never gave her another thought after her death (*GS* 113) because he had finally got what he wanted from her. Viewed in this light, Dowell corresponds not so much with the experimental modernist self as with the early modernist figure of the unreliable narrator, such as Mackellar in Robert Louis Stevenson's *The Master of Ballantrae* (1889). Rather as Mackellar's narrative both conceals and yet unwittingly discloses his desire for, and eventual attainment of, mastery,[22] so Dowell's narrative can likewise be read with respect to his eventual usurpation of Ashburnham's place as lord and master. This element of the story is indeed pathological but it is only linked by association to Dowell's complex relationship with imitative desire.

It is the way that these different narrative elements overlap that overdetermines the motivations and actions of the characters and makes critical interpretation difficult. This is hardly surprising given that Ford by his own admission, having exhaustively studied how novels are constructed, 'sat down to show what [he] could do' (*GS* 6). Contrary to Trotter's opinion, one might argue that it is precisely this complex and multilayered narrative construction that constitutes Ford's experiment rather than any will-to-abstraction. Furthermore, it is almost as though the particular strand of narrative construction, which associates unreliable narratorship with a certain form of modernist selfhood born out of opposition to the social mimesis of mass society, is expressly designed to show the link between will-to-abstraction and paranoia in order to subject it to ridicule. For it is only if Dowell is read monodimensionally as a diehard plotter and obsessive adherent of active values in the face of passive modernity, that his evident failure appears as absurd as the following admission implies:

> I am that absurd figure, an American millionaire, who has bought one of the ancient haunts of English peace. I sit here, in Edward's gun-room, all day and all day in a house that is absolutely quiet. No one visits me, for I visit no one. No one is interested in me, for I have no interests.... so life peters out. (*GS* 227)

The misdirection in this statement obscures the fact that Dowell is ultimately far more successful than this and guilty of neither paranoia nor will-to-abstraction. His distaste for normality, which Trotter correctly identifies, is motivated by an altogether different set of concerns. Trotter's argument is that Dowell paranoically 'remasculinizes' himself by identifying with Ashburnham, the 'exceptional man', and effecting a 'reduction of Leonora to normality ... as savage as his earlier disavowal of Florence' (*Paranoid Modernism* 218). Yet the whole point of the book is that Ashburnham is not in the least exceptional. Not only does Dowell explicitly label him as a 'normal man' (*GS* 214), but on the last page of the book he delivers the punch line that Ashburnham's 'mind was compounded of indifferent poems and novels' (*GS* 229). It is Dowell, himself, who is the exceptional person because he develops self awareness and an implicit critique of society:

> Mind, I am not preaching anything contrary to accepted morality. I am not advocating free love in this or any other case. Society must go on, I suppose, and society can only exist if the normal, if the virtuous, and the slightly deceitful flourish, and if the passionate, the headstrong, and the too-truthful are condemned to suicide and madness. But I guess that I myself, in my fainter way, come into the category of the passionate, of the headstrong, and the too-truthful. For I can't conceal from myself the fact that I loved Edward Ashburnham – and that I love him because he was just myself. (*GS* 227)

Far from being absurd, this is deeply and knowingly ironic because the Ashburnham that Dowell loves is his own invention: it is not the empty-headed 'good' soldier who occasionally shows through, but a courageous, virile figure whose agency both leads to, and derives from, Dowell's own agency as narrator. To borrow William Empson's terminology of 'Comic Primness', Dowell achieves this narrative trick by adopting a position of 'Ironical Humility':

> [this] is to say, 'I am not clever, educated, well born', or what not (as if you had a low standard to judge by), and then to imply that your standards are so high in the matter that the person you are humbling yourself before is quite out of sight.[23]

Another way of looking at it is to allow that Nicholls and Trotter are both half right: Dowell's closing confession that he loved Ashburnham 'because he was just myself' is equally absurdly sentimental and obsessionally paranoid:

> In full Comic Primness the enjoyer gets the joke at both levels. . . . It is a play of judgement which implies not so much doubt as a full understanding of issues between which the enjoyer, with the humility of impertinence, does not propose to decide. For this pleasure of effective momentary simplification the arguments of the two sides must be pulling their weight on the ironist, and though he might be sincerely indignant if told so it is fair to call him conscious of them. A character who accepts this way of thinking tends to be forced into isolation by sheer strength of mind, and so into a philosophy of Independence.[24]

This is what happens to Dowell. He ironically negotiates the boundaries between classical and romantic individualism and ends up forced into isolation and a philosophy of independence. As we have seen, Trotter had made a similar judgement of Ford before he went on to the arguments of *Paranoid Modernism*: '[Ford's] ironic measuring of "personal deterioration" establishes a critical attitude impervious both to sentimentality and to paranoia'.[25] Therefore, if Trotter's arguments (in this particular respect) may be more profitably read in reverse – a manoeuvre which the second half of this essay has attempted to carry out – the impertinent question arises as to whether Ford too (in this particular respect) might be more profitably read in reverse.

If we look back again from *The Good Soldier* to the source story in *The Spirit of the People*, and Ford's account of driving in the dog cart with P------ to the station in order to dispatch his ward Miss W------ safely out of the way on a round the world trip, we find Ford making a very Dowell-like comment which even includes a slightly absurd ambiguity: 'I won't say that I felt very emotional myself, for what of the spectacle I could see from my back seat was too interesting' (*SP* 314). Of course Ford is not talking about the landscape but the couple in front of him talking about the landscape and indeed anything else that might save them from having to acknowledge their own emotions and thereby from confronting society's norms. As we have seen, his dismissal of the characteristically English emotional horror of this scene as a 'hard case' by which to judge the English achievement of evolving a standard of manners that allow people to live together is unconvincing. By rewriting the story as *The Good Soldier*, he was able to create in his narrator, Dowell, an ironic accommodation between emotion and manners which allowed – indeed forced – a fully conscious engagement with everyday life in the modern world however absurd or paranoid that might appear. Therefore, not only does *The Good Soldier* owe as much to the penetration of Ford's sociological insight into the conditions of Englishness and modernity as *England and the English*, but also it demonstrates how modernist identity is formed by going beyond the social mimesis of mass society rather than by acting in opposition to it.[26]

NOTES

1   Ford Madox Ford, *England and the English* (1907), ed. Sara Haslam, Manchester: Carcanet, 2003: comprising *The Soul of London* (1905) – *SL*; The Heart of the Country (1906) – *HC*; and *The Spirit of the People* (1907) – *SP*; p. 10.

2   In Georg Simmel, *On Individuality and Social Forms: Selected Writings*, ed. Donald N. Levine, Chicago: University of Chicago Press, 1971 – henceforth 'Simmel'; p. 324.

3   Jürgen Habermas, *The Structural Transformation of the Public Sphere*, trs. Thomas Burger with Frederick Lawrence, Cambridge: Polity Press, 1992 – henceforth 'Habermas'; pp. 141-3.

4   David Trotter, *Paranoid Modernism: Literary Experiment, Psychosis, and the Professionalization of English Society*, Oxford: Oxford University Press, 2001 – henceforth *Paranoid Modernism*; p. 8.

5   David Trotter, *The English Novel in History 1895-1920*, London: Routledge, 1993, p. 166.

6   Giovanni Arrighi, *The Long Twentieth Century: Money, Power, and the Origins of Our Times*, London: Verso, 1994, p. 2.

7   See also Nick Hubble, *Mass-Observation and Everyday Life: Culture, History, Theory*, Basingstoke: Palgrave, 2006, pp. 17-37.

8   Cited by Ben Highmore, *Everyday Life and Cultural Theory: An Introduction*, London: Routledge, 2002, p. 40.

9   See John Roberts, 'Philosophising the Everyday: The Philosophy of Praxis and the Fate of Cultural Studies', *Radical Philosophy*, 98, November-December 1999, pp. 16-29.

10 Cited in Jeremy Paxman, *The English: A Portrait of a People*, London: Michael Joseph, 1998, p. 142.

11 Ross McKibbin, *Classes and Cultures: England 1918-1951*, Oxford: Oxford University Press, p. 533.

12 Cited in Paxman, *op. cit.*, p. 142.

13 George Orwell, *A Patriot After All: 1940-1941, Complete Works*, XII, revised edition, ed. Peter Davison, London: Secker & Warburg, 2000, p. 408.

14 David Goodhart, 'Discomfort of Strangers', *Guardian*, 24 February 2004, pp.24-5; available online at www.guardian.co.uk/race/story/0,11374,1154684,00.html.

15 *England and the English* (1907), ed. Sara Haslam, Manchester: Carcanet, 2003, p. xx.

16 Ford Madox Ford, *The Good Soldier*, Harmondsworth: Penguin, 1988 – henceforth *GS*; pp. 39-40.

17 Trotter, *The English Novel in History 1895-1920*, pp. 50, 60.

18 Peter Nicholls, *Modernisms: A Literary Guide*, Basingstoke: Macmillan, 1995, p. 186; quoting *GS* 227.

19 *Ibid.*

20 See Sigmund Freud, 'Remembering, Repeating and Working-Through' [1914] in *The Standard Edition of the Complete Psychological Works of Sigmund Freud: Volume XII*, ed. James Strachey, London: Hogarth Press, 1958, pp. 150-2.

21 See Roger Poole, 'The Unknown Ford Madox Ford', *Ford Madox Ford's Modernity*, ed. Robert Hampson and Max Saunders, Amsterdam and New York: Rodopi, 2003, pp. 117-36.

22 See Cairns Craig, *Out of History: Narrative Paradigms in Scottish and English Culture*, Edinburgh: Polygon, 1996, pp. 77-80.

23 William Empson, *Some Versions of Pastoral*, Harmondsworth: Penguin, 1995, p. 171.

24 *Ibid.*

25 Trotter, *The English Novel in History 1895-1920*, p. 166.

26 See Caroline Patey, 'Empire, Ethnology and *The Good Soldier*', *Ford Madox Ford's Modernity*, ed. Robert Hampson and Max Saunders, Amsterdam and New York: Rodopi, 2003, pp. 83-102.

WHEN PROPAGANDA IS YOUR ARGUMENT: FORD AND FIRST WORLD WAR PROPAGANDA

Anurag Jain

On September 2nd 1914, C. F. G. Masterman held a meeting with such leading authors as Thomas Hardy, Arnold Bennett, H. G. Wells, and Arthur Conan Doyle at Wellington House in Buckingham Gate, London, to discuss how these writers could contribute to the Government's war effort. The Government had just appointed Masterman as the head of their recently formed War Propaganda Bureau (WPB). The Government formed the WPB to respond to Germany's self-promotion and justification for their invasion of Belgium to neutral nations, particularly America. The architects of the War Propaganda Bureau sought a subtler form of influence that focused their efforts on the intellectual leaders of America as opposed to mass appeals to public opinion. While the Government also instituted negative propaganda domestically in the form of censorship, it considered positive propaganda to be crucial for getting the support that Britain would need in the war. As Britain's first official propaganda ministry, the WPB employed methods that were largely improvisational. Masterman believed that the prestige of distinguished writers would help bolster Britain's cause and recruited them to that end – commissioning, publishing, and distributing books and pamphlets without any trace of government involvement. Though he wasn't at the initial meeting, Ford, a personal connection of Masterman's, would go on to write in 1915 two such books of literary and cultural criticism for the WPB: *When Blood is their Argument* and *Between St. Dennis and St. George*. In this chapter I will situate Ford's propaganda work within the system of British propaganda, and examine how the arguments he makes in these books help to comprise the fight on the cultural front for British war propaganda. Though it is difficult to evaluate the effectiveness of these tracts in bringing America into the war, locating these two books within the system of British propaganda in the First World War can offer an understanding of the improvised nature of the developments of British propaganda and why the involvement of writers was considered important.

Ford responded to the war, continuing to write poetry, literary criticism, and prose for the duration as well as, most memorably, *Parade's End* once the war was over, but that writing should be distinguished from the work that was published under the auspices of the WPB. In strictly technical terms, when writing is solicited, printed, or distributed by a government agency for the purpose of influencing opinion, we can classify that writing as propaganda. This definition helps limit the term 'propaganda' to a particular type of speech or text which originates within the government. It does not apply to pro-war writing independently created by citizens or intellectuals away from government solicitation. Though there were independent writers all over the country who wrote in support of the war (in both fictional and non-fictional ways), to allow those types of speech and writing to be called propaganda would dilute the meaning of propaganda to apply to nearly all pro-war writing.

Ford's two books were utilised as part of a system of cultural denunciation of the savagery of Prussian culture as well as a refutation of the anti-war arguments; in particular, George Bernard Shaw's *Common Sense about the War*. George Robb posits that 'Britain's official propaganda was initially directed less at its own citizens, whose commitment was taken for granted, than to neutral nations especially the United States'.[1] Sanders and Taylor point to 1916, when Britain began conscription, as the time when propaganda became more of a priority on the home front.[2] The major analysts of British propaganda of the First World War[3] acknowledge that, while the methodologies were improvised as opposed to being premeditated and thought through, winning American opinion was seen to be crucial. Designed in opposition to German campaigns of propaganda – openly governmental, involving public meetings and petitioning of public opinion – British propaganda concealed its origin and the focus was 'opinion-makers rather than opinion itself'.[4]

It was Gilbert Parker's job at Wellington House to compile a list of names from *Who's Who* and send to the selected individuals books and articles that argued the British case. Ford's books were sent with personal notes from Parker which didn't mention Wellington House or the government at all.[5] Parker would simply pass on texts such as Ford's as if for the sake of interest and information. By approaching intellectuals, or those whose names had been selected from *Who's Who,* the British worked on the assumption that not only would the opinions they propagated be filtered down through publicity, book reviews, articles, university lectures, and magazine articles, but that it was leaders of opinion who made decisions in America, not the people. Ford's books, whether by intention or not, worked as part of the attempt to marshal American intellectual attitudes against Germany. To gain an understanding of these texts, we need to recognise the use to which they were put within the system of propaganda, rather than suppose them to offer objective insights into the European war.

In 'The Artist as Propagandist', L. L. Farrar Jr. evaluates Ford's propaganda in three ways. He writes that, as history, it displays a good grasp of the issues at stake in the war, but also demonstrates the limitations of his method. The books offer a strong contrast between literary and historical methods and 'approaches to reality'.[6] To the student of the oeuvre of Ford Madox Ford, these under-discussed works offer insight into the writer's mentality before becoming a soldier, and as some interesting links between his literary and non-literary work. Farrar places most emphasis on the comparatively less convincing discussion of this last point and far less on the texts as part of the British propaganda system. 'Ford's implication that Germany was solely responsible for the war (the Versailles verdict) is rejected by most historians – although, interestingly, not by all German historians.' Farrar's appeal to 'many historians' or 'most historians' draws too vast a variety of opinion into too reductive a consensus, denying the complexity of the relationship between writers, propaganda, democracy and the way the Allied governments conducted their war. Ford's analyses do not have the rigour or the method that Farrar attributes to them; his interest in Ford and in how the propaganda gives insight into his mindset at the period distorts his reading of these two polemics.

Beginning with Paul Fussell's important *The Great War and Modern Memory*, the canon of literary criticism on the First World War has tried to negotiate the discussion of war literature, memoirs, and trench poetry within and against the innovations of what is broadly known as 'High Modernism'. While the work of the past twenty years has seen the re-evaluation of this canon, particularly with the challenge to the privileging of male writing of war experience, Peter Buitenhuis's study *The Great War of Words: Literature as Propaganda 1914-1918 and after*[7] was the first dedicated to the propaganda written by the literary figures associated with the WPB. His attention to this helped expand the discussion of literature and the

First World War, but Buitenhuis shares with Farrar a tendency to prioritise the close reading of texts in relation to the other aesthetic productions of these literary artists, rather than looking at the way the texts worked within the British propaganda system. They were intended as a means to provide a cultural justification of the war to American intellectuals, to persuade them to break neutrality and support the Allies against Germany. In his biography, Max Saunders brings Ford's two texts closer to the system of British propaganda, but Saunders still emphasizes how these texts offer us not only the presence of the personality of Ford, but also of the 'necessity ... of a liberal, humane education'.[8] The emphasis on the psychology and aesthetic development of Ford, as can be read through these two books of propaganda, does not constitute an adequate examination of how these texts function as propaganda. Further, examining the tone, argument, and rhetoric of these texts will help us to see that they are not at all as reasonable, liberal nor humane as has been suggested by Ford's critical biographers.

Alan Judd writes that Ford's work isn't the 'normal run of propaganda, it is balanced, informed, lucid, wise, and readable'.[9] In his Introduction to Ford's *War Prose*, Max Saunders argues that Ford's propaganda is one of 'an unusually cultural and humane kind' while also acknowledging that Ford did get swept up in the patriotism of the time elevating the anger in the tone of his work.[10] Interestingly, Saunders suggests reading the work in the spirit of Ford's claim that his poem *On Heaven* was circulated to the troops by the Ministry of Information, to cheer them up. Saunders suggests that reading Ford's propaganda as intended to bolster the pride and vigilance of the troops may help us in approaching this unorthodox combination of historical, literary and cultural criticism (L. L. Farrar Jr. refers to the work as 'impressionist history').

When writing these books, Ford may not have known the particular way the WPB might have used them as propaganda. Though the WPB was improvising its methods, the internal record does illustrate that internal planning was aimed at neutral intellectuals, particularly in the United States. Ford knew he was writing propa-ganda but he may not have known to what audience and to what ends. At the end of *When Blood is Their Argument*, Ford writes that if he 'were a propagandist and tried to preach to the United States' and other neutrals, he would emphasize that a victory for Germany would mean their domination in the field of education and their monomania for detail (p. 317). Whether Ford knew it or not, the way his text was used was precisely as such preaching to neutrals and the WPB made use of his texts along with the other WPB writers and pamphleteers to this end. An increased awareness of these institutional and functional uses of the text will yield a better understanding of how propaganda worked in the early years of the WPB.

The thesis of *When Blood is their Argument* is that there is 'no such thing as "modern German culture"'.[11] Ford anticipates the obvious objection of an imaginary reader exclaiming 'What, no such thing as culture in the land that produced Beethoven and Goethe!' and answers by charting out the existence of two Germanys:

> If you will take a line from the mouth of the Elbe to a spot just north of the city of Dresden … you will discover that every German poet known beyond the confines of Germany, every musician, writer of fairy-tales, painter and the like – that every German who has contributed anything noteworthy towards German culture… was born to the south-west of that line, and that Prussian *Kultur* comes almost exclusively from the north and east of that line. (*WBTA* 20)

To address the difficult issue of German culture, Ford bases his reject-ion of it by dividing the cultured south from the barbarian Kultur of the Prussian North. Ford literally divides culture from war culture in the German people and counter-poses the beauty and genius of the south with the Prussian nature that initiated the invasion of Belgium. Culture has such an importance to Ford's understanding of a nation that he must reconcile his rejection of the country (and its actions) with his love for its culture. The contortion of this move reflects the kinds of aesthetic manoeuvring required in attempts to wage warfare on the cultural front. While Ford spends a considerable time discussing the economic, political, and educational aspects of the German state, all of these discussions are directed towards an understanding of the cultural sphere. His rejection is of the systematic, machine-like means of the Prussians. He assesses this mentality through a reading of Prussian culture and identifies it in their current attitude to warfare by regarding any of the possible contradictions offered to this view by German art and literature as separate from their war *Kultur* by definition (he dismisses Nietzsche as little more than a fad). The rhetorical move of creating such binaries could be read in the work of other WPB writers, for example Rudyard Kipling when he soberly states that 'However the world pretends to divide itself, there are only two divisions in the world today – human beings and Germans'.[12]

While delineating Prussians as materialist, militarist, and with a mania for organization, Ford saves his harshest critique for the German academic system. He states a hatred of its single-mindedness and its concentration on minutiae of literary insignificance. Impressionism shouldn't be far from our mind when we read Ford describing his book as 'sketchy, didactic, and insufficiently impersonal' (*WBTA* xix). He says that he commits himself to this style in order to make the book as readable and popular as possible. Ford rejects Prussian-academic hangovers of what the proper tone of a serious work should be, and asserts his right to write this book as a creative artist. It is his goal to make the issue of Prussian barbarism felt in his readers' hearts. If we lose the war, all of the western world including the Americans will fall under the system to become 'hopeless industrials ceaselessly toiling at the work of self-specialization in one cavern or another of the earth and their own souls' (*WBTA* 314). Whereas Gustave Le Bon's conception of European races is specific as a way of accounting for the war,[13] Ford's rhetoric on the relationship of a country's culture to national character bears uncomfortable similarities with those kinds of basic essentialisms expounded by Le Bon. The future of our race is at stake, he writes, between the 'organised, materialist egoism' of Prussia or what he describes as 'the all-round sportsmanship of altruistic culture' in Britain. Ford's early essays in *The Outlook* also echo his almost Victorian notions of chivalrous conduct in battle and conducting the war in terms of the 'gallant enemy'. In both *Zeppelin Nights*[14] (co-authored with Violet Hunt) and in *Between St. Dennis and St. George*, Ford makes a point of praising the old-fashioned values of honour in warfare, as demonstrated by Bertran de Born[15] when his castle was being besieged – sending food out to his attackers, for example.

The notion of the sportsmanship of British culture, propounded by Ford, is demonstrated in Michael Powell and Emeric Pressburger's 1943 movie *The Life and Death of Colonel Blimp*. In Powell's portrayal of the Great War, it is the Germans, according to the principal character Clive Candy, who bomb civilians, use gas, and have used unrestricted submarine warfare; the British win with good clean fighting. Powell's movie builds a case about the horror of war in relation to – or against – depictions of the particularly British sense of fair play. This is exemplified in a scene in which Candy's friend, the

German soldier Schuldorf, eats dinner with Candy and various members of the British Government who assure him that Britain will do all in their power to help rebuild Germany because they bear no grudge; war, like duelling or cricket, is a gentleman's game with gentlemen's rules. Acceptance of this sportsmanlike attitude is consistent with Candy's ignorance of the British concentration camps for women and children in the Boer War (24,000 dead). Candy fills his rooms with the mounted game trophies gathered from the colonies (along with a wife whose painting he similarly mounts after she died, not in a foreign country, Candy assures Schuldorf, but in Jamaica). The audience is led to a recognition of the fact that Candy's notions of colonialism and atrocity are kept in simple contradiction, separate and unresolved.

Near the beginning of *Common Sense About the War* Shaw explains that he retains his Irish capacity for critiquing England with the detachment of a foreigner and perhaps 'with a certain slightly malicious taste for taking the conceit out of her'.[16] Shaw brings attention to the position he critiques from better to explain his motivations in writing. Ford expresses his position as well, particularly as someone poised with a unique knowledge of English, French, and German culture, but he conceals the fact that he is writing not out of independent intellectual considerations of the argument and contradiction on both sides, but instead for the government. Ford's work was interested and directed writing, dedicated to the undermining of the German side while bolstering British civilization, democracy, and liberty. Ford decries the subjugation of the Irish by the English, more for the stupidity of such subjugation rather than the cruelty, and generalizes this hatred into a rejection of the idea of one race subjugating another (*BSDSG* 48-50). His passionate arguments against such subjugation, as driving the oppressed into madness, opens up a potential for a larger critique of war and Empire as came from the Union of Democratic Control. But, Ford transfers this outrage and potential self-critique of the English case, and in fact his expression of deep sympathy with subject peoples, into a condemnation of the particular brutality of the German Imperial war machine. He opens up the potential of finding a common ground of critique from which to discuss oppression as a whole, only to reinvest and redirect his argument towards its one goal: denouncing the artistic and militarist culture of Germany compared to that of England and France.

Whether discussing political or literary values, Ford establishes the issue as one he broadly considers as national culture. In his reduction to national types, he still refrains from drawing in how English Imperialism might destabilize the English case, for example, isolating instances of the greatest violence and evil not just in Germany, but in fact, in Prussia. When he undermines Germany on the cultural front, moreover, there are vitriolic moments when he demonstrates a kind of violence in his text that exceeds even the most extreme bounds of literary and cultural critique:

> That a rat has as great a moral right to exist as I myself I am ready to concede. But if I can kill it I will kill it, and its death seems to me to end its rights to existence. And in writing the present book I am attempting to cast such a stone at the rat of Prussianism, as posterity will not willingly... well, the reader may complete the simile. (*WBTA* xi)

Though we may accept the technique of leaving the simile in the reader's hands as impressionistic, the kind of de-humanizing that we read here, as in the Kipling reference above, reflects the rhetoric of an intellect far from objectivity or reasonable discourse about the war. Whatever passions may have ignited in Ford as a result of the German invasion of Belgium (a passion, we must note, that is not similarly inspired by British actions in the colonies, for example), they find a more compelling aesthetic expression in his poem 'Antwerp' than they do when he demonstrates this kind of anger. We cannot, for example, assent to Arthur Mizener's view that the argument of the book is conducted with intelligence and restraint. Critics, from Farrar to Max Saunders, argue for a reading of the propaganda text which give the kind of attention to drama and nuance that Impressionist writing requires, but what they fail to acknowledge is that, in addition to being a poorly argued book with a fanatically patriotic tone, the book most importantly was published by the WPB, to be given to American intellectuals as the opinions of an independent and objective writer in Britain. Farrar makes an interesting point when he notes that if the arguments in this book were separated into the mouths and consciousnesses of different characters of one of Ford's novels, then perhaps we may be able to better appreciate the subtlety of his analysis and his ability to capture the mood and emotions of people at the time; but this speculation, while interesting, takes the text too far out of its institutional parameters.

Not all writers were in support of the war or working for the WPB. There was significant protest against the war not only from

Fabian Society member George Bernard Shaw, but from the Union of Democratic Control, most dramatically and succinctly expressed by E. D. Morel and Bertrand Russell. *Between St. Dennis and St. George* was, in part, a response to the claims of these writers, to whom Ford referred as 'Anglo-Prussian Apologists'. The book has extended appendices that try and respond point by point to, in particular, Shaw's arguments. Though *St. Dennis* still has passages that refer to the Germans as savage Huns, it is less a rejection of German culture and more a promotion of French language and literature. One example of this is when Ford imagines leaders from the Prussian Royal State speaking:

> [l]et us at least go down amidst such waves of blood and such sounding of iron that future historians may at the least say we died splendidly true to our traditions. If we cannot keep the iron scepter for ever in our grasp, let us at least imprint upon the page of history such gory finger-marks of our Mailed Fist as the tides of oblivion shall never wash out. If we cannot reign in the memory along with Marcus Aurelius and Constantine let us at least be remembered as are Attila and Genghis Khan. (*BSDSG* 55)

Ford wanted to counter the anti-war polemics by using the hard facts and first-hand scrutiny required in the historian's craft. Shaw and company were 'intellectual fictionists' because they 'clothe dummy figures with ... the ideals that they pretend to portray ... [then] they proceed to foil, confute, and hopelessly confuse their puppets according to the traditions of Adelphic melodrama'.[17] Ford does not reflect on how close his own writing comes to fulfilling this description. Instead, he increasingly conceived of himself as closer to the hard facts of history than to the windy rhetoric of a gossip.

While posited as history, Ford's book is still a study of the importance of language, specifically that of Flaubert: 'we are, in the end, governed so much more by words than by deeds' (*BSDSG* 203). Ford argues that the fall of French monarchy had more to do with Henry IV of France saying 'Je veux que chaque paysan ait une poule au pot le dimanche' than with all that the Encyclopaedists did combined (*BSDSG* 67). Moreover, the genius that invented the phrase 'Honesty is the Best Policy' had had more of a material influence on England than the invention of the spinning jenny, in Ford's estimation. These claims highlight two things: his unflinching belief in the power of language to bring change to our personal and public lives; and his consequent refusal to offer a serious coherent cultural or fact-based history of the war.

To read Impressionist writing, we must be able to read contradictions, mood, and personality and the argument itself as interplay of a kind of dramatic unfolding in the text as opposed to a linear and logical process of argument. Thus, Max Saunders suggests that the purpose of this book is to help recreate the mindset of an Englishman in 1914. This argument ignores the fact that Ford's language did not only reflect a mindset but also helped to give a justification for this mindset to neutral intellectuals, particularly in America.[18] Ford may have employed irony, hesitation, and dramatic rhetoric, such as contradiction, or as Sara Haslam has suggested, outrage to provoke a response in his audience, but there are still moments in his text when Ford demonstrates a brash rejection of anything German:

> I wish Germany did not exist, and I hope it will not exist much longer... Burke said that you cannot indict a whole nation. But you can. (*BSDSG* 66)

Speculating as to why Ford wrote these texts, and how they related to his broader literary canon, may offer insights into his work, and into the development of modernist aesthetics during the war. They may help elucidate the war-time state of British intellectual opinion. However, the fact remains that these erratic texts demonstrate a chauvinistic support for the Allied cause, as it is seen through the lens of culture. These books cannot be considered coherent or as aesthetically important, beyond the need to understand Ford as a writer. Nor are they logical, fair, or insightful with regard to the historical situation of the war. The books are propaganda and to understand the meaning of that term – indeed, to understand how these texts were read and by whom – we need to pay attention to how British Propaganda of the First World War was conducted and why. Though 1917 finally saw the entry of America into the World War, it is debatable how far we may credit propaganda with that change. What isn't debatable is that, with their entry into the war, the Americans established their own propaganda ministry, the Committee on Public Information (CPI), to convince their own populace that it was the right thing to take the Allied side in the war, despite having voted Woodrow Wilson into office the year before on a 'he-kept-us-out-of-the-war' platform. When the Americans established the CPI, they didn't appeal to artists and writers in the same way that the WPB had done. Furthermore, a shake up in Britain resulted in the establishment of the Ministry of Information in 1917, with a brief to oversee W.W.I propaganda and reduce the influence of the WPB and what came to be seen as their too elite, and too literary, propaganda.

By 1917, and with the creation of the Ministry of Information and the CPI, propaganda had become an increasingly visual medium, and one that had developed more sophisticated methods. What the writers of the WPB could offer the government would become increasingly irrelevant as the war went on. Looking at these further changes could offer even greater insight into the changing role of writers in relation both to propaganda and to the First World War. For today's readers, Ford's propaganda books provide an insight into Ford the novelist and his relationship to the war. They are not as aesthetically sophisticated, nor as indeterminate, as his novels; they are artefacts of the improvisations of early British War Propaganda, and as readers, we should be aware of the need to place our close readings of the propaganda texts produced by literary figures within the context of the political and economic discourse of the time. Such located readings will give us a deeper insight into how the Great War was conducted and how it has continued to have an influence on notions of propaganda and psychological warfare. By examining the systems of First World War propaganda, we can develop greater insight into the way the government conducted its propaganda campaign. In 1916, when the Foreign Office said that propaganda would improve if they had more facts, the War Office's Sir Reginald Brade retorted that 'The really important thing is not the facts, but how they are presented'.[19]

NOTES

1   George Robb, *British Culture and the First World War*, London: Palgrave, 2002. p. 98.

2   Sanders, M. L., and Taylor, Philip. M., *British Propaganda During the First World War, 1914-18*, London: Macmillan, 1982, p. 11.

3   Major analysts include A. Ponsonby, *Falsehood in Wartime* (1928), H. Lasswell, *Propaganda Technique in the World War* (1927), J. M. Read, *Atrocity Propaganda* (1941); modern studies include Sanders and Taylor, *British*

Propaganda in the First World War (1982); Cate Haste, *Keep the Home Fires Burning: Propaganda in the First World War*. London: Allen Lane, 1977; Gary S. Messinger, *Propaganda and the State in the First World War,* Manchester: Manchester University Press, 1992; and most recently a chapter in Robb, *British Culture and the First World War* (2002).

4   Sanders and Taylor, p. 41.

5   A letter from Sir Gilbert Parker (Peterson, Horace Cornelius, *Propaganda for War: The Campaign Against American Neutrality, 1914-1917*, Norman: Oklahoma UP, 1939, p. 53):

> Dear Sir,
>
> I am well aware that American enterprise has made available reprints of the official papers relating to the present European war; but the original British prints of these publications may not be accessible to those persons of influence who would study them for a true history of the conflict. I am venturing to send to you under another cover several of these official documents. I am sure you will not consider this an impertinence, but will realize that Britishers are deeply anxious that their cause may be judged from Authoritative evidence. In common with the great majority of Americans, you have, no doubt, made up your mind as to what country should be held responsible for this tragedy, but these papers may be found useful for reference, and because they contain the incontrovertible facts, I feel that you will probably welcome them in this form.
>
> My long and intimate association with the United States through my writings gives me confidence to approach you, and I trust you will not think intrusive or misunderstood my motive.
>
> With all respect,
>
> I am,
>
> Yours very truly, Gilbert Parker

6   In *The Presence of Ford Madox Ford: A Memorial Volume of Essays, Poems, and Memoirs* ed. Sondra J. Stang, Philadelphia: University of Pennsylvania Press, 1981, pp. 145-60.

7   Buitenhuis, Peter, *The Great War of Words: Literature as Propaganda 1914-18 and after*, London: Batsford, 1987.

8   Max Saunders, *Ford Madox Ford: A Dual Life*, Vol. 1, Oxford: Oxford University Press, 1996, p. 469.

9   Alan Judd, *Ford Madox Ford*, London: Collins, 1990, p. 247.

10   Ford Madox Ford, *War Prose*, ed. Max Saunders, Manchester: Carcanet, 1999. p. 3.

11   Ford, *When Blood is their Argument*, London: Hodder and Stoughton, 1915 – henceforth *WBTA*; p. 19.

12   *Morning Post* on June 22nd 1915. Quoted in Haste, *Keep the Home Fires Burning*, p. 81.

13   Le Bon, Gustave, *Psychology of the Great War: The First World War & its Origins*, Brunswick, N. J.: Transaction Publishers, c1999. Originally published: London: T. Fisher Unwin, 1916.

14   Hunt, Violet, and Ford H. Madox Hueffer, *Zeppelin Nights: A London Entertainment*. John Lane: London, New York, 1916.

15   Bertran de Born (c. 1140 - before 1215) was a French soldier and a medieval troubadour poet.

16 Reprinted in *The European War*, Volume I, From Beginning to March 1915, New York: New York Times Company, 1915, p.11.

17 Ford, *Between St. Dennis and St. George,* London: Hodder and Stoughton, 1915 – henceforth *BSDSG*; p.9.

18 Saunders, *Ford Madox Ford: A Dual Life,* Vol. 1, p. 475.

19 Philip Taylor, *British Propaganda in the Twentieth Century: Selling Democracy.* Edinburgh: Edinburgh University Press, 1999, p. 31.

ENGLISHNESS AND WORK

Jenny Plastow

In reading the productions of Ford Madox Ford's long and prolific
writing career, one can discern a certain unchanging fascination with
the idea of *work*. From the early fairytales to those late portmanteaus,
The March of Literature and *Great Trade Route*, the reader can find
evidence of the concept of work, often not much stated but contin-
uously underpinning Ford's thinking. And often *work* is closely connected with *Englishness*. Ford's own true work was writing, and as a
writer he particularly valued internationalism. Yet he does seem to
have inherited from his grandfather and his Victorian associates an
idea that there was something distinctively English about other, more
physical, forms of labour. Unlike the concept of Englishness, however, which Ford consciously analyses and explores from different
standpoints (such as that of German-ness) and different class
constructions, his thinking about work and the Englishness of work
appears so deeply embedded in his conceptualisation that he does not
consciously challenge his own ideas about it. *Work* supports and
surrounds the idea of *Englishness* as a door-frame supports a door.

Where does it come from, this deep-rooted view of the
significance of work? The clearest indication as to its genesis can be
found in Ford's biography of his grandfather, published in 1896. It is,
of course, a homage; an outpouring of grief for a lost, and dearly
beloved, father-figure whose role in Ford's life cannot be underestimated. But it is a curious one. Where is the emotion located? Ford
calls the text by his grandfather's name, *Ford Madox Brown,* and
subtitles it 'a record of his life and works'. The term 'record' prepares
the reader for the absence of the author; appropriately, as it turns out,
for on a surface level, the book is just that. Ford quotes heavily from
Madox Brown's own work diaries, and holds the long sections of
quotations together by the barest of chronological narratives,
expressing no authorial opinion, no involvement, even in the
recounting of incidents involving himself. He even refers, on page
386, to: 'a couple of illustrations for a book of one of his grandsons' –

his own first published work of 1892, lovingly entitled *The Brown Owl*.

Throughout this biography Ford never states his relationship to his subject, makes no reference to his reason for writing, and abstains absolutely from anecdote or evaluation of the man or his approach to his 'life and works' until he reaches p 390, when the style quite suddenly changes and becomes a personal account of Brown. Max Saunders remarks, 'he could not bear to write in too personal a way about him' and that 'its ending is extremely moving, as only then does he reveal ... the act of self-suppression that has kept the writing so subdued.'[1] But in fact, even after this shift, the writing is still bald, though personal. Ford gives us access to Brown's Spartan thinking: 'Madox Brown, rightly or wrongly, considered anything that was not strictly useful as a trouble and a hindrance';[2] and gives evidence of his own belief in Brown's deep egalitarianism, describing Brown as respectful both of the younger men who were coming to replace him and to those from different orders of society. According to Ford, 'The utterances of a navvy had as much weight with him as those of many distinguished philosophers, and seemed to him infinitely more picturesque' (*FMB* 400). In both these ways, Ford chose to follow in what he regarded as his grandfather's footsteps. He also comments on Brown's religious belief, saying that:

> In his early days he was a conventional member of the Church of England; in later years he was an absolute agnostic, with a great dislike for anything in the nature of priestcraft.... his intellect made him a Socialist of an extreme type. To this, of course, his desire to better the lot of the poor contributed largely. (*FMB* 401)

Ford does not say so, but we can assume that this change came about ultimately under the influence of Carlyle.

The book, written in 'as critical and unimpassioned style as I could command', could hardly be more different from the anecdotal style of *Ancient Lights and Certain New Reflections* (1911) in which Madox Brown appears again in an altogether different, and thoroughly Fordian, representation. Max Saunders compares Ford to a jazz musician in his approach to anecdote; 'he would highlight, embellish, and often transform those tales which had been most formative'[3] and it is Ford's jamming style which is most familiar, and which inspires the affection that Ford *aficionados* feel for their man. Ford's tales of his grandfather recount incidents among the most formative of Ford's life.

Ford's stated desire to keep himself 'out of it' in writing, and his self-professed inability to do so,[4] are signatures of his form, which makes his absence from the text of *Ford Madox Brown* the more remarkable.

He had already begun to develop his style. A reading of any of his fairy tales, most of which were written before Brown's death and brought to public attention at Brown's behest – 'Fordie has written a book, too. Go and fetch your book, Fordie!'[5] – reveals precisely that charming allusive, conversational narrative which seems to take the reader into the drawing room at Fitzroy Square, and on the imaginative flights thence, as a fascinated observer. But when Madox Brown died only four years after Ford's father Francis Hueffer, the mantle of the eldest male in this extraordinary family fell upon Ford (Brown's son Oliver had died aged 17 in the year of Ford's own birth). It is possible that the deep seriousness of this proposition affected Ford's creative process for a time, leaving him with a writing identity only as the chronicler of his grandfather's life. At any rate, the grief and loss he felt at Brown's demise are submerged utterly in the language of the text; even after he reveals his interest in the subject. They find expression instead in the metaphorical espousal of Brown's own style and values. For a time, just in the manner of a man mourning a lost father, Ford puts on his grandfather's shoes, or takes on his grandfather's voice, as a creative artist, and Brown's view's and values become his own.

Stylistically, this does not last. The unembellished and unemotional voice of *Ford Madox Brown*, copied from the style of Brown's own diaries, rapidly receives the descant and improvisations of amused detachment which characterise Ford's own jazz approach. By 1899, Ford was working on *The Inheritors,* and considering, through Conrad's excitement about the X-ray machine, the internal and external, the existence of dimension, and the significance of perception, solidity and mirage,[6] all relative to his own ideas about writing. The writing of *Rossetti* (1902), though also an *homage*, does not demonstrate the same immersion in the viewpoint of the subject as that of the Brown book, and Ford's own personality, as well as that of Rossetti, is present in the text.

The dominant feature of the Madox Brown book is the insistence upon work as the redeeming feature of life. Brown was not a successful painter. His immense importance to British nineteenth century art was in his lifetime undervalued, and is so still, despite the prominence of his work, and its use for the poster, at a recent (2005) exhibition at the Royal Academy. He struggled desperately all his working life for the money to keep himself painting and his family alive, and Ford's 'record' is filled with accounts in Brown's own voice of the difficulty of selling work and the disappointments attendant upon exhibitions and sales. Yet he keeps working. One of the models for his picture *Work* in 1857 was his son Arthur, the beautiful naked baby. During July, Brown writes: 'About this time I painted in the swell Martineau and his horse; also the little girl on her pony. Then, till July 13 (when our poor little Arthur sickened and died in one painful week), I was occupied with four things' – he relates four work projects, including the adjustments to the picture which had to be made, Arthur being no longer available as a model. In 1874, on the approaching death of his son Nolly from blood poisoning, he writes: 'Of course I have lost three or four weeks work, but that and the expense is nothing at all in the scale'. After the death:

> 'What seemed likely to turn out the crowning reward of a life not overstocked with successes otherwise is suddenly turned into a mockery and illusion, and yet we are strangely calm, after our wont, and indeed, my belief; it is of no use arguing with the whirlwind. . . . There is nothing for it but to patch up what remains of hope in other directions and get to work again; but the savour is gone, *unless in the work for itself.*' (my italics, *FMB* 295)

From Brown's own diaries and from Ford's handling of his material, the overwhelming impression is that Brown's life was completely dedicated to the English philosophy of his time: the doctrine of salvation through work, established by Thomas Carlyle. Brown is gently satiric about Carlyle the man – 'Browning said that one evening he was at Carlyle's, and that sage teacher, after abusing Mozart, Beethoven and modern music generally, set Mrs. Carlyle to show Browning what was the right sort of music; which was some Scotch tune on an old piano' and also about the style of delivery of Ruskin and Maurice – 'At night went with Gabriel to the Working Men's College. There was a public meeting, and we heard Professor Maurice and Ruskin spouting. Ruskin was as eloquent as ever, and as wildly popular with the men' (*FMB* 139). But he was deeply committed to the 'religion' which took hold of the minds of British thinkers as Darwinism introduced doubt to Christian belief. For Brown, as for Carlyle, 'all true work is religion'[7] as evidenced by his astonishing, dedicated life. 'Work, and do not despair' Carlyle demanded, and

Brown, like Carlyle himself, (and like Ford after him) subject to despair, made this peculiarly English doctrine the centre of his inner world and brought up his children and grandchildren in that belief. The predominance of Carlyle's doctrine at this time creates a curious link between Work and Englishness. The successful development and application of a number of inventions during the second half of the eighteenth century – Kay's Flying Shuttle, Hargreaves' Spinning Jenny, Arkwright's water frame, Crompton's Mule and Cartwright's power loom – led to the revolution of industry in Britain and transformed British cities, especially those in the north. This located Britain at the forefront of the European Industrial Revolution, and Britannia without any doubt ruled the waves as the richest and most successful nation on earth. As, for the working man, work became brutally mechanised and relentless, work itself achieved a new philosophical status, partly in recognition of its locus at the centre of such economic success; it must be the hard work of the British people that has led to such reward. To be 'English', and to share in that economic well-being, is to believe in the industrious application of energy; therefore, *work* is *English*. In fact many of the luminaries of the early Industrial period, including Carlyle himself, were not English but Scottish; this fact seems to have been glossed over in the national consciousness as 'Englishness' assumed the greater part in the construction of 'Britain'. Such high-handed elisions inspired the discontent that led, much later, to devolution.

Gradually, alongside the material success and the admiration for the work that achieved it came a recognition of its cost. With the rise of economic success came the rise of philanthropic thinking. The first People's Charter, was presented as early as 1838. Its ideas for the reform of franchise were so radical that one hundred years later only five of its six tenets had been achieved; the sixth – annual parliaments – might well be welcome, in 2006. Due to Carlyle, Dickens and other passionate reformers such as Henry Mayhew, chronicler of the lives of the London poor, the plight of the worker was foremost in philanthropic thought. Ford Madox Brown was young at this time, and, like William Morris, an idealistic socialist with a belief in the spiritually redemptive qualities of work; aligned by nature to Carlyle's mode of thought. 'Men are grown mechanical in head and in heart, as well as in hand' said Carlyle; a rallying call to Morris and Brown.[8]

Manchester – nicknamed 'Cottonopolis' – came in for particular opprobrium from the philanthropists. Famed for the massacre at St.

Peter's Fields in 1819, Manchester also had a formidable history of
working class politics, even by the 1850s. Friedrich Engels' father was
a mill-owner there, and it was the working class of Manchester who
inspired the writing of *The Condition of the Working Class in England*
(1845). The city, notoriously polluted even by Victorian standards,
had great significance for thinkers of the period, and Ford Madox
Brown was the painter commissioned, in 1880, to paint the history of
the town in a series of frescoes in the Town Hall. This was largely on
the strength of his most famous painting, now in the Manchester City
Art Galleries. *Work,* begun in 1852, was eleven years in the painting,
and is an extraordinary testament to an extraordinary time. It is the
pictorial representation of the whole Carlylean doctrine. Set in
Hampstead and inspired by Brown's observation of a navvy who is the
central character, the picture is a visual representation of a complex
intellectual construct, described here in my part-paraphrase of
Brown's own words as quoted by Ford.

The navvy, in 'the full swing of his activity … in the pride of
manly health and beauty' is with other navvies; one strong and fully
developed who 'does his work and loves his beer, a tough older man,
one, significantly of strong animal nature, who, but that he was when
young *taught* to work, might even now be working at the *useless
crank'*. (He means the treadmill; this man represents the type who
might easily get on the wrong side of the law were it not for the
salvation of work.) Near this group of saved navvies is another man
less fortunate: 'the ragged wretch who has never been *taught* to *work;*
with his restless, gleaming eyes he doubts and despairs of everyone'.
This man, though, is gentle and no criminal; he collects plants to sell
to botanists and his basket is protected from violence: 'the bread-
winning implements are sacred with the very poor'. Also in the picture
are two men who appear to have nothing to do but are in fact 'brain-
workers, who, seeming to be idle, work, and are the cause of well-
ordained work and happiness in others – sages, such as in ancient
Greece published their opinions in the market square'. These two are
in fact Thomas Carlyle himself and F. D. Maurice. Maurice was the
first principal of the Working Man's College founded in 1854 to
provide a liberal arts education for the Victorian skilled artisan class,
and associated with the Co-operative movement. A poster for the
college, where Ruskin, Rossetti, Morris and Brown himself taught, is
on the wall in the picture. Brown describes these, in his account of his
picture, as a wild Socratean philosopher who has 'reversed men's

thinking ... on many things' and a clergyman 'a gentleman without pride, much in communion with the working classes'. Near to them are depictions of those out of work; haymakers with an old sailor and two young peasants, in quest of harvest work, a young Irishman with his wife and baby, an Irish 'stoic', a 'Pariah, who has never learned to work' and others who 'have not been sufficiently used to work either – the rich ... A pastry-cook's tray, a symbol of superfluity, accompanies these'. There is also a trio of children, newly orphaned, cared for by the eldest girl, and other characters representing work or lack of it in different manifestations. The picture, and Brown's commentary accompanying it, are the fullest expression of the doctrine of Work and is, as Brown says about the pastry-cook's tray 'peculiarly English ... I could never get over a certain socialistic twinge on seeing it pass'. Indeed.

Ford Madox Brown is not quite the first evidence we have of Ford's own adherence to the idea of the Englishness of work; nor is his attendance at William Morris's Socialist gatherings. Many of the adherents of the Carlylean doctrine were also writers of works for children; and Ford's fairy tales, influenced as they are by the Scottish Presbyterianism of George MacDonald, whose badly behaved children must find salvation through learning how to clear up after themselves,[9] also show evidence of his reading of Kingsley's *Water Babies* and *Hereward the Wake*, and Dickens' *Christmas Carol*. We can also assume later readings of Mrs Gaskell and Browning. Even Ford's scatty princes and princesses know that to find salvation they must work, and that bad behaviour is that which neglects tasks and causes serious consequences for the protagonists and their friends. In *The Queen who Flew*, the regent's advances towards marriage with the Queen are rebuffed by her practicality:

> "Well, who's to be my tutor, then?" the Queen said.
> "I had purposed according that inestimable honour to myself," the Regent answered.
> "Oh, I say! You'll never do!" the Queen remarked. "You could never darn a pair of stockings, or comb my hair. You'd be so awfully clumsy."
> "Your Majesty has no need to have your royal stockings darned; you can always have a new pair."
> "But that would be so fearfully wasteful!" the Queen said.
> "Your Majesty might give the other pairs to the poor."
> "But what *are* 'the poor'?"
> "The poor are wicked, idle people – too wicked to work and earn the money, and too dirty to wear stockings," the Regent said.

"But what would be the good of my stockings to them?" the Queen asked.[10]

The principles of intelligence and thrift, and the attitude to work as regarded in the Fitzroy Street household – these stories were originally written for Juliet, Ford's younger sister – are clear.

Ford's least fictional expression of his ideal of work as a peculiarly English quality is perhaps to be found in *The Heart of the Country,* 1906; volume two of *England and the English.* In his third chapter *In the Cottages* we are introduced to Meary Walker, an English working-woman of what in France would be called the peasant class. Of her he says:

> I think I cared for her more than any friend I have made before or since, and now that she has been dead for a year or so her memory seems to make sacred and to typify all those patient and good-humoured toilers of the field that, for me, are the heart of the country. If you saw her at work in the hop-fields, with her hands and arms stained walnut-green to the elbows; in her own potato-patch, stooping, in immense boots, to drop the seed potatoes into the rows; striding through the dewy grass of the field to do a job of monthly nursing; or standing with one hand over her eyes in the doorway that she fitted so exactly that her thin hair was brushed by the four-foot thatch, she had one unfailing form of words, one unfailing smile upon her lips – 'Ah keep all on going!' That was her philosophy and her reason for existence.[11] (*HC* 169-70)

Meary Walker's approach to life and her philosophy become quintessentially and explicitly English as Ford contrasts the thinking of her type with that of the French peasant – in many ways similar. Discussing a kind of rural myth that arises at the death of the impecunious old, that they have a hoard of secret wealth concealed somewhere, he explains a difference in the expectations of the neighbours depending on whether they are French or English. This becomes a vehicle for his view that the English way is 'more patient', 'more law-abiding' in the face of the fact that there is, in fact, no wealth; that there is nothing. His respect for Meary is inspired by 'a certain original genius, such as that which prompted her to keep fowls for profit at a time when no labourers had ever thought of such a thing' (*HC* 172). The ability to think outside the groove was always the mark of creative intelligence for Ford, and he held in high esteem its application to practical work. He completes the chapter as a meditation on the disappearance of Meary and her class, as new prospects open up in the towns for the, now-lettered, children of the labouring classes. He is not hypocrite enough to lament the passing of a way of life which deforms the bodies of the labourers by the hardness of physical toil, yet he makes explicit his thought that, though the body may be deformed, the mind retains a straightness and a simplicity that will not, in the future, be found in 'the young shop-assistant, with her preserved figure, her gayer laugh, her brighter complexion, her courtships, her ideals and her aspirations for a villa in a row, with a brass knocker and an illustrated Bible on the parlour table' (*HC* 181). In the true Morris tradition, Ford believes that it is work with the hands that dignifies labour and makes it a spiritual necessity. He quotes:

> 'By hammer and hand
> All art shall stand'

the motto of the blacksmith, evidence of 'the corporate consciousness of the other nearly indispensable crafts' (*HC* 178).

He is a good enough socialist to understand, though, how to the agricultural labourer the tilling of the soil in itself can seem a pointless activity. In his 1904 collection of poems *The Face of the Night*, 'The Small Farmer Soliloquises' muses in persona on whether there is some being beneath the earth watching as 'us futile toilers scratching little lines and doing nothing'.[12] The shadow of the workhouse broods over him all his working life until at last 'I am here'. Yet Ford has not put these words into his mouth while he *is* working. It is without work, now that his working life has come to an end, that he has succumbed to despair, as Carlyle might have predicted.

As Ford's writing develops and his idea of what constitutes Englishness becomes more complex, the idealisation of work and its essential connection with Englishness remains at the heart of his thinking. In *A Call* (1910) he creates the character of Dudley Leicester, a figure in London society, whose social position and his inactivity, having absolutely nothing whatever to do, result in his extreme vulnerability to manipulation by a clever woman and a bizarre breakdown in his mental health. The cast of characters in this dark carnival, living ludicrously among the trappings of upper-class life, foreshadow those later created by P. G. Wodehouse, (who at the time of *A Call* was still writing school stories) and Dudley's essential vapidity is encapsulated in the moment at which he finds himself at a loose end:

> He hadn't a visit to pay to his tailor; there wouldn't be at his club or in the Park anyone he wanted to talk to or be talked to by. The one bright spot in his

day was the P-exercise that he would take just before lunch in his bathroom before the open window.[13]

Later, in discussing Dudley's wife and her effect upon him, Dudley's alter-ego Robert Grimshaw comments:

> 'She'll make a man of him. She'll give him a career. He'll be her life's work. And if you can't have what you want, the next best thing is to have a life's work that's worth doing, that's engrossing, and that keeps you from thinking about what you haven't got.' (*Call* 23)

This is straight from the lips of Ford Madox Brown, as quoted by Ford above after the death of his son, and the figure of Carlyle – 'Work, and don't despair!' – stands firmly behind him. The failure of any of the characters in *A Call* to 'get what they want' is explicitly due to their failure to work. For all his empowering words, Robert Grimshaw fails to take his own advice and although he has a profession, as a lawyer, he is insufficiently industrious in it to prevent his being drawn into a coil of silliness which destroys even the possibility of happiness for him. The women in the novel, like the unusual women of Ford's family and social group, Madox Brown's wife and daughters, think of themselves as *working*. Katya is a psychotherapist; Pauline Leicester's life's work is her husband. They are much more robust in their application of the principles than the men.

In Ford's fictions, work in professions such as the law continue to have much less redemptive power than work in 'honest trades'. The figure of William Morris, later joined by Conrad in Ford's imagination as a sea-captain, a master mariner from, perhaps, an Icelandic saga, takes his place beside Carlyle and Brown as the backbone of Ford's thinking about work:

> He walked up and down in the aisle between the rows of chairs, his hands in his jacket pockets with the air of a rather melancholy sea-captain on the quarter deck.[14]

This description of Morris comes from a chapter in *Return to Yesterday* devoted to left-wing politics, but Morris, as well as being a Romantic Socialist and tireless worker for his vision of the well-being of mankind, was a legendary worker at his own trades. His idealism related entirely to the regenerative power of working with the hands. The famous Morris designs, reproduced in every imaginable form almost a century after his death, owed their originality at the time partly to his insistence that every mechanical process in the production of his work, whether it was type-setting at the Kelmscott Press or silk-screen printing through Morris and Co. in Oxford Street, should be performed by hand out of respect for the dignity of the craftsman's labour. In this he set himself firmly against the tide of workers pouring in from the countryside to take up dehumanising mechanical work which, while it might pay the rent, did nothing for the soul. Factory labour was not what Carlyle and his followers meant by work, though they recognised that to work at all was empowering and better than idleness. Morris, Brown's closest friend, was himself a prodigious labourer by nature, and attempted to apply Carlyle's doctrine of work to his own incipient despair after the betrayal of his wife and friend (Janey Burden-Morris and Dante Gabriel Rossetti were lovers). With Morris among Ford's cast of substitute fathers, it is hardly surprising that the redemptive doctrine of manual work becomes increasingly evident in Ford's writing as his own optimism darkens.

Sadly, despite the faith he places in it, Ford doesn't seem to have been much good at working with his hands. Stella Bowen recounts Ford's attempts to repair and paint the house in which he and she lived in Sussex after the war, in humorously disparaging terms; he seems to have had much less luck with chickens than one might suppose from the frequency with which his characters take up chicken-care.

In the years of the War, Ford was determined, though over-age, to get work in the army, and it is clear from his writing that soldiering, to him, constituted a trade with redemptive power. He was not alone in this; soldiers still speak of their activity as 'having a job to do' whatever the ethics of the conflict. In his first post-war novel, the unjustly neglected *The Marsden Case,* Ford's subject is another coil of silliness which destroys a man, this time around a suspicion of illegitimacy. The central character is George Heimann, as he is known at the start of the novel, who, despite his German-sounding name, and as the matter of the story, turns out to be the legitimate son of an earl and essentially English. Not only essentially, but quintessentially English; this much is apparent to the narrator from George's manner of conducting himself, his code of honour and his decency in speech, from their first encounter. He is certainly decent in speech and code; he sounds exactly like the boys of E. Nesbit in *Five Children and It*, striking heroic poses, or the protagonists of P. G. Wodehouse's school-stories.[15] His peace of mind compromised by uncomfortable publicity surrounding his name and provenance, George is contrasted throughout the novel with the peaceful Fred, brother of the narrator. A man of clear certainties, Fred is competent, of the land, a chicken-farmer who loves the view from his property and makes his personal sacrifices with no comment or fuss; one of Ford's archetypal English workers. He goes quietly away to be killed at the Front. The narrator Jessop, who at the beginning of the novel is a successful writer, busy with the public life of a London celebrity, speaking at women's meetings and concerned with the staging of a shadow-play, overtires himself during a long working day with not enough to eat and too much excitement and suffers a kind of nervous collapse. He convalesces at his brother's chicken-farm, while Fred takes charge. Jessop, however, is himself transformed by taking up the work of war, despite the fact that he is appalled by the war and by the muddle that results from increased bureaucracy, getting in the way of people trying to do a worthwhile job. Jessop has a role looking after his men, as later, does Christopher Tietjens, and becomes powerfully authorit-ative, being spoken to deferentially on – and off – the telephone by people with 'Governing class' voices. We have little detail of Jessop's new work but enough to see that it suits him to have his mind occupied with it. Entertaining George in his rooms while he is attending a course on machine guns, he reflects:

> I suppose, just because I was in my own rooms [. . .] I had resumed a good deal of my old attitude of rather depressed irritation – at the stupidity of life and the irrational muddlesomeness of humanity.[16]

He goes on to rage about the waste of George as a soldier, as an im-pressive physical specimen who should be allowed to do the work he has selected. For George wants to find his own salvation through work, and though still supposed to be German, joins the Guards as a private. Jessop finds him there, exulting in his work and physically gleaming:

> 'I'm going to tell you all about the Huns. There's our Adjutant. The company officer is putting my name forward for lance-stripe unpaid; so I may be in the corporal's mess. After six weeks. Not bad . . . .'
> He went on like that, rejoicing in his strength until we reached the archway. (*MC* 204)

Oddly, though opposed to the war and horrified by the distance that grows between like-minded people, here represented by George and his friend, the German poet Curtius, as soon as war has become a reality, Jessop does not comment on the potential waste of a fine physical specimen through being lost in the trenches. He refers only to the waste of that man in not being allowed to do his work; clearly the salvation through work matters more than life. And again, work has a curiously English quality. In this novel George does not meet any Germans who work, during his attempt to escape Germany. He meets people of the quality of the fat assessor who seems unable to keep his clothes done up, and sees wives at a railway station bidding farewell to husbands who travel in soap-substitutes, but we see none of these closely enough to recognise any nobility in their calling. Later, in *The Rash Act*, Henry Martin similarly fails to find any dignity of labour in 'travelling in Pisto-Brittle' for his father's firm of pistachio flavoured toffee. He is appalled when his father tells him:

> 'You will be going to learn the business from the bottom. American fashion. Stoking. Boiling. Cutting. Packing. Carting, travelling, retail selling. Boy clerk. Head cashier.... Partner.... Sole owner.' [17]

Ford seems by the time of writing to have sufficiently caught the American habit of mind to see travelling salesmen as tragic, but not to descry the nobility of work in such a calling, as Arthur Miller perhaps did.

As a worker – in this case, working at his business in the Army – George is completely English to the extent of referring to 'the Huns' though he is only weeks returned from the Germany he had supposed to be the land of his nationality. The work he has sought is his complete redemption, but he is taken from it by the interference of his sister and the muddle-headed approach of those in high office who have agreed to help her. When he is kept from his work, his identity – his true identity as a human being, which lies beneath the spurious Heimann/Marsden dual identity (a theme Ford returns to continually, especially later in the *Henry for Hugh* sequence) – is compromised to the extent that he cannot live, and attempts a suicide that imitates his father's, and for a similar reason. Of the third Earl Marsden, George's father, Jessop remarks: 'Of course Mr. Heimann had to hang himself: he had experienced the breakdown of a moral ideal' (*MC* 208). He hangs himself from a beech tree, significantly in the Philosophen Wald – a place found in most German cities 'so that philosophers might feel at home'. George's moral ideal has been to work in the army and fight for England and Englishness; it has a puissance for

George, greater than that for most Englishmen, in that he has deliberately chosen his side; having failed, like his father, to achieve his ideal he feels he has no other resort than to emulate him also in death, having found a handy parade of beech trees similar to those in the Philosophen Wald. Luckily for him, he fails again in not calculating his method correctly.

Towards the conclusion of the novel, George's subsequent moral – and mental – salvation is assured by this. Despite his morbid fear of publicity, his indignation about being misrepresented in his practical competence over the suicide empowers him once again to take charge of his life.

He was faced by the article that Mr. Plowright had contributed to every journal in the British Empire. He exclaimed violently:

> "But, Good God! What's all this about...He says I walked with a rope! And slipped down a bank! I!"
> Mr. Plowright... had written an amazing account of an accident to a British peer. It combined the feudal spirit of a member of our ancient aristocracy with an amazing ignorance of how a three hundred year old beech tree can be felled.
> George said:
> "Am I such an incompetent ass? Is it imaginable? To take a plough-rope to pull down an ancestral oak. It would have to be an oak. And to mislay – mislay, you understand – my crosscut saw!"
> He threw the paper down. And then – and that was what put final tranquillity into the heart of Clarice! – he took it up and read it all over again, with a sort of fascination. (*MC* 322)

It is the fact that he does know his work as a peer and a landowner that assures him of his rightful place in society. He is next seen at a different aspect of his work, concerned with the re-establishment of national boundaries, his personal concerns and public role at last melding into one:

> A section of the fate of a section of the world was in the hands of that young man and his party. That is to say that they were representing Great Britain at some meeting or other of some or other League for the settling of certain boundaries. (*MC* 323)

The scene in which this observation occurs brings together the three different types of the work with which the book deals. There is Heimann's – Marsden's – diplomatic work, ludicrously juxtaposed in that characteristically Fordian manner with the work concerns of the little waiter who has just upset a dish of sauce over George's boots, weeping with shame and the fear of losing his job as the now splendid, confident George puts in a plea for him. Then there is Jessop's work; once his role in the Army, which allowed him not to despair, is over, he takes up again the work of the theatre. After months and years of horrible depression, he is beginning to be able to perceive the theatricality of such an incident, and relates to it as to a piece of theatre. It takes place upon a kind of stage, a dais; and Jessop notes where he is standing in relation to the main action, the position of the orchestra, and the fact that 'all the people are looking'. *The Marsden Case* is a vehicle then for the exploration of Ford's version of his grandfather's belief in the redemptive power of work.

This theme of a man's salvation through work is explored even more fully in the four volumes of *Parade's End*. Christopher Tietjens, like George Heimann subject to despair and harrowed by incessant gossip about him, gradually works through a series of manifestations. Despite Tietjens' extraordinary brain, he moves from an initial position of unrealised potential, aligned to that of Dudley Leicester, to that of engaged existence as an army officer; work which allows him to develop an almost maternal attitude of care for 'his' men. This helps him to hold in balance his rage against a system of well-intentioned muddle, by which many of them are destroyed either physically or emotionally, and his need to be contributing to something which is clearly worth while i.e. their well-being, however temporary his effect. This success gives him a modicum of inner peace, despite being generated by conflict. This is a matter of great importance to Ford. The emotional peace secured by Jessop in *The Mardsen Case*, while he has a job to do and men to care for during the conflict, comes horribly unstuck in peace-time when he has no task of such immediacy. In the scene mentioned above, Jessop describes himself as having 'at last gone through what, thank God! – proved to be the last stage of a mental pilgrimage I began among beastly horrors, lasting for horrible years' (*MC* 324). Despite the contradiction of a peace engendered by conflict, the sense of being engaged in a job well done is necessary for emotional stability. This may sound like pure Carlyle, but it would seem that for Ford, it was very much a reality.

Like Brown he was a tireless and prodigious worker at the craft he had made his own, but was not very successful in the world's terms. He continued undeterred, but it would seem that it was his experience at the Front, when he was as much an 'uncle' as when editing the *English Review*, which gave him one of his greatest feelings of a job well done; and when it was no longer required of him it was very difficult to believe enough in writing-as-work to keep despair at bay. He chronicles this for us in *The Marsden Case,* but Jessop and his war experience are not the centre of this story. It is Tietjens' progress, in *Parade's End*, which traces to its end the process of salvation through work. Tietjens finds a self he can bear to be during his war experience, but after the war, he has to find another kind of resolution. When he finds it, it is a resignation, literally and emotionally. He resigns his ancestral rights and his position in society – the responsibility for which has caused him endless problems, both grave and ludicrous, during his progress through the war – in favour of a William Morris-like craftsman's existence as a restorer of furniture. He becomes, we are led to believe, a peace-loving man of his trade; Ford's ideal of the English working-craftsman-thinker is achieved for Tietjens. He takes his place alongside William Morris and Ford Madox Brown, working and not despairing, keeping his mind on what is next to be done, so as to 'keep all on going' despite the work of mourning. Flaring moments of interest like little epiphanies, interspersed throughout the first three volumes, when Tietjens notices and reflects upon furniture in need of repair, have prepared the reader to accept this solution as right and comfortable, though we see little of Tietjens at work. The fascinated desire to represent the technicalities of the work process (in this case of printing) which threaten to overwhelm the reader in the early chapters of *The Fifth Queen,* are held in check in *Last Post*, with a discipline redolent of *Ford Madox Brown.*

For in this final volume of the tetralogy, Tietjens is almost absent from the text. Though the matter is entirely about his choices, and how little they can be understood by – American – others, being entirely English, he himself has disappeared, no more evident than is Ford himself, in the writing of *Ford Madox Brown*. Living an English working life, as engaged as Meary Walker or any of Ford's other workers, he has achieved the anonymity of the worker despite his class origins. In Ford's formulation, the fully engaged worker seems to experience a blissful, meditative, disappearance of the self; a concept of sublimation of the personal into the work which stands between Madox Brown and that fugitive from American nationality to English, T. S. Eliot. As Tietjens' common-law wife Valentine, in that stage of preparedness for giving birth when the veil between everyday and spiritual realities grows thin, reflects in a fantasy Nativity scene which brings the work of workers and the birth of new hope of salvation into the same humble space:

> But she did not know what she wished because she did not know what was to become of England or the world. . . . . But if [the baby] became what Christopher wished, he would be a contemplative parson farming his own tythe-fields and with a Greek testament in folio under his arm. . . . A sort of White of Selborne. . . . Selborne was only thirty miles away, but they had never had the time to go there...As who should say: *Je n'ai jamais vu Carcassonne*. . . . For if they had never found time, because of pigs, hens, pea-sticking, sales, selling, mending all-wool undergarments [. . .] if they had never found time now, before, how in the world would there be time when, added on to all the other, there should be the bottles, and the bandagings, and the bathings before the fire with warm, warm water and feeling the slubbing of the soap-saturated flannel on the adorable, adorable limbs [. . . .] Never! Never![18]

NOTES

1 Max Saunders, *Ford Madox Ford: A Dual Life,* Oxford: Oxford University Press, 1996, Volume 1, p. 61.
2 Ford, *Ford Madox Brown: A Record of his Life and Work*, London: Longmans, Green, 1896 – henceforth *FMB*; p. 391.
3 Saunders, Volume 1, p. 5.
4 Famously, his statement in his late memoir *Return to Yesterday* (1931): 'So, if one can keep oneself out of it, one may present a picture of a sort of world and time. I have tried to keep myself out of this work as much as I could – but try as hard as one may after self-effacement the great "I", like cheerfulness will come creeping in'. Dedication to Dr. Michael and Mrs. Eileen Hall Lake, *Return to Yesterday,* Manchester: Carcanet Press, 1999.
5 Ford, *Mightier Than the Sword,* London: Allen and Unwin, 1938, p. 92, reprinted in *Memories and Impressions*, Harmondsworth: Penguin 1979, p. 93.
6 Saunders, Volume 1, p. 119.
7 Thomas Carlyle, *Past and Present* (1843), New York: Houghton Mifflin, 1965: '"Religion", I said, "for properly speaking all true Work is Religion; and whatsoever Religion is not work may go and dwell among the Brahmins, Antinomians, Spinning Dervishes, or where it will; with me it shall have no harbour. Admirable was that of the old Monks, 'Laborare est Orare, Work is Worship'" Book 3 Chapter 12: Reward.
8 Chapter 2 of Tristram Hunt's *Building Jerusalem,* entitled 'Carlyle and Coketown' gives an excellent analysis of Carlyle's reaction to the ills of industrialization and his philosophic influence on the thinking of the period. He quotes 'Men are grown mechanical . . .' without attribution to a specific text:

Building Jerusalem; the Rise and Fall of the Victorian City, Phoenix, London 2005, p. 62.

9   See especially Macdonald's 1875 story *The Wise Woman,* also called *The Obstinate Princess: A Double Story,* in which a princess and the even more over-indulged daughter of a shepherd learn to manage their own behaviour through tackling housework.

10 Ford, *The Queen Who Flew,* London: Bliss, Sands and Foster, 1894, pp. 14-15.

11 Ford, *England and the English*, ed. Sara Haslam, Manchester: Carcanet, 2003, pp. 169-170.

12 Ford, 'The Small Farmer Soliloquizes' from *The Face of the Night,*1904, reprinted in *Ford Madox Ford, Selected Poems*, ed. Max Saunders, Manchester: Carcanet 1997, p. 27.

13 Ford, *A Call*, Carcanet, 1984, – henceforth *Call;* p. 90. P-exercise is physical exercise – P.E.

14 Ford, *Return to Yesterday*, Part II, chapter II; 'Farthest Left'. Carcanet 1999, p. 88.

15 See for example *The Gold Bat,* 1904, reprinted by Penguin 1986.

16 Ford, *The Marsden Case*, London: Duckworth, 1923 – henceforth *MC*; p. 206.

17 Ford, *The Rash Act*, London: Jonathan Cape, 1933, p. 29.

18 Ford, *Parade's End*, London: Penguin, 2002, p. 812.

A MODERNIST ELEGY TO THE GENTLEMAN? ENGLISHNESS AND THE IDEA OF THE GENTLEMAN IN FORD'S *THE GOOD SOLDIER*

Christine Berberich

This chapter's title rather grandly lines up three terms that do not necessarily come hand in hand or complement each other: modernism, Englishness and the idea of the gentleman. While *Englishness* and *gentleman* seem inextricably linked – the gentleman has always, and as will be elaborated on below, been considered a quintessentially *English* phenomenon – the term *modernist* seems the odd one out here. Surely modernism in all its radical newness – Andrzej Gasiorek points out that 'an oft-articulated critical view urges that modernism be defined in terms of a break with tradition'[1] – must counteract notions of English gentlemanliness that evoke musty smells of stiff collars, top hats and tails and pictures of Trollopian squires. Ford himself was aware of these contradictions – and not only relished but nourished them. In the spring of 1914, he gave a lecture on modernism at Wyndham Lewis's new Rebel Art Centre. That in itself would not necessarily merit mention; but Ford gave the lecture dressed in a tailcoat.[2] Ford, who believed that the 'the novelist ... must be the historian of his own time'[3] clearly saw that his was an era of rapid change and transition, and considered himself 'the bridging figure that would be part of the "revolution in Art" dressed as an Edwardian gentleman'.[4] As such, it could be argued, Ford consciously constructed himself, and his work, in a captivating and challenging combination of old and new, of traditional and modern; as, in other words, a modernist gentleman.

Literary anecdotes are often highly successful in introducing a topic, and the following one is an admirable example. Picture this: the scene is a street café in Paris; two men, both leading lights on the literary scene, are engaged in deep conversation. The men are Ford Madox Ford and a young Ernest Hemingway:

> "Tell me why one cuts people," I asked. Until then I had thought it was something only done in novels by Ouida ... "A gentleman," Ford

explained, "will always cut a cad." I took a quick drink of brandy.
"Would he cut a bounder?" ... "It would be impossible for a
gentleman to know a bounder." "Then you can only cut someone you
have known on terms of equality?" ... "Naturally." "How would one
ever meet a cad?" "You might not know it, or the fellow could have
become a cad." "What is a cad? ... Isn't he someone that one has to
thrash within an inch of his life?" "Not necessarily." ... "Is Ezra a
gentleman?" I asked. "Of course not. ... He's an American." "Can't
an American be a gentleman?" "Perhaps John Quinn," Ford explained.
"Certain of your ambassadors." "Myron T. Herrick?" "Possibly."
"Was Henry James a gentleman?" "Very nearly." "Are you a
gentleman?" "Naturally. I have held His Majesty's commission." "It's
very complicated," I said. "Am I a gentleman?" "Absolutely not,"
Ford said. "Then why are you drinking with me?" "I'm drinking with
you as a promising young writer. As a fellow writer in fact." "Good of
you," I said. "You might be considered a gentleman in Italy," Ford
said magnanimously. "But I'm not a cad?" "Of course not, dear boy.
Who ever said such a thing?" "I might become one," I said sadly.
"Drinking brandy and all. That was what did for Lord Harry Hotspur
in Trollope. Tell me, was Trollope a gentleman?" "Of course not."
"You're sure?" "There might be two opinions. But not in mine." "Was
Fielding? He was a judge." "Technically perhaps." "Marlowe?" "Of
course not." "John Donne?" "He was a parson." "It's fascinating," I
said. "I'm glad you're interested," Ford said. "I'll have a brandy and
water with you before I go."[5]

Why have I started with this anecdote? First of all, because it is funny.
Ford, of course, mercilessly teases his younger colleague. Secondly,
because it is interesting. Interesting mainly because we have to ask
ourselves: 'why does Ford pick on Hemingway in this way?' Is this
merely a case of an older man playfully provoking a younger? Or a
case of cultural differences with the benevolent would-be English
gentleman Ford teasing an, in his eyes, ignorant yankee? Or is it
something altogether different? Does, possibly, Ford's bantering
display his own deep-seated insecurity about the term 'gentleman', his
own incomprehension of a term that had evolved over centuries and
that had always been successful at adapting itself to changing times?
Can we maybe say that Ford's inability to pinpoint the term
'gentleman' in any way is representative of a typical modernist
fragmentation, indicative of a changing world where nothing seems
certain anymore?

    Max Saunders writes that 'there are continuities of mannerism
and preoccupation [in Ford's work] that make his prose recognizably
Fordian: vivid slight exaggerations; stoical ironic falling cadences; the
preoccupation with "Englishnesses"'.[6] Patrick Parrinder asserts that

'of all [Ford's] literary contemporaries only Kipling ... is so ostensibly concerned with English national identity'.[7] To investigate Ford's Englishness, it is vital that one look at some of his non-fiction texts first. Here, his trilogy *England and the English*[8] is of the utmost importance. Vincent J. Cheng writes that 'in dealing with the relations between religion, repressed passion, behaviour, and "good English form", these three volumes of non-fiction are also revealing and suggestive for the light they shed on Ford's later novels – most notably *The Good Soldier ...*'.[9] In the final volume of the trilogy, *The Spirit of the People*, Ford sets out to present the reader with his own, personal interpretation of 'The Englishman' which, and he is aware of this, is by force biased and subjective: 'he has dwelt, for instance, very much on the fact that his "Englishman" has appeared to have the characteristics of a poet.... That may be because he has been attracted to the contemplative, pleasant, kindly, romantic, active – but quite unreflective – individuals of this nation' (*SP* 232). This sentence already contains enough value statements – 'pleasant', 'kindly', 'romantic' – to ring warning bells in attentive readers' minds. The above mentioned characteristics of English kindness that so appealed to Ford, but also the interestingly placed and largely negative adjective 'unreflective', will be of the utmost importance in Ford's construction of Edward Ashburnham in *The Good Soldier*[10] as will be shown later. This combination of positive and negative descriptions of English identity already point towards the quandary Ford was in with regard to Englishness: neither whole-hearted admiration, nor complete condemnation; neither total identification with values of the past, nor with those of the modern.

Consequently, Ford's preoccupation with Englishness has to be problematised straight away. One of the complicating factors is his own position: due to his mixed Anglo-German ancestry, he considered himself sometimes an insider – 'that part of me that was English'[11] – sometimes an outsider in England – 'a man of no race and few ties' (*SP* 325) – but always an observer and a chronicler. Ford was deeply fascinated with the idea of Englishness in general and that of the English gentleman in particular. He not only engaged with both subjects in most of his writing, but also attempted to set himself up as a country gentleman as many of his friends and contemporaries observed, often in a non-sympathetic and even scathing manner as it seemed so out of character with his other, and seemingly conflicting interest in modernism. Hemingway complained to Ezra Pound in 1924 that Ford 'could "explain stuff" – but "in private life he is so goddam involved in being the dregs of an English country gentleman that you get no good out of him"'.[12] Similarly, Pound believed that 'Ford's impersonation of an English country gentleman had distorted not only his private life but his writing as well'.[13] While Pound did clearly not approve, Ford appeared proud of this: Allen Tate recalls him explaining that he 'wrote his novels in the tone of one English gentleman whispering into the ear of another English gentleman'.[14] This attitude towards writing might consequently account for the unusually restrained style of *The Good Soldier* where so much remains unsaid and below the surface for so long.

Ford's attempts at self-fashioning – Parrinder even talks about Ford's 'huge talent for self-dramatization'[15] – pose another problem as they seem to challenge his claim to be the objective and impassive observer *per se*. Setting himself up in the guise of the traditional English gentleman seemed the easiest way to prove that Englishness was, for Ford, a 'willed identity rather than a settled character'.[16] This, in itself, is also a telling statement: it shows that, in Ford's case, Englishness is something that can be assumed and discarded at will, a cloak that can be worn, and a marker of identity that can be divorced from the very nation it seems to represent. In other words, Ford did not consider Englishness as an innate birthright, but rather as a conscious, personal choice. One could argue that this attitude is reflected, in *The Good Soldier*, by the character of the narrator Dowell, a self-styled 'Philadelphia gentleman,' (*GS* 80) who vainly tries to copy the attributes of an English country gentleman.

Despite those attempts at fashioning himself in a traditionally English mould, Ford was clearly divided between the lure of nostalgia and the call of the modern – remember the lecture on the Modern in a tailcoat. R. W. Lid points out that:

> in his treatment of the post-Victorian gentleman, Ford was not concerned with writing a propagandistic attack.... In the course of his literary career Ford was involved for largely personal reasons in a long romance with the concept of the English gentleman.[17]

The conversation quoted above between him and Hemingway also points at Ford's internal struggle of traditional versus new: two prominent names in that passage are those of Trollope, representing the past, and Pound, representing the modern. In his work, Ford himself attempted to recreate a past world with chivalric and gentlemanly heroes – but he gave them a new twist which clearly shows his own ambivalence between pure nostalgia and admiration of the modern.

The history of the 'gentleman', of course, has always been closely linked to 'Englishness'. In *The Enigma of Arrival* V. S. Naipaul writes that 'you cannot say you know England until you know the English Gentleman',[18] thus marking the gentleman as a uniquely 'English' – as opposed to 'British' – idea. And this has been the predominant notion for centuries. Wilhelm Dibelius's voice is one among many considering the gentleman as a quintessentially English phenomenon:

> [the gentleman is] something specially English in all the course of its manifestation from the age of the mediaeval knight to the age of the public-schoolboy of the reign of Queen Victoria. 'Among the things every Englishman is proud of … is the fact that the idea of the gentleman is peculiar to England.'[19]

Shirley Letwin confirms this particular 'Englishness' of the ideal:

> everyone agrees that the gentleman is a traditional English phenomenon. Dr. Arnold reported "a total absence" in France and though Coleridge taught England to admire Germany, he found that the species was unknown there. Foreigners have endorsed this view by just importing the English word.[20]

In 1883, a 'distinguished German jurist' wrote to two friends in England: 'Do you know any good treatise on the duties and characters of a *gentleman*? It is a peculiarly English social type'.[21] The American Dixon described the idea of the gentleman as 'characteristically and admittedly English' and elaborated, as late as 1931, that 'every one in England, if not in wealth or position, at least in his actions, desires to be thought a gentleman'.[22] Before him, his compatriot Emerson stressed the Englishness of the ideal by favourably comparing the gentleman to his European counterparts: 'I much prefer the condition of the English gentleman … to that of any potentate in Europe – whether for travel, or for opportunity of society, or for access to means of science or study, or for mere comfort and easy healthy relation to people at home'.[23] Harold Laski stated in 1939 that 'it is the boast of England that the idea of being a gentleman is peculiar to her people, and I think there is solid substance in the boast,'[24] and Kazantzakis affirmed this in the 1960s when he wrote that 'after centuries, over the rocks and green hills and harbours of England, three great English monuments were erected: Magna Carta, the

Gentleman, and Shakespeare. These are the three great triumphs of man *made in England*.[25]

Roger Scruton similarly explains that the ideal of the gentleman was 'so frequently proclaimed and acted upon that ... it has attracted both commentary and emulation from foreigners, many of whom have adopted the word "gentleman" into their language as an explicit acknowledgement that it names a peculiarly English condition and a peculiarly English virtue'.[26] Thus the German historian V. A. Huber wrote in 1843 that '[the Germans] have nothing of the kind',[27] and the French author Hippolyte Taine famously commented that 'in France we have not got the word because we have not got the thing, and those three syllables ... sum up the whole history of English society'.[28]

The idea of the English gentleman looms large in Ford's 1914 novel *The Good Soldier*. Several important attributes of the potential 'hero' are explicitly stated from the beginning. Edward Ashburnham was:

> very well built, carried himself well, was moderate at the table and led a
> regular life . . . he had, in fact, all the virtues that are usually accounted
> English. . . . They were the things that one would set upon his tombstone.
> They will, indeed, be set upon his tombstone by his widow. (*GS* 140)

These are the words that, in the opinion of *The Good Soldier*'s narrator Dowell, admirably describe the object of the title, Edward Ashburnham, the good soldier, good sport and quintessential English gentleman. And the words thus *seem* to set the scene, painting Ashburnham as the perfect gentleman. 'Seem' is here, of course, the crucial word. *The Good Soldier* is, after all, a modernist text and, as such, one that has several surprises in store for its readers. Gasiorek claims that Ford's novel 'dismantles the codes by which conventional narratives proceed',[29] and, as I shall argue in the further course of this chapter, it also mantles traditional codes of gentlemanliness. At a superficial reading, *The Good Soldier* presents its readers with 'good people', with impeccable manners in its lead character, the English gentleman Edward Ashburnham. But this apparent social stability is undermined by the subtext of the novel: instead of the traditional image of the perfect country gentleman, it presents us with the crumbling façade of a landed gentry which can no longer present an opposition to the onslaught of modernity. And this, crucially, reflects social realities in Britain at the beginning of the First World War which has always been considered a watershed for the British class system.

On careful reading of the novel, it becomes apparent that the idealised image of Edward Ashburnham as the perfect English gentleman is queried, challenged and problematised from the very beginning of the novel. First of all, Ashburnham is presented to us through the eyes of the narrator Dowell, a highly subjective observer who places Ashburnham on a pedestal. Despite this, we have to take a few factors into consideration: first of all Dowell is an American, and thus an outsider to the very English way of life he describes. And secondly, of course, Dowell writes with the knowledge that his own wife conducted a year-long affair with Ashburnham. Although he repeatedly confirms that he blames his wife rather than the allegedly saintly Ashburnham, the discerning reader cannot but wonder at the reliability of his narration.

But the most important point to consider when looking at Ashburnham and his apparent 'gentlemanliness' is the very fact that he is such a careful and conscious 'construct'. He has clearly been devised according to existing notions and discourses on gentlemanliness: good officer, good landlord, good lover. As such, *The Good Soldier* follows in the established tradition of drawing from stock characters not only for instant recognition by the readers but also their moral edification. At first glance, Edward Ashburnham resembles Steele and Addison's Sir Roger de Coverley, the perfect country squire, who admirably looks after his estate and his tenants, an image later recreated by Trollope in Sir Roger Carbury in *The Way We Live Now*. Ford was thus aware of conceptions of gentlemanliness in society that had been inherited from the Victorians and earlier, and he very carefully tried to incorporate them in his novels. David Eggenschwiler confirms:

> Edward seems a perfect replica of a nineteenth century fictional type: the attractive and not overly bright career officer (and cavalry, at that). He would have been quite at home in *Vanity Fair*. He is handsome in a conventionally manly way (fair hair, sunburnt complexion, blue eyes, bristling moustache); he dresses elegantly but not foppishly (the pigskin cases – for guns and collars and helmets and hats – strike the right balance); the way he talks of clothes, horses, and artillery; to women he "gurgles" the ideals about love's redemption which he has picked up from popular novels; he is common-sensical about common-sensical things and sentimental about "all children, puppies and the feeble generally"; above all, with his physique, his composure, his perfectly stupid blue eyes, he is decidedly attractive to women.[30]

Looking at the existing criticism on *The Good Soldier*, one particular article appears helpful in trying to assess the importance of the gentlemanly ideal for Ford. Mary Cohen's 1973 '*The Good Soldier*: Outworn Codes'[31] tries to link *The Good Soldier*, and particularly the character of Edward Ashburnham, to mediaeval notions of chivalry. More than that, however, it claims that Ford, when writing the novel, had a particular thirteenth-century Provençal chivalric romance in mind, *Flamenca*, which was even discussed in a study of Provençal poets by Ford's father, Francis Hueffer, in *The Troubadours* of 1878. This seems a clear case of Foucauldian in-doctrination in the cradle, as Ford clearly inherited, or learnt, his interest in all things chivalric from his father. With his interest in chivalric mythology Ford also shows himself as indebted to much nineteenth-century writing and culture which always showed a strong preoccupation with the days of mediaeval knights.[32] Cohen explains that *Flamenca* is the story of a love triangle between the noble but very jealous Archambaud of Bourbon, his beautiful and long-suffering wife Flamenca and the chivalric William of Nevers. She lists similarities between the cuckolds of either work – Archambaud and Dowell who, incidentally, both guard their wife's locked room with an axe – and claims that Ashburnham is William's counterpart, albeit a rather pale one. *Flamenca*, Cohen suggests, establishes the kind of mediaeval chivalric code that Edward desperately wants to live up to but fails in the turbulent times of change just before the Great War. And it has, of course, been commonly claimed that the Great War saw the, quite literal, death of the gentleman-ideal in the trenches of Flanders. In her opinion, Ford uses these mediaeval chivalric virtues to show the rottenness of his contemporary society. She writes that 'it is the discordance of the two forces, the medieval code and the morals of pre-war England, which forms the basis for the condemnation of society offered by *The Good Soldier*'.[33] To enforce this 'construct' of Ashburnham, Dowell, and through him, Ford illustrates it with chivalric and gentlemanly images, for example describing his interest in chivalric literature: 'Even when he was twenty-two he would pass hours reading one of Scott's novels or the Chronicles of Froissart' (*GS* 128). This was a popular device in that kind of twentieth-century literature that dealt with the demise of contemporary society in one way or another. One example for this is Evelyn Waugh's aptly named Tony Last in *A Handful of Dust*.[34] Tony is both captivated by – and captive to – the mediaeval atmosphere that enshrouds his estate,

Hetton, where even the bedrooms are named after chivalric heroes and heroines of mediaeval mythology. This clouds Tony's outlook on life. Sleeping in a room named after a gallant knight all his life, he has fully absorbed – in a Foucauldian manner – chivalric notions and ideas. Chivalric heroes and heroines recur throughout Waugh's work and clearly show this author's preoccupation with the manners and morals of an earlier (and better?) world. Both in *Brideshead Revisited* and the *Sword of Honour* trilogy the chief protagonists show an almost unhealthy – as it means they move against rather than with their times – preoccupation with and veneration for historic battles that have become part of a chivalric myth.[35]

The perfect mediaeval knight had to fulfil three basic requirements: he had to be a good soldier, a fair and compassionate landlord and a passionate lover. This three-way division is adhered to in *The Good Soldier*, but Edward Ashburnham's initial appearance as the perfect English gentleman, and with it his roles as soldier, landlord and lover are being slowly but steadily undermined, and it is this that forms the modernist element of the novel. In the army, he was admired by his men, but he lacked actual battle experience and consequently could not prove himself in that field. As a landlord, he is *over*generous rather than just. A comment such as "'Oh well, he's an old fellow and his family have been our tenants for over two hundred years. Let him off altogether'" (*GS* 134), about an impoverished tenant who cannot pay his rent, is typical for him and arguably an admirable trend, worthy of a gentleman and a magnanimous landlord. But Ford here also shows the reverse side of the coin with Leonora's grief at Ashburnham's over-charity which endangers the estate – and consequently the future of the tenants altogether. Leonora clearly perceives that 'his generosities were almost fantastic. He subscribed much too much to things connected with his mess, he pensioned off his father's servants, old or new, much too generously. They had a large income, but every now and then they would find themselves hard up' (*GS* 132). Good soldier and good landlord, or rather reckless spendthrift who throws about his money for lack of a proper occupation or a more structured lifestyle? The line seems to be a very thin one. Andrew Radford, in a discussion of the Tietjens tetralogy, talks about 'the trivialising dilettantism of a superfluous country gentleman',[36] a term that can clearly be applied to Ashburnham as well. Bereft of a more coherent social role in a world dominated by the upheaval of 'the Modern', Ashburnham is left without a clear-cut role, duty or responsibility.

   In the context of the three chivalric characteristics, Cohen talks bluntly about Ashburnham's 'incompetence'[37] and his failure in two of his three chivalric categories. It almost appears as if Ashburnham is trying to redeem himself with his efforts as a courtly lover. He tries to cast himself in the guise of the over-sentimental man but his affection for one woman is quickly succeeded by that for another. His wife Leonora is replaced by first La Dolciquita, then Mrs Basil, Maisie Maidan, Florence, and finally Nancy. His chivalric attitude towards women is consequently revealed as nothing deeper than serial womanising. At the same time, his attempts at keeping a 'stiff upper lip' at all cost shows his inherent inability to express emotion. One can thus say that Ford challenges very English ideals: chivalric ideals are undermined, the idea of emotional control highlighted as nothing but emotional frigidity.

In *The Spirit of the People* Ford narrates a key-scene from his life which made an indelible impression on him and which he incorporated into his novel *The Good Soldier*: it is the story of a friend who had grown very, not to say 'too', attached to his young female ward. Ford himself witnessed to stoic leave-taking between his friend and the young girl which is, of course, echoed in the farewell scene between Ashburnham and Nancy in *The Good Soldier*.[38] Ford elaborates on the scene in *The Spirit of the People*:

> Now, in its particular way, this was a fine achievement; it was playing the game to the bitter end. . . . what was most impressive in the otherwise commonplace affair, was the silence of the parting. I am not concerned to discuss the essential ethics of such positions, but it seems to me that at the moment of separation a word or two might have saved the girl's life and the man's misery without infringing eternal verities. . . . a silence so utter, a so demonstrative lack of tenderness, seems to me to be a manifestation of a national characteristic that is almost appalling. (*SP* 314-5)

This quotation again shows Ford's own ambivalence with regard to 'Englishness' and his own sense of 'belonging'. On the one hand, he admires the ability to keep a stiff upper lip – a quintessential English characteristic, and one commonly attributed in particular to the English gentleman. On the other hand, though, he shows the appalled reaction of the, perhaps, more effusive continental. Ford's attitude is echoed in E. M. Forster's 1936 diatribe against his compatriots, in which he bemoaned the fact that Englishmen have:

> well-developed bodies, fairly developed minds, and undeveloped hearts. And it is this undeveloped heart that is largely responsible for the difficulties of the Englishman abroad. An undeveloped heart – not a cold one. . . . For it is not that the Englishman can't feel – it is that he is afraid to feel. He has been taught at his public school that feeling is bad form. He must not express great joy or sorrow, or even open his mouth too wide when he talks – his pipe might fall out if he did. He must bottle up his emotion, or let them out only on a very special occasion.[39]

In *The Good Soldier*, Ford's narrator Dowell again and again emphasises the fact that they are all 'good people'. 'Good people', and some of them *English* good people at that, they have to live and behave according to unwritten laws. And these unwritten laws prove to be the downfall for all of them. Scenes of any kind in public have to be avoided at all cost; emotions and passions have to be repressed, a stiff upper-lip has to be kept. In *The Spirit of the People* Ford had come to the telling conclusion that:

> not being to the English manner born, I did not know just what 'things' were.... Nowadays I know very well what 'things' are; they include, in fact, religious topics, questions of the relations of the sexes, the conditions of poverty-stricken districts – every subject from which one can digress into anything moving. That, in fact, is the crux, the Rubicon that one must never cross. And that is what makes English conversations so profoundly, so portentously, troublesome to maintain. It is a question of a very fine game, the rules of which you must observe. (*SP* 312)

Dowell's experiences in *The Good Soldier* are similar: as the foreigner, he is clearly the puzzled outsider when it comes to the nuances of English behaviour. With both publications Ford clearly criticises the ingrained English conception of the 'stiff upper lip' and advocates more emotional freedom.

With *The Good Soldier*, Ford highlights the problems that social expectations can place upon a character. Edward Ashburnham was born into a privileged family and consequently had expectations with regard to conduct heaped upon him from infancy onwards. He was educated with the clear aim of grooming him for his socially priv-ileged position – but as an adult he realises that he cannot live up to that pressure. He fails – in the same way that in later twentieth-century novels, Evelyn Waugh's Tony Last and Sebastian Flyte, or Anthony Powell's Charles Stringham, the latter two examples of upper-class 'alcoholic futilitarian[s]', fail.[40] It thus became a new popular theme in twentieth-century literature to show men who had all the outward trappings and requirements of the gentlemanly lifestyle but who could not live up to society's – and possibly their own – expectations. This, of course, also has to do with the general sense of displacement and fragmentation that came hand in hand with the onset of modernism: Victorian values were discarded, the class system began to crumble – and people began to cast around for new ideals. *The Good Soldier* is thus about the conflicts between passion and convention, being and appearing that were in keeping with the turbulent times the book was conceived in. The novel's characters are shown to be puzzled and lost at the events unfolding around them – we here only have to think of narrator Dowell's many uncertainties and constant admissions that he 'does not know', 'did not know' or 'does not understand'[41] – and the novel's subtext in every way contradicts its surface appearance: the Ashburnhams seem to be good people; but in fact they are not even on speaking-terms; Edward Ashburnham appears the perfect gentleman, but in fact he is not.

At the end of the novel, Edward's suicide again complicates the message of the book. Why did he kill himself? Because he can't have what he wants? Because he is unable to cope with the pressure of conforming to society's expectations? Because it is the decent thing to do? Again, Ashburnham's end has its parallels in later fiction: Tony Last in Waugh's *A Handful of Dust* disappears in the Brazilian jungle, for ever condemned to reading Dickens to a madman which, of course, represents his social, if not his literal, death; Sebastian Flyte in *Brideshead Revisited* slowly drinks himself to death in a North African monastery; Charles Stringham in Powell's *Dance to the Music of Time* foregoes his social role, joins the army in the ranks and dies in a Japanese POW camp. All these characters are initially drawn according to chivalric notions – Stringham, for example, is said to resemble a 'version of Veronese's Alexander';[42] and they all fall foul of modern society.

As far as the image of the gentleman is concerned, Ford's novel at first reading appears very nostalgic, seemingly yearning for the ideal of a bygone era. But at the same time, as previously pointed out, it dismantles traditional codes of gentlemanliness by subverting the ideal through bitter irony. During Ashburnham's affair with Mrs Basil,

Ford shows that it appears acceptable for gentlemen to cheat on each other with each other's wives but, at the same time, blackmail each other with that knowledge. While the tacit acceptance of a spouse's adultery with a fellow gentleman could possibly be construed in terms of gentlemanly 'fair play' coupled with snobbishness – all is allowed as long as the other is a gentleman, too – blackmail, of course, is a cowardly act that blatantly goes against any gentlemanly values. Ford here is quick in pointing out the hypocrisy of his contemporaries.

And then, of course, there is the superb episode of the Kilsyte case, in which a frightened servant girl, kissed by Ashburnham for 'comfort', remembers with horror that:

> all her life, by her mother, by other girls, by school-teachers, by the whole tradition of her class she had been warned against gentlemen. She was being kissed by a gentleman. She screamed, tore herself away; sprang up and pulled a communication cord. (*GS* 139)

This incident also has its roots in earlier literature and shows that servant girls, too, have had their share of emancipation from lordly rights of caddish gentlemen since the days of Richardson's *Pamela*. Society is here shown as having moved on from the days of gentlemen having the freedom to take whatever took their fancy. Ashburnham, for once well-meaning rather than selfish and caddish, falls victim to that.

At the beginning of the novel, Dowell ponders: 'Permanence? Stability? I can't believe it's gone. I can't believe that that long, tranquil life, which was just stepping a minuet, vanished in four crashing days at the end of nine years and six weeks' (*GS* 13). In 1995, W. G. Sebald pondered that 'now there was nothing anymore, nobody, no stationmaster in gleaming peaked cap, no servants, no coachman, no house guests, no shooting parties, neither gentlemen in indestructible tweeds nor ladies in stylish travelling clothes. It takes just one awful second, I often think, and an entire epoch passes'.[43] In *The Good Soldier* Ford presents us with the end of this epoch. The novel is his epitaph to the ideal of the Victorian gentleman. But his modern twist to an old tale is that he shows us a gentleman who is, despite appearances, not perfect and hailed as the epitome of society, but a character who is deeply flawed. Perfect gentlemen drawn in the Trollopian mould, Ford might have been saying, can no longer exist in the fragmented modern world.[44] Perhaps they never could.

NOTES

1   Andrzej Gasiorek, 'Ford Madox Ford's Modernism and the Question of Tradition,' *English Literature in Transition,* 44:1 (2001), 3.
2   For full details on this story see Jeffrey Mathes McCarthy, '*The Good Soldier* and the War for British Modernism,' *Modern Fiction Studies* 45:2 (1999), pp. 303 ff.
3   Ford Madox Ford, *A History of Our Own Times,* ed. Solon Beinfeld & Sondra J. Stang, Manchester: Carcanet Press, 1989, p. xvi.
4   McCarthy, p. 312.
5   Ernest Hemingway, *A Moveable Feast* (1936), London: Arrow Books, 1996, pp. 73-74.
6   Max Saunders, 'Ford Madox Ford and European Culture,' in Robert Clark & Piero Boitani (eds.), *English Studies in Transition. Papers from the ESSE Inaugural Conference,* London: Routledge, 1993, p. 208.
7   Patrick Parrinder, '"All that is Solid Melts into Air": Ford and the Spirit of Edwardian England,' in Joseph Wiesenfarth (ed.), *History and Representation in Ford Madox Ford's Writing,* Amsterdam: Rodopi, 2004, p. 6.
8   All references to Ford's England Trilogy in this paper come from *England and the English,* ed. Sara Haslam, Manchester: Carcanet, 2003; comprising *The Soul of London* (*SL* – 1905); *The Heart of the Country* (*HC* – 1906) and *The Spirit of the People* (*SP* – 1907).
9   Vincent J. Cheng, 'The Spirit of *The Good Soldier* and *The Spirit of the People,*' *English Literature in Transition* 32:3 (1989), p. 304.
10 Ford Madox Ford, *The Good Soldier* (1915) – henceforth *GS*; London: Penguin, 1981, p. 80.
11 Ford Madox Ford, *It Was the Nightingale,* London: Heinemann, 1934, p. 85.
12 Ernest Hemingway, quoted in: David Trotter, 'Hueffer's Englishness', *Agenda* 27:4/28:1 (Winter 1989-Spring 1990), 148.
13 Ezra Pound, quoted in Trotter, p. 148.
14 Allen Tate, quoted in Samuel Hynes, 'Ford and the Spirit of Romance,' *Modern Fiction Studies,* 9:1 (Spring 1963), 20.
15 Patrick Parrinder, '"All that is solid melts into Air": Ford and the Spirit of Edwardian England', p. 5.
16 *Ibid.,* p. 7.
17 R. W. Lid, *Ford Madox Ford, The Essence of His Art,* Berkeley: University of California Press, 1964, p. 32.
18 V. S. Naipaul, *The Enigma of Arrival,* London: Penguin Books, 1987, p. 161.
19 Quoted by Sir Ernest Barker in *Traditions of Civility. Eight Essays,* Cambridge: Cambridge University Press, 1948, p. 124..
20 Shirley Robin Letwin, 'Tradition II: The Morality of the Gentleman,' *The Cambridge Review* (7 May 1976), p. 142.
21 W. R. Browne, 'The English Gentleman', *National Review* (April 1886), 261.
22 Macneile W. Dixon, *The Englishman,* London: Edward Arnold & Co. Ltd., 1931, pp. 78, 82.
23 Ralph Waldo Emerson, *English Traits and Representative Men,* London: Macmillan & Co., 1888, p. 135.

24 Harold Laski, *The Danger of Being a Gentleman and Other Essays,* London: George Allen & Unwin Ltd., 1939, p. 13.
25 Nikos Kazantzakis, *England,* Oxford: Cassirer, 1965, p. 14.
26 Roger Scruton, *England: An Elegy,* London: Chatto & Windus, 2000, p. 64.
27 V. A. Huber, quoted in Shirley Robin Letwin, 'The Idea of a Gentleman: Englishmen in Search of a Character', *Encounter,* 57:5 (1981), 18.
28 Hippolyte Taine, *Taine's Notes on England* (1860–1870); London: Thames and Hudson, 1957, p. 144.
29 Gasiorek, 'Ford Madox Ford's Modernism and the Question of Tradition', p. 15.
30 David Eggenschwiler, 'Comic-Tragical Illusions,' in Ford Madox Ford, *The Good Soldier, A Norton Critical Edition,* ed. Martin Stannard, New York: W. W. Norton & Comp., 1995, p. 345.
31 Mary Cohen, '*The Good Soldier*: Outworn Codes', *Studies in the Novel,* 5 (1973), 284-97.
32 The nineteenth century saw frequent chivalric revivals, for example the splendid Victorian extravaganza, the Eglinton Tournament of 1839. For an admirable description of the origins of the gentleman in the Middle Ages see Maurice Keen, *Origins of the English Gentleman. Heraldry, Chivalry and Gentility in Medieval England, c.1300-c.1500,* Stroud: Tempus Publishing Ltd., 2002. For the importance of chivalry for the image of the English gentleman, see also Mark Girouard, *The Return to Camelot. Chivalry and the English Gentleman,* New Haven, CT: Yale University Press, 1981.
33 Cohen, p. 287.
34 Evelyn Waugh, *A Handful of Dust* (1934), London: Penguin Classics, 2000.
35 For more information on this see, for example, Evelyn Waugh, *Brideshead Revisited* (1945), London: Penguin Books, 1962, pp. 14-15 and *Men at Arms* (1952), London: Penguin Classics, 2001, p. 166.
36 Andrew Radford, 'The Gentleman's Estate in Ford's *Parade's End,*' *Essays in Criticism,* 52:4 (2002), 317.
37 Cohen, p. 289.
38 See *SP* 313-4 and *GS* 224-5 for more details. The episode from SP is discussed elsewhere in this volume, by Sara Haslam (p. 53), by Nick Hubble (especially pp. 154-5), and by Austin Riede (p. 215).
39 E. M. Forster, 'Notes on the English Character,' in *Abinger Harvest* (1936), London: Edward Arnold Ltd., 1961, p. 13.
40 Edward Pearce, 'Brideshead Resisted', *Quadrant,* 26:7 (July 1982), 60. For more details, see Evelyn Waugh, *A Handful of Dust* and *Brideshead Revisited* and Anthony Powell, *Dance to the Music of Time, 4 Volumes: Spring, Summer, Autumn, Winter* (1951-75) London: Mandarin, 1997.
41 See, for example, *GS* 14, 16, 18, 19, 20.
42 Anthony Powell, *Dance to the Music of Time, Vol. 1, A Question of Upbringing,* p. 8.
43 W. G. Sebald, *The Rings of Saturn* trans. Michael Hulse, 1995; London: The Harvill Press, 1999, p. 31.
44 Ford developed this notion further in his Tietjens tetralogy *Parade's End* in which he presents us with yet another deeply troubled gentleman.

THE DECLINE OF ENGLISH DISCOURSE AND THE AMERICAN INVASION IN *THE GOOD SOLDIER* AND *PARADE'S END*

Austin Riede

Ford's 1915 novel *The Good Soldier*, the capstone to his pre-war career, has been read as symbolic of the close of the pre-war era, and it adumbrates not only the First World War, but also the socio-political and cultural aftermath of that war. *The Good Soldier* predicts both the decline of English imperialism and the American Invasion of England that are central themes in *Parade's End*, Ford's post-war tetralogy. Both works deal with relations between England and the US, and the competition between the entrenched ideologies of the first, and the emerging imperial inclinations of the latter. The English protagonists of the novels, Edward Ashburnham and Christopher Tietjens, are archetypes of certain kinds of anachronistic English subjects, constructed by English national and imperial discourse; they are both princely feudalists who try to hold on to idealized notions of Englishness which seem to have no place in the twentieth century. It is the construction of their characters by the discourse of the metaphorical game of Englishness that is the impetus of their passions and their tragedies. Both are made to pay dearly for their lack of ability, or of volition, to hear the voices of their own time, and while they differ markedly in intelligence, articulation, and recognition of the changes happening in the world around them, they share a monomaniacal devotion to taciturnity and to properly 'playing the game'.

Both Tietjens and Ashburnham lose power at the end of the novels, and their places are taken over by Americans; Ashburnham commits suicide and Bramshaw Teleragh is bought by the American millionaire John Dowell. Likewise, at the end of *Parade's End*, the Tietjens estate, Groby, has been occupied by Mrs. de Bray Pape, a ceaselessly chattering rich American woman. Through these symbolic displacements of imperial and collective English archetypes by hyper-individualist Americans, Ford dramatizes the displacement of reticent insular Englishness by a verbose American expansiveness. The contrast between the old 'feudal' landowners and the Americans who replace them demonstrates that, for Ford, relations between England and its commonwealth and ex-colonies were defined by differing patterns of discourse. Very specific rules of discourse govern and create Englishness, and Englishness is kept intact by strict adherence to these rules. These rules are the distillation of English politics and literary tradition, which are present to Ford's characters in a clearly parodied fashion as either rigid rules of etiquette and conformity (e.g., rare roast beef and cold baths), or as sentimental Romance drawing uncritically on feudal notions of chivalry and masculine prowess. In these parodically reduced forms, the rules of Englishness are offered in a Bakhtinian monoglossia and cannot realistically sustain an idea of nationality as shared community.[1] As Bakhtin argues, the discourse of epic is sustained univocally in a language assumed capable of sustaining a whole and coherent world view; as long as Englishness seemed able to subordinate and silence all other cultural discourse, the English point of view remained untroubled and uncontaminated by other voices. The story of English triumphalism and empire is epic, and like ancient epics, sufficiently authoritative to silence debate and even to 'go without saying'. Under this dispensation, Englishness is a closed system, a game played by absolute, defined rules learned on the playing fields of Eton, and is characterized by a laconic disposition to rest upon received opinions. With the world upheaval of the Great War, the challenge to insular English assumption – the univocal epic of imperialism – gives way to the many contending discourses of heteroglossia. In Ford's representation of national character, the reserved English gentleman gives way to a talkative new world power, aggressively represented by American garrulousness.[2] The English community that might once have shared parochial customs has been over-extended in the expansion of empire, and the dissonant voices of the no-longer English colonizers make themselves heard when the American empire rises as a threat from the former colonies.[3]

English colonizers and their descendants (particularly, though not exclusively Americans) who have lost contact with these unspoken rules, threaten and destroy Englishness by entering into its discourse, and adding the kind of heteroglossia that is fatal to the single-voiced (actually tacit – even more than other national ideologies, Ford has argued – the discourse of Englishness is under-stood but unspoken) notion of nationality as a presumably closed and finished system. If, as Benedict Anderson argues in *Imagined Comm-unities*, 'the nation is always conceived as a deep, horizontal comradeship',[4] then the coherence of a national character is necessary for the preservation of the nation itself, either as island or as empire.

It seems, from Ford's definitions in his three-part study *England and the English*, published between 1905 and 1907, that the first rule of this metaphorical game is to keep a stiff upper lip, that is, to refrain from displaying emotion, and to speak only in the most precise terms and only when speaking is necessary to convey meaning or to properly fulfil the duties of etiquette.[5] This is how the national discourse that formed Ashburnham and Tietjens preserves and perpetuates itself, by shutting out competing or seemingly incom-prehensible or indelicate modes of speech. This is essential to a discourse of imperialism, as imperialism and nationalism function through the assumption that theirs is the only discourse adequate to the subject; that is to say, they are monoglossic. This, loosely, worked for Imperial England through the nineteenth century. When the Great War forced this ideological moment to its crisis, however, the imposed boundaries of acceptable expression that had defined English discourse rendered competition with the clamour of other national voices nearly impossible, and this is, largely, what *Parade's End* is about. As Dennis Brown has argued '*Parade's End* stands out as perhaps the most comprehensive fictive exploration of Englishness which the twentieth century produced, and one highly relevant to current multi-ethnic and post-devolution Britain'.[6] In *Parade's End* Ford is chronicling, through Tietjens, the rapid decline of Englishness.

Returning from his first round of warfare, as Tietjens faces the imminent prospect of complete mental breakdown, he realizes what a shifting economic and cultural global power structure means for the English Empire, and why the English in general and he in particular, are ill-equipped to cope with the emerging conflicts of the twentieth century:

> In electing to be peculiarly English in habits and in as much of his temperament as he could control . . . Tietjens had . . . adopted a habit of behaviour that he considered to be the best in the world for normal life. If every day and all day long you chatter at high pitch and with the logic and lucidity of the Frenchman; if you shout in self assertion, with your hat on your stomach, bowing from a stiff spine and by implication threaten all day long to

shoot your interlocutor, like the Prussian; if you are lachrymally emotional as
the Italian, or as drily and epigrammatically imbecile over inessentials as the
American, you will have a noisy, troublesome and thoughtless society without
any of the surface calm that should distinguish the atmosphere of men when
they are together.[7]

While this idealized and calm English society of 'deep arm-chairs in
which to sit for hours in clubs thinking of nothing at all' (*SDN* 178) is
what he believes he is fighting the war to protect and preserve,
Tietjens has made an inherently anti-imperial realization about the
limits of the discourse that has created him and which he has had his
small part in creating. Englishness allows for no release, no high-
pitched chatter, no self-assertive shouting, no lachrymose displays or
imbecile verbosity, and thus for no release of the immense pressures
with which a subject may be burdened, and also no space for
accepting or incorporating new ideas or points of view. Tietjens still
sees taciturn English existence as an ideal, but he also sees that
modernity has made a less perfect discourse necessary. He concludes
that occasions demanding the discursive release that he sees in other
national characters are so rare in any one life that 'the great advantage
would seem to have lain with English society; at any rate before the
later months of the year 1914' (*SDN* 179).

    Tietjens's dedication to the English land-owning model is so
complete that he sees it as a structure that transcends this world; for
him, the English feudal model is quite literally heavenly. He sees 'the
almighty as, on a colossal scale, a great English Landowner,
benevolently awful'. Christ is 'an almost too benevolent Land-
steward, son of the Owner, knowing all about the estate'. In this
trinity, Tietjens conceives of the Holy Ghost as 'the spirit of the
estate, the Game, as it were, as distinct from the players of the game'
(*NMP* 365-6). Tietjens, here, is half joking with himself, but his good
natured joke reveals that his ideal image of heaven essentially posits
Englishness, or English national discourse, as a perfect state of being,
and the English social model as perfect in the most spiritually exact
sense of the word, although he also understands that this material
notion of heaven is antiquated, and he only hopes that he can get there
before the ascendant conception of God as 'a real estate agent with
Marxist views' (*NMP* 366) can abolish it completely. Ashburnham,
for all his sentimentality, would probably share Tietjens's view of the
hereafter if he had the brain to formulate it, but he would not
understand, as Tietjens does, that it is the pursuit of empire and

expansion that have ruined this closed system of Englishness and its possibility of attaining perfection.

Ford gives a lengthy description of 'the game' in *The Spirit of the People*, the third volume of *England and the English*. It is here that he defines Englishness as a certain manner of discourse that perpetuates itself by rendering impossible the introduction of new concepts into the lexicon, thus insuring the stability of the current power structure, but also rendering it impotent and unable to assert itself amongst the din of contending voices from other power structures. The avoidance of talk pertaining to what Ford and his American parody Dowell both refer to as 'things', is the primary objective of Englishness, for to discuss 'things', or even to say what those 'things' are, would be to open the gates of Englishness, rendering dialectic the designedly unilateral and hierarchical structure of Ashburnham's imperialist and Tietjens's feudalist paradigms. Ford writes that

> 'delicacy' is the note of the English character – a delicacy that is almost the only really ferocious note that remains in the gamut. It is retained at the risk of honour and self-sacrifice, at the cost of sufferings that may be life-long; so that we are presented with the spectacle of a whole nation bearing every appearance of being extraordinarily tongue-tied and extraordinarily unable to repress its emotions. (*SP* 313)

The paradoxical conjunction of delicacy and ferocity is highly significant here: the laconic manner of the English gentleman masks a disciplinary regime of unspeakable and unspoken violence to suppress unruly emotions and unruly subjects. This is certainly a blueprint for Ashburnham, who is tongue-tied to the point that Dowell is more likely to write that he 'groans' or 'gurgles' his utterances, rather than saying them. This perceived delicacy is also the source of life-long suffering for Ashburnham and Tietjens, whose refusals, in the name of decency or convention, to pursue their desires result in heartbreak. This is the essence of the scene that Ford relates at the close of *The Spirit of the People*, and which is the inspiration for *The Good Soldier*. Ford is astonished by the power of repression that he witnesses from a dog-cart as he sees a man, the model for Ashburnham, part forever with his love, the model for Nancy Rufford. In the anecdote, Ford, an Englishman, is the observer, but it is necessary for Ford to make the observer American in his novel so that Englishness may be discussed from a more alien point of view, for

Ford sees in the anecdote something particular of the English, and not of universal humanity. Dowell says of Edward and Nancy's unemotional parting 'it was the most horrible performance I have ever seen' (*GS* 159). To Dowell, this performance of repression is horrible, and not in the least bit noble or chivalrous. 'The Game' is purely English and incomprehensible to outside observers, making the extension of a shared community of Englishness impossible, even as the empire attempts to sustain the idea of a 'Greater Britain'.[8]

Paul Fussell, author of *The Great War and Modern Memory* also discusses how important, and how antiquated, this notion of 'The Game' was for English soldiers in the Great War.[9] The perfect player of 'The Game', Fussell argues, was defined by Sir Henry Newbolt in his poem 'Vitaï Lampada', which equates the imperialist spirit with the winning spirit of the cricketer, and would have been known to almost every British public schoolboy. Fussell defines the player described in the poem as 'honourable, stoic, brave, loyal', like Christopher Tietjens, 'and unaesthetic, unironic, unintellectual and devoid of wit,' like Edward Ashburnham. This hypothetical phlegmatic Englishman is constructed by the codes of conduct that he has explicitly learned in school and that he has seen implicit in the behaviour of romantic characters from literature. In an Althuserrian sense, his Englishness is constructed in him as his unconscious, the unrealized motivation behind his conscious thought and action, by the ideological discourse within which he exists and of which he is a part before he forms any perception of discourse or of himself. Fussell demonstrates that, unlike any subsequent war, the Great War was defined by its soldiers in literary terms. While it seems, initially, that this is because the Great War was anomalous as a modern/industrial war in which the ruling class had an active role in the fighting, literary allusion was not only a pervasive mode of communication for the officers, but for the regular Tommies in the trenches, as well, who were not only literate, but unusually schooled in their nation's literary traditions. Christopher Tietjens and most of the other English characters whose minds are revealed in *Parade's End* tend to think in literary quotation and to organize their minds in terms of literary convention. In order to save his sanity from invasive thoughts of his thoroughly and enigmatically cruel wife, Sylvia, Tietjens writes a bout-rimé sonnet. By forcing his mind to express itself in the regular, closed form of a sonnet, he is able to keep his mind in order. Also, it is the recollection of a snatch of George Herbert's poem 'Virtue' that helps him to get through the later stress that he will encounter when he moves up the line. This bit of verse defines for Tietjens the England for which he is fighting, an ideal of peace that is heavenly: 'Sweet day, so calm, so cool, so bright / The bridal of the earth and sky' (quoted in *MCSU* 565). In the novel, Tietjens never pursues the next lines that close the stanza: 'The dew shall weep thy fall tonight/ For thou must die'. The first three stanzas of the poem develop the idea that death is the universal fate of beauty, so the lines are fitting for Tietjens, whose meticulous mind is constantly elegising the passing of the ostensibly beautiful Englishness which has created his subjectivity, and around which he constructs his ego-ideal. Also, his repetition of just the first two lines demonstrates that his unconscious desire cannot see beyond his prelapsarian seventeenth century principles. The fourth stanza of the poem, however, suggests that virtue can overcome death:

> Only a sweet and virtuous soul,
> Like seasoned timber, never gives;
> But though the whole world turn to coal,
> Then chiefly lives. (13-16)[10]

Tietjens is either Christly, or has Christliness thrust upon him, throughout *Parade's End*. He also knows that his fantasy of English-ness is a fantasy, but his ability to live by his fantasized code is how he retains his virtue and his sanity. For Tietjens, the test of character which he must pass, whether the world turns to coal or not, is the ability to touch pitch and not be defiled. It is Tietjens's willingness to withdraw from the Englishness that he loves, and that he sees is over, that saves him, and saves, for Valentine Wannop, his pregnant mistress, the notion that the Herbertian ideal may still survive in the world for their unborn son.

Ashburnham, who is more thoroughly a creation of the senti-mentally chivalrous Romance that preceded and formed his subject-ivity, talks, when he becomes 'deucedly vocal'[11] at the end of *The Good Soldier:* 'like a cheap novelist. Or like a very good novelist for the matter of that, if it's the business of a novelist to make you see things clearly' (*GS* 76). Although this shoring up of familiar utterances against the crumbling ruins of an Anglo-centric era of cultural expansion is common to all of Ford's English characters, Ashburnham and Tietjens are the only two Englishmen still to take the game of Englishness entirely seriously, or, if not taking it entirely seriously, at least not to cheat. In *No More Parades*, Tietjens says as much to General Edward Campion when, in realizing that Campion means to send him up the line to his likely death, he unlooses his tongue in a moment of weakness: 'it is not good to have taken one's public school's ethical system seriously. I am really, sir, the English public schoolboy. That's an eighteenth-century product [. . . .] Other men get over their schooling. I never have' (*NMP* 490). Tietjens, unlike Ashburnham, realizes that his ideal, although he can't give it up, has no place in modern England, and none in the world. It is because of this realization that 'the game' is a construction that Tietjens can survive a lapse of attentiveness to its rules, and Ashburnham cannot. If Tietjens is a genius, he is of the absent-minded variety, and he is often inattentive; he is frequently described as being mentally absent from conversations in which he is engaged, forgetting what his interlocutor is talking about, and sometimes forgetting what he is talking about himself. But because he has recognized that his parsimonious discourse is outdated, Tietjens's lapses are harmless. Tietjens willingly cedes power, and so survives. Ashburnham does not and so does not.

As Carol Jacobs has pointed out, talk is the germ of all ruin and abomination in *The Good Soldier*. The passion for talk creates all other passions, and it is talk that destroys Edward Ashburnham. 'Language', Jacobs argues, 'the talk of desire, does not mediate an already existing passion, but rather generates it. And it's not simply that language generates passion: the fatal driving passion of the tale becomes this desire for talk'.[12] Jacobs points out that it is Edward Ashburnham's perfectly innocent accolade to Nancy Rufford in the garden at Nauheim that makes him realize that he could develop a sexual attraction to her. Also, to take Jacobs's argument a step further, and apply it to the Kilsyte case, it is the discourse that surrounds Ashburnham during the trial that leads him to the notion that, although he hadn't meant to molest the chambermaid, he could have meant to. And so he could again. The discourse of the Kilsyte Case constructs and interpellates Ashburnham as a passionate Romantic. He realizes that he may pursue his naïve passions and, in so doing, he is not at all defying the circumscribed rules of the game. For it is quite normal, in romantic or sentimental English tales of passion, to pursue the ideal of courtly love, and courtly love is always Ashburnham's sentimental ideal.

While talk, here, is dangerous to the imperialist Tory ideal as embodied by Ashburnham, it is both good and bad for Dowell, the Yankee Conquistador. After Ashburnham is talked to death, in long and tortured night-time conversations at Bramshaw Teleragh, by the Anglo-Irish Leonora and the Anglo-Indian Nancy, the Anglo-American Dowell is able to sweep up the estate and live a pale imitation of the feudal life. But talk is dangerous for Dowell, too; through his imagined fortnight of fireside narration, he begins to realize the implications of the adulterous minuet in which he danced. Talk, like 'things', draws the most pure idealism into the material world of actuality. Throughout Dowell's narration of *The Good Soldier* he represents himself as having been a quiet and calm member of the minuet, but when he begins telling the story in retrospect, even if he is only talking to an imagined listener, the discussion of 'things', unavoidable in the telling, creates in Dowell a realization of his own potential passions. As he moves through his narrative, his trivial peccadilloes – a gluttony for caviar and an impatience with Belgian trains – lose their privileged position as the boundaries of his capacity for lust and passion. By the novel's close, his talk of 'things' has generated in him a desire to 'be a polygamist; with Nancy, and with Leonora and with Maisie Maidan and possibly even with Florence' (*GS* 151).

Dowell's slight insights into Edward Ashburnham's behaviour, compared to his greater blindnesses, make *The Good Soldier* a tale of distinctly European passions told by an American idiot. The grandiose feudal notions of a dying British aristocracy are filtered through and re-configured by the narrow conventions of the United States, a country with less history and culture of its own. Dowell never comprehends the significance of realizing Florence's dream of buying Bramshaw Teleragh. In his bumbling way, and without exactly meaning to, he has begun the reverse financial conquest of Europe, predicted by Tietjens early in *Some Do Not . . .*, which would dominate relations between Europe and the US for the rest of the century. He is, ironically, the prodigal son as returned conqueror, whose family has acquired a tremendous fortune at the expense of an indigenous population. John Dowell comes from Philadelphia,

> where, it is historically true, there are more old English families than you would find in any six English counties taken together.... I carry about with me, indeed – as if it were the only thing that invisibly anchored me to any spot on the globe – the title deeds of my farm, which once covered several blocks

between Chestnut and Walnut Streets. These title deeds are of wampum, the
grant of an Indian chief to the first Dowell, who left Farnham in Surrey in
company with William Penn. (*GS* 10)

Florence's family, the Hurlbirds, hail, originally, from Fordingbridge,
the location of Bramshaw Teleragh, and had been a blue-blooded
family there before the Ashburnhams had even established residency.
Although Dowell's is new money, it is not altogether different, in how
it was acquired, than is Ashburnham's. Dowell's family made its
fortune in exploiting the indigenous peoples of America, much as
Ashburnham's money comes from his role as imperialist officer in
India. Similarly, Groby in *Parade's End* is essentially stolen property,
the Tietjenses having acquired it when Catholics were persecuted and
run off their land with the succession of William III.

By the end of *The Good Soldier*, the conquest of what became
the United States has come full circle as Dowell occupies Edward
Ashburnham's gun room, the estate's locus of masculine imperial
power. Similarly, at the end of *The Last Post*, a vacuous and garrulous
American woman has occupied Groby, and Groby Great Tree, a massive and obviously phallic representation of the rooted power of the
Tietjenses, has been cut down, knocking down the section of the
estate that contained Christopher's boyhood bedroom. Additionally,
Groby is legally set to pass once more into the hands of a Catholic,
thus ending the presumed curse upon the Tietjenses, and, in effect,
ending Englishness at Groby, since, as Linda Colley has argued, Englishness was, in large part, defined as the antithesis of Catholicism.[13]

As the destruction of Groby Great Tree suggests, Ford is
representing not simply the demise of Englishness, but of specifically
English ruling class masculinity. At the beginning of Dowell's
narration, he is aware, if perhaps only unconsciously, that
Ashburnham's 'passion' is really his enacting of storybook romances.
Dowell, who has been interpellated and created by American ideological discourse just as Ashburnham has by English, is envious of
what he sees as the romantic passion that Englishness allows
Ashburnham. He is envious of Ashburnham's sexual and social
prowess, and delusionally thinks of himself as a 'fainter' version of
his passionate friend. But Dowell was not, and will never be, like
Edward Ashburnham. Ashburnham's massive sexual potency is
intimidating, even terrifying, to the 'eunuch' Dowell, and here, again,
Dowell is representative of a general trend in his nation: around the
turn of the century, there was (as it could be argued there has been

ever since) a crisis in American masculinity. With Manifest Destiny complete, the rugged frontiers of the land were becoming less rugged, as was the national character. Dowell engages in the 'shaky reconstructions of manliness' that critic Gail Bederman has defined as representative of turn-of-the-century American men.[14] Dowell's extremely shaky reconstruction of manliness in Ashburnham's shadow, nevertheless, displaces the seemingly confident and knowingly epic feudal paradigm of Englishness with the serendipitous and unknowingly epic American expansionism that would define global politics in the twentieth century. Because what he saw as the passionate characters of the novel have burned themselves out with their fighting, Dowell was in a position to pick up the pieces, glue them together with the inheritance money won from stripping American Indians of their land, and pervert them into a vague travesty of the anachronistic passion which he still wants to see in himself, despite the wealth of evidence demonstrating that it has never been there: the narrative of Dowell's takeover is, in miniature, the narrative of the trans-Atlantic power-shift which is still, in many ways, the Great War's legacy.

Although Dowell has defined and constructed himself in Ashburnham's image, taking over the space, if not exactly the role, of an administrator to the world, he has been able to do so only through the use of his New World capital, which is actually Old World capital that has accrued a massive interest, his lands having been bought in wampum, and their value inflated by the tremendously exploitative expansion of America's Manifest Destiny. Dowell, in keeping with his American national discourse, is an isolationist. His values are individual rather than collective, like Ashburnham's, because American character has always been violently anti-collective, and the seemingly limitless room for expansion of American territory made individual acquisition the primary impetus of the American subject.[15] This hyper-individualization easily accounts for American loquacity: there is only a need to preserve delicacy when one cares about, or is aware of, the possible ramifications of a breach in manners, when the goal of society seems to be for people to live together in peace. If the discourse that defines a national subject emphasizes the importance of individual desire, rather than of propriety, those subjects will necessarily think, usually, of their own desires without comprehending the effects that their desires may have on others. As it is an inability to accommodate other voices that subverts English identity, it is essentially an indifference to other voices or people that causes the

American characters in these novels, particularly Florence and Mrs. de Bray Pape, to prattle on so endlessly, and to such harmful effect.

Both Florence and Mrs. de Bray Pape are described as women who desire, with their self-involved discourse 'to clear up the dark places of the earth'. The conspicuous reference to *Heart of Darkness* makes the imperial implications of their actions, and of their discourse, clear.[16] While the imperial epic of Englishness is ending, moneyed Americans are beginning a new, equally condescending and equally epic effort to bring their national discourse to bear on the world as they go about their civilizing mission. Mrs. de Bray Pape is an exaggerated, worse version of Florence; exactly like Florence, she is (ironically) described as 'hop[ing] to leave the world a better place before she passed over' (*LP* 711). Unlike Florence, she gets her way in the end, demonstrating that Ford's convictions about Americans, and about the likelihood of their taking over, from Europe, the role of global administrator and exploitative 'improver' must have been intensified in the long years between *The Good Soldier* and *The Last Post*, and after the role of the US in the post World War I era (as well as the decline of English imperialism) became more apparent.

Both *The Good Soldier* and *Parade's End* have been criticized for being inconclusive. Many critics have read *The Last Post* as no more than an epilogue to a *Parade's End* trilogy. In his introduction to the 1982 edition, Robie Macauley defended *The Last Post* as a necessary part of the novel as a whole, but also called it a 'strangely inconclusive conclusion'.[17] The apparent inconclusiveness of both works, though, is, in fact, an emphatic conclusion, and the only one that Ford could honestly draw. They both conclude with the end of a paradigm of Englishness as a viable ruling ideological and discursive force in the world. One archetypal Englishman has cut his throat in the pursuit of 'a bit of a rest' (*GS* 162) from a vulgar and unsentimental, unromantic, loquacity. The other has galumphed off in obscurity, at the moment of his older brother's death, to look after some insignificant old drawings that he needs (for money from Americans!), while clinging to a chunk of the extraordinarily mighty tree, now felled, which was the symbol of his family, their power, and, by extension, the power of the English Empire. Groby Great Tree was cut down by a vulgar, un-entitled and typically hyper-individualist American (for the matter of that) and Ashburnham's death has been witnessed by Dowell, who now embodies a voluble and unwitting American expansionist epic, and will soon tell Ashburnham's story, without excluding the 'things', over the course of a fortnight's imagined babbling – the babbling that would constitute the end of phlegmatic Englishness, and would define the so-called American century.

NOTES

1   Mikhail Bakhtin, 'Discourse in the Novel', *Literary Theory: An Anthology*. eds. Julie Rivkin, Michael Ryan. Malden, MA: Blackwell Publishers, 1998, pp. 32-44.

2   Although this is true for the themes in the novel, it does not reflect Ford's personal feelings. Indeed, at the time that he was writing these novels, he was increasingly attracted to American authors and what he perceived as American outspokenness.

3   Although WWI devastated European populations and economies and gave the US an advantage over Europe in the global power structure, the American doctrine of isolationism had been falling apart for some time. The most notable example of burgeoning US imperialism may be the turn of the century war for the Philippines.

4   Benedict Anderson, *Imagined Communities,* London: Verso, 1991, p. 7.

5   All references to Ford's England Trilogy in this paper come from *England and the English*, ed. Sara Haslam, Manchester: Carcanet, 2003; comprising *The Soul of London* (*SL* – 1905); *The Heart of the Country* (*HC* – 1906) and *The Spirit of the People* (*SP* – 1907).

6   Dennis Brown, 'Remains of the Day: Tietjens the Englishman', *Ford Madox Ford's Modernity,* International Ford Madox Ford Studies, 2, ed. Robert Hampson and Max Saunders, Amsterdam: Rodopi, 2003, p. 169. *The Good Soldier* is engaged in exactly the same kind of exploration, but because it comes through the voice of Dowell, a parody of American hyper-individuality, the exploration is not as direct or as thorough.

7   Throughout this paper, references to *Some Do Not. . .* (1924) – *SDN; No More Parades* (1925) – *NMP; A Man Could Stand Up* – (1926) – *MCSU;* and *The Last Post* (1928) – *LP;* are to the Penguin edition, 1982, entitled *Parade's End. SDN* 178.

8   Charles Dilke's *Greater Britain* (1868) argues that the colonies are English and extensions of Englishness.

9   Paul Fussell, *The Great War and Modern Memory*. Oxford: Oxford University Press, 1975, p. 26.

10 George Herbert, 'Virtue', lines 13-16: *The Norton Anthology of English Literature vol. I B: The Sixteenth Century/The Early Seventeenth Century*, ed. M. H. Abrams et al., New York: Norton, 1999.

11 Ford Madox Ford, *The Good Soldier*, ed. Martin Stannard, New York: Norton, 1995 – henceforth *GS*; p. 76.

12 Carol Jacobs, 'The Passion for Talk', *GS* 337.

13 Linda Colley, *Britons: Forging the Nation, 1707-1837.* New Haven: Yale University Press, 1992.

14 Gail Bederman, 'Civilization, the Decline of Middle-Class Manliness, and Ida B. Wells's Anti-Lynching Campaign', *Gender and American History Since 1890*, ed. Barbara Melosh. New York: Routledge, 1992, p. 211.
15 Paradoxically, the room for Western expansion created a generally imperial American national discourse, while defining the US as a strictly isolationist nation. The political doctrine of isolation was bound to conflict with the expansionist spirit after the West was settled.
16 Joseph Conrad, *Heart of Darkness*. ed. Robert Kimbrough, New York: Norton, 1988, p. 9.
17 Robie Macauley, 'Introduction' *Parade's End*, New York: Penguin, 1982, p. xvii.

FORD MADOX FORD'S ENGLISHNESS AS TRANSLATED INTO GERMAN IN *SOME DO NOT . . .* AND *NO MORE PARADES*

Jörg W. Rademacher

> The message was:
> 'Righto. But arrange for certain Hullo Central travels with you. Sylvia Hopside Germany.'
> [. . . .]
> 'It means I go to my wife on Tuesday and take her maid with me.'
> 'Lucky you!' the girl said, 'I wish I was you. I've never been in the Fatherland of Goethe and Rosa Luxemburg.'[1] (*SDN* 128-9)

In a novel full to the brim with allusions to things German, and quotations from German texts, these are but two of the most striking instances of Ford's Germanophilia which meets the eye long before 1914 but also, much more surprising, in this post-war tetralogy about Christopher Tietjens, the quintessential English gentleman. His Englishness, though, is like that 'composite photograph', a mental image, that is, which Ford had tried to present of the English countryside in *The Heart of the Country* (1906), using the same simile also in its sequel, *The Spirit of the People* (1907)[2], to outline his concept of the English (*HC* 109 & *SP* 232). Still a traveller between the Münster of his ancestors and both Western Europe and the United States, Ford in 1907 seems to be far less generous with his snippets of German civilisation than in *Some Do Not . . .* (1924) and *No More Parades* (1925), where he looks back on the pre-war and war periods.

So as the editor, translator, and commentator of an anthology of writings by Franz Hüffer and Ford Madox Ford, I have a professional interest in how colleagues approach the problem of bridging both the temporal and linguistic gaps as well as the cultural one separating German readers today from their English counterparts in the early twentieth century. There is no space here to expatiate on the economic reasons, but it must be noted that five of Ford's books so far translated into German – *The Good Soldier* (1962), *Romance* (2000), *Some Do Not . . .* (2003), *No More Parades* (2004) and *A Man Could Stand Up* – (2006) – have not been annotated at all. Thus,

despite the academic background of some translators, the general
German reading-public must come to terms with Ford presented not in
terms of 'a modern classic, but as an unknown young writer once
again'.[3]

Here I concentrate on *Some Do Not . . .*[4] and *No More
Parades*[5]. An avid reader even of *The Good Soldier* in German, I also
enjoyed the first two instalments of Ford's war novel – for the reason
that all of these simply 'work' in German translation, which as such is
well-written and accurate as to sense. If, however, one starts to read
the original and the translation side by side, it quickly becomes obvious that the latter lacks the textures and contexts of Ford's German
roots as well as the allusions both to his modernism and to his other
works. Such a point being ever difficult to prove unless as part of a
sustained argument within an academic monograph, I prefer to select
some significant passages for detailed discussion.

Openings and endings of novels are particularly pertinent parts
for such an analysis, given that any writer would work on them with
special care to make sure that his readers have good first and last
impressions of the narrative. Since German and English are contig-
uous languages – semantically and morphologically speaking, that is –
it is often the syntactical disparity, most conspicuously realised in the
word order, that makes for striking differences between English
original and German translation. So I juxtapose the opening and
closing passages of *Some Do Not . . .* and *No More Parades* with
versions of my own in order to assess the degree to which Joachim
Utz has succeeded in rendering Ford's English Modernist text in
German before discussing briefly the amount of annotation necessary
for making Ford's novels accessible to present-day readers.

Some Do Not . . . p. 3: The two young men – they were of the English public official class – sat in the perfectly appointed railway carriage	**Sentence structure:** S[ubject] – S V[erb] C[omplement]–V C
Utz – Manche tun es nicht, p. 3: Die beiden jungen Herren – sie gehörten dem englischen höheren Staatsdienst an – saßen in ihrem perfekt ausgestatteten Eisenbahnabteil.	**Sentence structure:** S – S V O[bject] –V C

Here the contiguity of English and German allows for a perfectly
parallel sentence structure but the devil is in the detail, and I have

misgivings about 'Herren' because the equivalent of the French 'Messieurs' precludes the correlation on the level of the signifier of 'men' and 'gentlemen' which, in German, is normally expressed by 'Männer' and 'Edelmänner'. (There is, however, a problem in this, for 'gentleman' has become a natural part of German vocabulary. In any case, there is no need to give up the use of 'Männer' for 'men'.) Euphonics apart, this opening sentence of the novel is also indicative of the difficulty any translator faces of finding the *mot juste* in both a semantic and a cultural sense. The 'English public official class', probably a coinage of Ford's just as 'administrative class' (*SP* 299), becomes, in Utz's words, the higher tiers of the state service which, in English, must be termed *civil service*, the antonym of *military service*. Thus a socially descriptive term as class, albeit used in an idiosyncratic Fordian manner, is turned into a term relating to the basically meritocratic system of officialdom established in Prussia after the defeat at the hands of Napoleon's armies in October 1806 with a view to rebuilding the state. You are 'of' a class since you are born into, or co-opted by it, but you 'belong to' a service after having successfully sat an entrance examination (*SL* 68-69). Therefore I think a more nuanced rendering would have been:

Rademacher – Some Do Not . . .	**Sentence structure:**
Die zwei jungen Männer – sie zählten zur	S - S V
staatstragenden Klasse Englands – saßen in	C - V
dem perfekt ausgestatteten Eisenbahnwaggon.	C

For me, it is unnecessary to explicate at once that, at the time, every compartment had a door of its own, as Utz does, but I prefer to make the reader gather information from the text as it proceeds. It is a complex mosaic that Ford presents to us – as if it were being pieced together by the principal characters themselves throughout the tetralogy. This is why a translator of this English Modernist novel both needs to be aware of the complete work and to be able to follow patiently in the writer's footsteps by withholding, in translation, the same or at least similar pieces of information that Ford keeps to himself at this stage of the narrative.

Annotating even such a vital part as the opening of a tetralogy asks for concentration, since reading should remain a pleasure rather than be stifled by all too learned notes. What, however, meets the eye in the first paragraph in the translation is the juxtaposition of Germany and Britain: 'a geometrician in Cologne' who designed the 'intricate, minute dragon pattern'. It can be seen in the upholstery, whereas the smoothness of the train's running – 'Tietjens remembered thinking' – was likened to that of 'British gilt-edged securities'. A palpable sample of primarily Catholic German craftsmanship – just like the 'windows in imitation of stained glass', also from Cologne and environs, mentioned in *The Spirit of the People* (*SP* 285) – the upholstery contrasts sharply with the kinetic image of correlating the British money market with the functioning of the train. On the one hand Germany stands for stability, with Britain standing for mobility, while the English society consists of classes and Germany has medieval guilds of craftsmen on the other hand. There is no remembrance of words spoken in this first paragraph but a remembrance of quite a few things past on Tietjens's part, both seen, smelt, and touched; and it needs an awareness of the Modernist tradition – of the Proustian, Joycean, Woolfian order – in order not to destroy the fragile structure of past impressions as Tietjens tries to regain consciousness of them.

The last sentence of *Some Do Not . . .* corroborates this view since, by contrast to the opening sentence, it is in the past perfect, as if, by now, Tietjens felt more at ease in his rôle as recorder of his own past actions:

Some Do Not . . . (SDN 309): He had caught, outside the gates of his old office, a transport lorry that had given him a lift to Holborn.	**Sentence structure:** S V – parenthesis C – O; S V O O C
Utz – Manche tun es nicht (*MTN* 404) Vor dem Eingang zu dem Gebäude, in dem sich sein ehemaliges Büro befand, hatte er auf einen Lastwagen steigen können, der ihn mitnahm bis Holborn.	**Sentence structure:** C; C S V V S C; S O V C

It is true that, albeit convoluted, this German sentence runs smoothly, but it is separated from Tietjens's reflections about his farewell from Valentine Wannop by a block of complements and a relative clause, so that there is a sense of closure in the translation where Ford in the original had managed both to end his book and keep his writing open for the sequel *No More Parades*. I would suggest retaining Ford's sentence structure, thereby rendering his 21 typically brief English words by just 16 longer German words:

Rademacher – Some Do Not . . . Er hatte, vor dem Eingang seines alten Büros, einen Lastwagen bestiegen, der ihn mitnahm bis Holborn.	Sentence structure: S V – parenthesis C – O V; S O V C

One may quibble about English as a language which allows the juxtaposition of clauses and phrases – the latter lacking the verb – and German as a language which asks for the subordination of clauses, but I think that a translator of *Some Do Not . . .* is required to render the movement of Tietjens's mind and body, as well as a merely logical hierarchy of observations on the page which prevents the reader from reconstructing the events as they occurred in the protagonist's mind. Reading the translation would thus enable us both properly to enter Tietjens' theatre of memory and to perceive what actually happened to him externally.

To facilitate this process, maps of the United Kingdom, France, and Germany as well as city plans of London and Rouen should be part of any annotated edition of *Parade's End* (as introduced, for example, into Martin Stannard's 1995 edition of *The Good Soldier*), so as to ensure that readers can follow the peregrinations of Ford's characters. Though Lobscheid is presented only in *Some Do Not . . .* as a place of action contemporary with the narrated time, it is regularly re-invoked in *No More Parades* just as are the execution of Father Consett and Roger Casement[6] or the small village in Brittany where Sylvia Tietjens set off to rejoin her mother at Lobscheid. The dissociation of the places of action both in reality and in the characters' memories is suggestive of the Modernist quality of Ford's novel, and it also reflects the degree to which the intrusion of Sylvia Tietjens, née Satterthwaite, into the life of her husband's family has contributed to destroying the gilt-edged securities, so to speak, of Ibsenite pillars of English society such as the country gentleman, his code of honour, and his idiom – the understatement. A translation of Ford's history of decay which fails to convey the impression of the Empire as it crumbles far from realises the Modernist potential of the text.

Apart from its motto, *No More Parades* opens with a sentence the *in-medias-res* quality of which becomes obvious with the second word, the subject:

No More Parades (*NMP* 313):	Sentence structure:
When you came in the space was desultory,	Conj. S V; SV
rectangular, warm after the drip of the winter	C
night and transfused with a brown-orange dust	and C;
that was light.	
It was shaped like the house a child draws.	S V C S V
Utz – Keine Paraden mehr (*KPM* 7):	Sentence structure:
Wer hier eintrat, fand sich in einem	S V; V
unaufgeräumten, rechteckigen Raum, feucht	C
vom warmen Schwitzwasser einer Winternacht	
und erfüllt von dem braun-orangenen Staub des	
Lichts.	
Es hatte die Form eines von einem Kind	S V O C
gezeichneten Hauses.	

Again, as at the end of *Some Do Not . . .*, this opening defies easy access, not because Utz fails to write a good German sentence, but because he doesn't dare follow Ford. What needs to be realised in translation is the movement of one's eyes with which the reader mentally enters the text as Tietjens entered it *physically*, and, indeed, may have entered the loading space of the lorry at the end of *Some Do Not . . .*. This movement is not palpable in a German sentence that ends with several lines of verbless complements. The same applies to the second sentence. Once more, I would propose to stick to Ford's sentence structure:

Rademacher – No More Parades	Sentence structure:
Der Raum, den man betrat, war unaufgeräumt,	S; O S V; V
rechteckig, warm nach den	C
Kondenswasserströmen der Winternacht und	
durchdrungen vom braun-orangefarbenen	
Staub des Lichts.	
Er sah aus wie ein Haus, wie es Kinder	S V C;
zeichnen.	conjunction O S V

As a language inflecting nouns and pronouns, adjectives and determiners as well as verbs, German is quite flexible in terms of word order. Hence it is easy to render Ford's English here, provided the translator is prepared to give up the stylistic dogma that German sentences mustn't contain too many auxiliaries. With the use of 'was', however, instead of no verb at all, it is also possible to avoid the abundance of inflected adjectives which, to my mind, is even less beautiful and certainly less effective than a series of epithets dependent on a single copula. English and German, two Germanic languages, transfused with Latin syntax and Romance vocabulary, must be deemed parallel worlds in order to create similar effects. The space, to paraphrase my translation, looks like a house that children draw. Tietjens, putative father of Michael, thus has found another analogy which I'd render by using a main clause, plus a relative clause construction, which is the closest you can get to imitate contact clauses in German. A past participle as employed by Utz stifles the impression of activity associated with children who draw houses.

No More Parades ends with General Campion inspecting the kitchen, which triggers an image in Tietjens's mind:

No More Parades (*NMP* 539): To Tietjens this was like the sudden bursting out of the regimental quick-step, as after a funeral with military honours the band and drums march away, back to barracks.	**Sentence structure:** C S V C conjunction C S V C
Utz – Keine Paraden mehr (*KPM* 326) Tietjens kam das alles vor wie der Augenblick nach einer Beerdigung mit militärischen Ehren, in dem das Musikkorps mit den Trommeln plötzlich in den schnellen Regimentsschritt fällt und zurückmarschiert in die Kaserne.	**Sentence structure:** S V C O S C V and V C

Similes open and close *No More Parades*, and Ford is all for brevity, while Utz produces a German sentence which confirms the prejudices about the long-windedness of Teutonic syntax. He does so, perhaps, to avoid annotating the text just for very few footnotes. There is no bursting out in the translation as remembered by Tietjens but a rational reconstruction as an omniscient narrator might formulate it. I am grateful to Utz and his publisher for having taken the first three steps in producing a German *Parade's End*, which, however, would need revising to be more critically and historically sensitive:

Rademacher – Keine Paraden mehr	Sentence structure:
Für Tietjens war das so, als höre er jäh den Regimentsschritt, wenn nach einem Begräbnis mit militärischen Ehren die Bläser und Trommler abmarschieren, zurück zur Kaserne.	C V S – conj V S O; conj C S V C

Where Utz adds 'moment' to visualise the scene, I would opt for the verb 'to hear' in order to ensure the aural effect. Thus I'd verbalise Ford's nominal sentence structure. A regular attendant of the German equivalent of bandstand concerts as a boy, I have never witnessed a 'Musikkorps' without drums, hence I'd choose to render 'band and drums' by 'Bläser und Trommler': the German generic term for wind and brass instruments accompanied by drums.

It would have been interesting to discuss all this with the translator and his editor since my view – that *Parade's End* should preferably be translated and published as a whole so as better to relate it to Ford's oeuvre – has been confirmed. As things stand, I'm willing to share the material slumbering in my notes in order to help render Ford the English Modernist into German. Since the books have appeared, we should try to profit from the lessons to be drawn from the translations:

1) Since annotating Ford is part of an international research project, it would be both valuable and profitable for commercially conducted translation projects if cooperation between translators, editors, and critics became possible for the simple reason that it is highly improbable that a second version of a work such as *Parade's End* will appear in the near future.

2) Extant translations should be examined in terms of how faithfully they render the movement of Ford's prose.

3) Translators are practitioners of various arts of writing and experts on any work they have rendered, so it would be valuable if they attended conferences – perhaps funded by their publishers – to share their superior knowledge of and about the texts with the critics and, in

turn, to profit from the latters' superior knowledge of the writer's overall output.

NOTES

1   All references to Ford's Great War Tetralogy in this chapter come from the Everyman's Library edition, London, 1992, comprising *Some Do Not . . . (SDN –* 1924); *No More Parades (NMP –* 1925); *A Man Could Stand Up – (MCSU –* 1926) and *Last Post (LP –* 1928).

2   All references to Ford's England trilogy in this chapter come from *England and the English*, ed. Sara Haslam, Manchester: Carcanet, 2003; comprising *The Soul of London (SL –* 1905); *The Heart of the Country (HC –* 1906) and *The Spirit of the People (SP –* 1907).

3   'Towards Editing and Translating Parade's End' in *Modernism and the Individual Talent: Moderne und Besondere Begabung*, ed. Jörg W. Rademacher, Münster: Lit, 2002, pp. 173-175.

4   *Manche tun es nicht,* tr. Joachim Utz, Berlin: Eichborn, 2003 – henceforth *MTN.*

5   *Keine Paraden mehr*, tr. Joachim Utz, Berlin: Eichborn, 2004 – henceforth *KPM. Der Mann, der aufrecht blieb,* tr. Joachim Utz, Berlin: Eichborn, 2006, appeared too late to be considered in this chapter.

6   See *The Spirit of the People*, pp. 310-11, for a muted reference to Casement's uncovering of the atrocities committed by the Belgians in the Congo Free State.

ESCAPE FROM ENGLISHNESS: *THE RASH ACT* AND *HENRY FOR HUGH*

Robert E. McDonough

What might be called the second Anglicisation[1] of Henry Martin Aluin Smith, American protagonist of *The Rash Act* (1933) and *Henry for Hugh* (1934), his transformation into his English cousin Hugh Monckton Allard Smith, takes the form of a 90° rotation, from upstanding and battling as an American to supine, passive, and almost mute as an Englishman. And yet only by *having been* an Englishman can Henry Martin find success as an American once again, this time an American with a voice, social and economic power, and a mate, all of which he had been lacking.

On the morning he has planned to commit suicide, a sudden storm changes Henry Martin's course of action. Rather than step off his rented boat to drown, he is compelled by instinct to save the boat and of course himself from the storm. Stunned and bleeding from two blows from the boat's boom that have implausibly reproduced a wound on the exact site of a scar of Hugh Monckton's and have changed his voice so as to disguise it, Henry Martin now confusedly, without explicit intention, and even more implausibly switches his own passport with that of his look-alike distant cousin Hugh Monckton, so as to convince almost everyone that it is the impoverished American and not the wealthy Englishman who has carried his suicide through to its conclusion (*RA* 226-28). And as Hugh Monckton he must lie down.

The first words of Chapter I of Part Four of *The Rash Act,* when Henry Martin has been established as Hugh Monckton, are 'Henry Martin lay looking at the grey Mediterranean' (*RA* 313). The first words of *Henry for Hugh* are 'Henry Martin, on his terrace, lay in his deck chair' (*HH* 7). He lies there for two chapters, and then in Chapter 3 he lies in bed, unable to sleep, thinking. And much of the rest of the novel occurs or is recollected when Henry Martin is being an invalid in a chair.

The French doctor who has prescribed all this supineness has first made Henry Martin comatose. Examining him after his injuries from the boom, the doctor gives him exactly the same advice that had once been given to Hugh Monckton. The doctor prescribes abstinence from women and alcohol, with the threat of '"the most distressing mental symptoms" . . . heralded by excruciating pains in the head' (*RA* 308), and then in effect knocks him out. After he awakes, Henry Martin contemplates the missing 'Twenty days. . . . For three of them that doctor had kept him under with a strong opiate. Then for twelve more he had bromided him into a moron' (*RA* 366). Thus Henry Martin is temporarily extinguished so that he can be reborn as Hugh Monckton.

Henry Martin comes to blame his condition on his new identity: 'And, damnation, wasn't he, Henry Martin, just as Hugh Monckton had been, shut off from all sexual relations with any woman? . . . For fear of that blinding pain in the head! . . .' (*HH* 102). (These restrictions will be removed by an English doctor right before Henry Martin is ready to become an American again.)

On the night before his own aborted suicide and Hugh Monckton's completed one, Henry Martin has had contradictory feelings about Hugh Monckton: he wants to be him, but he also feels Americans should dislike the English, on principle as it were. 'He had never liked Englishmen. He could never see how any American could ever like any Englishman. The English sometimes liked Americans. But the other way around, never!' The English, he continues in a racialist, even racist vein, 'were worse than negroes because they were whiter and colder' (*RA* 144).

The reasons for wanting to be Hugh Monckton are obvious enough. Hugh Monckton is rich, the director and principal shareholder of the wildly successful Monckton automobile company, while Henry Martin is almost penniless. Just that day he has received a jeering telegram from his father, refusing him any support unless Henry Martin returns to America to work for the family candy company. In the past few years Henry Martin has also been cheated by a publisher of the royalties of a successful book he has written and has lost all his investments in the Crash. Then, Hugh Monckton is accompanied by the beautiful singer Gloria Sorenson,[2] of 'glorious bare shoulders' (*RA* 36) and 'blazing flesh' (*RA* 70), while the principal feature of Henry Martin's romantic history is a dismal marriage that ended when another woman took his wife away from him. Hugh Monckton also seems to have had a glamorous war, complete with a sabre wound to the skull when 'Other men had to be hit by pieces of shell or old tin'

(*RA* 69); Henry Martin's war was boring and inglorious, far from any fighting. And Hugh Monckton seems physically graceful. Henry Martin has been impressed by the terse Latin eloquence of a tribute to a dancer inscribed on the wall of the Roman Theatre in nearby Antibes: 'SALTAVIT. PLACUIT. MORTUUS EST' (*RA* 33). He glumly reflects that his own dancing has never given pleasure to anyone, and soon he will be dead, but that the opposite must be true of the wealthy Hugh Monckton: 'No wonder you could give pleasure with your dancing. . . . There was not a thin, numbing stream of lead within all your limbs' (*RA* 40).

None of this is as it seems. Though the wealth is genuine, it makes everything else even more bitter for Hugh Monckton. The physical well-being is illusory. The glamorous sabre wound has disabled him for life, unmanned him; he can never have a drink or have sexual relations. Gloria Sorenson refuses him and he will commit suicide. First, however, he writes a will and a letter that Henry Martin will only receive almost three weeks after Hugh Monckton's death. In the letter he asks Henry Martin to do whatever is possible to delay or suppress the news of Hugh Monckton's suicide, for the sake of the company's stock, and leaves him a large sum of money, which he is to use living Hugh Monckton's life for him:

> He begged Henry Martin to hire *Le Secret* [a luxury yacht] – or any equivalent abode of bliss . . . And to take any little piece . . . and so to prolong for Hugh Monckton, here on earth, the jolly old beanfeast that, by all odds, his own mortal career should have witnessed. . . . (*RA* 380)

But, as we have seen, that is not at all what it means for Henry Martin to be Hugh Monckton. Early on in Henry Martin's impersonation of Hugh Monckton, he sets himself ethical limits, deciding that he will not assert a claim to the false identity but will not correct people who mistakenly attribute it to him. These involve what he will say, but also concern his physical position. Because everyone except the woman he loves, Eudoxie, assumes he is Hugh Monckton, and she will not reveal his secret, he can allow himself to be taken for Hugh Monckton without

> active, false pretences. It was one thing to lie in a bed nearly voiceless, and have people call you Asch Emma Smith. [That is how Henry Martin hears the French pronunciation of his and Hugh Monckton's initials.] It would be quite another to sit, say, in a terrace in one of the Riviera palaces and amidst crowds, boldly to declare:

'I am Hugh Monckton Allard Smith!' (*RA* 302)

Thus if he only lies (down) in a modest villa he is not lying (deliberately deceiving) as he would be if he sat in a palace. And for most of *Henry for Hugh* he does lie down.

Several times in *Henry for Hugh*, Henry Martin feels that he is what we would today call 'channelling' Hugh, and he doesn't like it. He misses American speech: 'He could have screamed at that moment to hear a real American voice. His life was unbearable for want of that' (*HH* 134). He wants to be an American, 'free, male, and twenty-one' (*RA* 42) and 'six feet in his stockings' (*RA* 63), to use two of his favourite phrases, but instead he must lie on his back surrounded by English and French people.

Henry Martin continues his racist thinking in a way that should offend just about everyone reading this essay. 'The French,' he thinks, 'are of course really niggers. Just like niggers with their eternal "Messieurs-Mesdames" and hand-shakings' (*HH* 330). The English, as we have seen, are worse. 'You were taught in the United States' schools that the English were to be regarded as all one with the Poor Whites of the South' (*HH* 147-8). Ford and Henry Martin stop short of adding the one word to make the American phrase 'poor white trash', but that is clearly the tone intended.

What Henry Martin seems to hate about the English are a perceived coldness and a disinterested sense of obligation – perhaps we could think of it as 'chivalry'– that, for Henry Martin at least, also partakes of coldness. When Hugh Monckton's Aunt Elizabeth, who is also Henry Martin's more distant relative, appears early in *Henry for Hugh* and accepts Henry Martin as Hugh Monckton, Henry Martin comes to love her. Fear for her frail health if his impersonation is revealed becomes one of Henry Martin's strongest motives for retaining his role. Nevertheless, even this love does not impede Henry Martin's hatred of Englishness. When he thinks that Aunt Elizabeth will not want him to marry Eudoxie at the cost of abandoning Jeanne Becquerel, Hugh Monckton's *maitresse en titre* with whom neither Hugh Monckton nor Henry Martin has had sexual relations, because Aunt Elizabeth 'might believe that he had given to Jeanne Becquerel pledges that, as an English gentleman, he could not get out of', he comes to a round conclusion: 'Damn English gentlemen!' (*HH* 268). After Aunt Elizabeth's death he realizes that he is grieving for it more than he had done for his mother's, and reflects sourly that his mother would probably have wanted him to be an 'English country gentleman' too. 'It was the sort of thing that your women wished for you' (*HH* 296).

Just before the final abandonment of his impersonation of Hugh Monckton, Henry Martin talks to Eustace Monckton, Hugh's cousin and the inheritor of his wealth until there is an official declaration of Hugh Monckton's death. Henry Martin for the last time has a feeling appropriate to Hugh Monckton, which he angrily rejects for more American attitudes. When Eustace Monckton says that the newly poor English living abroad should not be given special consideration even if they could not have foreseen the fall of the pound, Henry Martin's

> first reaction had been the thought that he must do something for all those harassed people. . . . He had mentioned only Miss Pettifer, the Elkingtons, the Hamish's. . . . But he had had an image of hundreds of the destitute. . . . That he must help! . . . He *wasn't* an English squire with his tenantry and poor! He was a down and out American. . . . (*HH* 316-17)

Even Aunt Elizabeth is not excluded from Henry Martin's objections to the English. Henry Martin believes that for a country to secure a monopoly of gold holdings would be fatal to its economy; therefore, somewhat paradoxically, he believes it is not in America's interest for Britain to repay its war debt. Aunt Elizabeth believes

> in the first place that England ought to pay her debts whatever happened and, in addition . . . she could not but feel that anything that hurt the United States – at any rate in the realms of currency – must be of advantage to the world as proving that you cannot with impunity ride rough shod over the faces of all the nations of the earth. . . . (*HH* 311)

Henry Martin reacts by seeing in his mind

> the English governing classes fixed like weasels at the throat of his country – cold creatures with fiendish intelligences. . . . And his aunt – with *her* cool intelligence – he suddenly saw as one of that ruling class that had achieved the ruin of his country. . . . (*HH* 312)

Despite Henry Martin's belief in the development of a kind of mid-Atlantic way of talking, with Americans trying to sound English and English affecting American slang, language and its conventions cause him the most difficulty in his impersonation and finally lead to his discovery. Though his belief that the thoroughly English response to any situation is not to say a word (*HH* 314) helps him to maintain his impersonation for a long time, he ultimately gives himself away through a convention of language. He insists to his private secretary, Macdonald, who is a communist and thus bitterly resentful of Hugh Monckton's wealth and power, that a letter should be dated American-fashion, with the number representing the month coming first (*HH* 89-90). That is enough for Macdonald to realize that his employer must be an American, and thus not Hugh Monckton but Henry Martin. Macdonald is happy to reveal the truth.[3]

However, it is also through language that Henry Martin achieves the closest and most productive identification with Hugh Monckton. Henry Martin and Hugh Monckton are able to co-author a book. Two American publishers make an offer to Hugh Monckton, as they think he is, but Henry Martin is able to persuade them to accept a book by Henry Martin, of whose death they are not convinced, with an introduction by Hugh Monckton. (It is only speaking as Hugh Monckton that Henry Martin is able to get fair treatment for himself from publishers.) When Eudoxie returns from a stay in England, she brings with her masses of manuscript Hugh Monckton had left behind, from which they will be able to pull together an introduction to the book Henry Martin has been writing 'that would at last give poor dear Hughie a chance to express himself. . . . They could not refuse to the poor fellow the opportunity to make his voice heard. . . . From beyond the cold grave. . .' (*HH* 320). So, Henry Martin and Eudoxie will marry, Henry Martin will run the Monckton automotive company while Eustace Monckton receives the profits, and both the English Hugh Monckton and the American Henry Martin will be heard in their book.

Of course, like Hugh Monckton and Henry Martin, the English Ford Madox Ford (and Hueffer) preceded the American Ford. *The Rash Act* and *Henry for Hugh* continue his project of writing himself into America. We can accept the satisfaction in his writing to Ezra Pound that *The Rash Act* is his best book 'for years', but we should reject his later removal of qualification when he tells Caroline Gordon it is simply 'my best book', 'better than anything I have yet done'.[4] *The Rash Act is* Ford's best novel after the first three volumes of *Parade's End*. If *Henry for Hugh*, though interesting, is decidedly less so than *The Rash Act*, just as *Last Post* is inferior to its three preceding volumes, that is due to the inability even of Ford to make completely fascinating a book-length presentation of Englishness as a form of impotence and paralysis – of supineness.

NOTES

1   The first Anglicisation is recalled, not acted out within the time frame of the two
     books. Near the beginning of *The Rash Act* (a coroner's phrase for suicide), when
     he is planning to kill himself on the next morning, Henry Martin remembers that
     as a student in war-time Oxford he had been 'a lanky giant amongst copper,
     coffee, or saffron-hued midgets – from Paraguay, the hinterlands of Bengal or
     Monrovia'. After 'the more truculent spirits of Magdalen' (Henry Martin's
     college) had paraded before Balliol demanding 'Bring out your black man' ('the
     coal blackest negro that those climes had ever seen'), Balliol reciprocated,
     demanding 'Bring out your white man, Magdalen' and capturing and then
     dragging 'tall, white Henry Martin . . . along the High whilst little, yellow and
     parti-colored fellows had tried to rescue him'. Ford Madox Ford, *The Rash Act* –
     henceforth *RA*; Manchester: Carcanet, 1982, pp. 27-28. Thus Henry Martin
     became 'White Man Smith of Magdalen'.
2   It is some comfort to a critic struggling to keep straight in his mind the complex
     narration and abundant cast of characters of these two novels to realize that
     neither Ford nor his editor could entirely manage the task either. 'Gloria
     Sorenson' here becomes 'Gloria Malmström' in *Henry for Hugh* – henceforth
     HH; Philadelphia: J. B. Lippincott Company, 1934. So, too, Hugh Monckton's
     cousin 'Cyril Monckton', who will receive Hugh Monckton's share of the profits
     after his disappearance and until the legal declaration of his death, becomes
     'Eustace Monckton' in the second novel. In this essay characters will be given the
     name they carry in whichever of the novels is being referred to.
3   Of course the characters of Henry Martin and of Eudoxie when she is speaking
     English are themselves exercises in dialect by an author who as recently as 1927
     had boasted himself 'as English as they make them' – *New York Is Not America*,
     London: Duckworth, 1927, p. 122. Ford does this well, though not perfectly. For
     example, 'bundle-stiffs' (*RA 76*) should be 'bindle stiffs'; and, although it is not
     possible to point to a glaring error in Ford's rendering of Eudoxie's American
     slang, the overall effect is unconvincing. Her speech seems sub-Runyonesque, as
     though reproduced from the page rather than from life.
4   Quoted by C. H. Sisson, 'Introduction' to Ford Madox Ford's *The Rash Act,*
     Manchester: Carcanet, 1982, p. 1.

HISTORY, IDENTITY AND NATIONALITY
IN FORD'S *GREAT TRADE ROUTE*

Christopher MacGowan

Ford Madox Ford's *Great Trade Route* describes a physical journey from France, via a barely glimpsed English coastline, to the New World – and back. Its account of history, culture, and writing is an attempt to account both historically and personally for the divisions between the three cultures that rob the New World in particular of a potential that, on a personal level, would solve Ford's own problems as a writer: problems of identity and audience that shadow almost every page of the broader social and historical commentary in the book.

The Western part of Ford's Great Trade Route crosses the Mediterranean, moves up through France to the English Channel and 'along the South coast of England to Cornwall and the Court of Arthur'[1] (*GTR* 88). The ancient civilizations covered by the route include Samarkand, Ispahan, Damascus, Venice, Paris and Tintagel, and in this book Ford traces the line westward to the American South. The transatlantic voyage outward that Ford describes takes him past the south coast of England, and it is an England that reminds him of the past, of exile, and of personal loss. He records: 'The North Foreland glides by... Eventually a grey hillside with clumps of coppices on the shoulder. I used to own that land once. Slowly it glides by too [. . . .] Conrad used to groan after he had left that place and mood' (*GTR* 40). Although this is close to 'Cornwall and the Court of Arthur', the only Knight in this scene is an aged German steward on the boat, 'a mild, aged man, like the White Knight, with a grey face and tender feet' (*GTR* 41) – a knight from a story quite different from Malory's. Ford's account conflates Lewis Carroll's teller, the White Knight, and the subject of his song, the 'aged aged man / ... Whose look was mild' and perhaps Conrad's groan too – 'Who seemed distracted with his woe / ... That summer evening long ago'.[2] Fiction, loss, the past, and the contemporary realities of a boat associated with the Third Reich come together as the voyage continues on.

England is only glimpsed in passing on the voyage out, but its associations with King Arthur and Malory's tale haunt the book's account of the full journey. But this is an association more complex and ambivalent than the feudal nostalgia associated with the Fugitive poets Ford had arranged to meet up with in Tennessee. Ford had recently reexamined what experiencing a medieval past could teach a man of integrity in revising his *Ladies Whose Bright Eyes* of 1911 for U. S. publication in 1935. The revised version had concluded that such history and myth finally offered little to the task of finding a solution for how to live in the contemporary world, a world that Ford was finding increasingly inhumane. And a United States racked by economic depression, and a feudal idealism transported to part of its more rural south, did not offer a promising background for finding such a solution. But *Great Trade Route* is, on one level, Ford's try. The American market offered him a potential readership. He might find there a way to integrate a self-sufficient integrity with a personal future, within a country having the vast spaces to shelter at least a version perhaps of an English past. And France offered a common bond with both. Thus Ford's journey is at once more quietly desperate and rootless than just an account of a transatlantic visit. And in his description of the journey Virginia plays a pivotal role in the breakdown of the continuities that Ford would like to establish, and France is finally the refuge and home from which he can look back on lost possibilities, and on such promise as still might be. King Arthur's martial Virginian surrogates Robert E. Lee and Stonewall Jackson are defeated heroes, the journey itself is not completed as planned, and the production of the book is compromised by the very economics of value and scarcity that its pages condemn. On the voyage back the writer is isolated, his exile ended only back in France, in the company of the 'Little English girl' (*GTR* 408), who represents not only his past (she is, or is based on, Julie, Ford's daughter from his relationship with Stella Bowen), but also through her youth, and her French education, a possible future English identity mirroring the international values of Ford himself. But importantly in this particular possible resolution there is no place for the recently visited New World.

A characteristic of travel writing is the foregrounding of the account being produced, and in a number of ways Ford uses this characteristic as part of his account of the relationships of England, America, and France. Ford notes the temptations to self-indulgence for anyone writing on Virginia ('or almost any neighbourhood on the Great Route'):

> Virginia glamour has been overdone because it makes such easy writing [.
> . . .] it makes easy writing just because it is authentic. You don't have to bother
> about getting in an atmosphere; it is done all ready for you. So you overdo it...
> unless you are a very good writer indeed. (*GTR* 294)

But writing is most centrally foregrounded – and linked through Arthur to England, the New World, and France – in Ford's account of an incident in New York. Ford has a feverish temperature of 103, and somebody knocks at the door and drunkenly enters, 'to offer' Ford writes, 'his shining sword in my service'. This would-be knight has come to defend Ford's literary reputation against the slights of such English novelists as H. G. Wells, J. B. Priestley, and Frank Swinnerton. 'He says: "The critics are treating you shamelessly. Shamefully." [. . . .] If I will permit him to use his shining sword he will bring me the heads of a hundred English novelists every one of whom wants mine.' Immediately following this unwanted if gallant offer of service, the 'patient New Yorker', as *Great Trade Route* calls this figure, begins to read from Malory while outside in the street the 'shining blue knights' of the New York Police Department perform some mysterious investigative rituals (*GTR* 61-63).

The passage from *Le Morte D'Arthur* (Chapter XXI) that the New Yorker reads begins with paper and ink being brought to the now contrite, but mortally wounded, Sir Gawaine, who writes to Sir Lancelot pleading with him to return from France and save Arthur's civilization – a plea that is answered too late: 'And when paper and ink was brought, then Sir Gawaine was set up weakly by Sir Arthur... and then he wrote thus as the French book makyth mention'. Thus the allusion, set in New York, encapsulates Ford's themes of loss in England, a possible salvation in France – and the potential, but finally not realized, power of pen and ink. Later Ford as narrator paraphrases the words that Gawaine writes to Lancelot when, while still in Pennsylvania, he looks forward to reaching Lexington, Virginia, where Robert E. Lee is buried. But in *Great Trade Route* Virginia is as lost a cause as was Camelot. As Ford anticipates reaching the state, Malory's 'wherefore I beseech thee, Sir Launcelot, to return again unto this realm', quoted by the New Yorker in the city, now becomes Ford's 'And I pray thee, Sir Lancelot that thou come again to this land and bring Jefferson with thee...' (*GTR* 63-64, 200).

Ford writes of British America that Virginia was 'the only one of its colonies to deserve the name of civilized' (*GTR* 334). The association of Jefferson and Lancelot in this prayer brings together the two doomed cultures, both failed links in the personal and cultural connection that Ford wants his trade route to forge. Jefferson is importantly an artist and writer, with close links to France. Washington and Jefferson, for Ford, are respectively 'the first farmer of his country' and 'the first artist-craftsman' (*GTR* 152). Although both men were born in Virginia, Washington, for Ford, is a product of England despite his birthplace, a farmer who is 'the best individual man that the country of my birth ever produced' (*GTR* 334). The more international 'artist-craftsman' Jefferson, however, is for Ford among 'the best in the modern world that began when the Golden Age came finally to an end' (*GTR* 296). Ford singles out Washington for criticism for his role in the tensions in 1797-98 between France and the United States – Ford terms it 'the little war' – and comments on this 'want of taste on the part of Washington and Virginia', naming the state rather than the newly formed nation (*GTR* 333-34).

Ford contrasts the Virginians Lee and Jackson with the victor-ious northern generals Grant and Sherman – the last two 'murderers' as far as he is concerned. The comparison is again foregrounded within acts of writing and reading, for Ford is actually discussing a book on Grant: 'when you read about Lee you feel better... and it is good for the world that you should feel better like that. But if you read about Sherman you might say: "After all that is the way wars should be waged"'. The ruthlessness of the northern generals, Ford argues, won them victory and destroyed a civilization. In contrast, for him, 'Lee deserves well of mankind because he observed the laws of war and the dictates of humanity'. Lee's stature in Ford's eyes is reinforc-ed by Ford's setting him alongside Sir Philip Sidney, in a further con-textualising of these generals within the act of writing (*GTR* 300-01).

The Virginia that Ford sees as at once embodying the best of what characterized the England of Arthur is tied to the political vision of self-sufficient communities and the agricultural ideal of the small producer. But this is a condition achieved for a relatively short period in Ford's account of Virginia history, and for Ford is a promise de-stroyed by the materialist motivations of those in power in England. He argues that 'the English' had 'for a short moment in Virginia' the potential to create a society in which, true to the values of the Great Trade Route, 'peace should be interminable and crime still unknown in the habitable world' (*GTR* 115). This potential falls to the greed of 'the rulers in Whitehall' – initially for gold, 'the dreams of El Dorado', and then for quick rewards from agriculture (*GTR* 137). Just as Jefferson stands for Ford at the forefront of the modern age, Ford argues that the beginnings of 'the struggle between cash-farming and mass industrial production', a struggle that he sees behind the American Civil War, 'must in the modern world be looked for in the establishment of the Virginia Company in seventeenth century England' (*GTR* 324-5).

The lost past that unites England and Virginia is both a personal and an historical past. As a personal example, Ford describes childhood adventures with playmate Walter Atterbury, his nurse's grandson, the two boys on an upturned table imagining voyages across the Atlantic to Norfolk, Virginia. And Ford's favourite house in Virginia, Gunston Hall, has among its attractions 'its red brick suggestion of the age of Queen Anne' (*GTR* 291). But the childhood memory, and the Eighteenth Century house also have associations with the Mediterranean, the destination that returns Ford to the present in this book. The memory of voyaging on the upturned table with Atterbury also includes an account of Ford arguing with his playmate – young Ford sometimes wanted to sail the Mediterranean, as well as the Atlantic (*GTR* 12, 24-25). As for Gunston Hall, the plantation was the home of George Mason, friend of Washington and Jefferson, and composer of the Virginia Declaration of Rights (1776), which Jefferson drew upon for the opening paragraphs of the Declaration of Independence, and which is often cited as a source document for the French Declaration of the Rights of Man (1789).

There are other examples of the positive associations of Virginia, always in the past, being linked to France. Lexington, Lee's burial place, Ford calls 'the loveliest town in the New World' (*GTR* 262), but also, a little later, 'that Carcassonne of the West.' This later reference comes in a paragraph where Ford recalls a pre-war visit to Virginia and having thoughts 'of going [. . .] into tobacco'. The suggestion of this unrealised alternative future arose, Ford recalls, from watching 'the representative of a relative [. . . who] was buying tobacco for the French Régie', the French Government's tobacco monopoly (*GTR* 314). As if to warn that sentiment might overtake reality in Ford's sense of what Virginia could represent for him he has his companions make fun of his self-indulgence early in the book:

'We shall have, the patient New Yorker said, to do something about it [. . . .] He will be talking about his cousins in Richmond, Va. And their aunts in the Shenandoah Valley. He's been talking about Monticello, and the Capitol at Richmond. . . .' (*GTR* 124)

However, Ford describes the historical houses of Virginia as now museum pieces rather than the centres of a vibrant culture that they once were. (No doubt Ford knew that the last private owner of Gunston Hall had donated the house and grounds to the state in the early 1930s.) Ford does find 'traces' of 'the inhabitants of the great houses' and their connection to a lost England and Virginia in the Delmarva Peninsula that joins easternmost Virginia, Maryland and Delaware – calling the inhabitants 'those squires with the traditions and much more than the opportunities of the squirearchy of the old country' (*GTR* 148). For Ford this particular remnant of 'the old country' will contain a 'hundred' of the survivors who will, in Ford's momentary vision here, begin the renewal of the values of the Great Trade Route (*GTR* 107). But even this somewhat positive note about Virginia's future potential is qualified. The peninsula was the premier location in the U.S. for truck farming of vegetables during the nineteenth and early twentieth centuries, and for this reason Ford had planned a slow return from the South to New York via this route. But he is obliged to return quickly – 'the telegram said imperiously' – to sign an agreement for the very book that he is writing, and to 'take ship' or lose a last possible reservation to cross the Atlantic. Thus there is no account of a trip along the peninsula in a book so concerned with truck farming and with what 'traces' there might be of an order and hierarchy elsewhere consigned to history – only notice of the reasons for its absence, reasons closely tied to the book's central themes of the need to return home, and to the process of the book's composition and production (*GTR* 376-77).

The South has some important creative figures for Ford in this book, as do other parts of the United States, but Virginia's pre-eminent artist-craftsman for Ford is the long-dead Jefferson – the Jefferson associated with Lancelot's doomed mission. Ford had earlier given another reason for not being able to return via the Delmarva Peninsula, this time a non-commercial one that foregrounds France and artistic activity. He writes – 'I had to hurry back to New York to be present at the opening of an exhibition of pictures of Provence' (*GTR* 335). The choice here is Art or the 'traces' of old Virginia. The artists and writers that Ford records meeting in this book are not from

Virginia, a place for Ford of Queen Anne landscaping, grand houses now empty, and lost eighteenth-century hopes of civilized reform. The meetings with contemporary artists occur in Tennessee – Allen Tate and Caroline Gordon – in New Jersey, where Ford meets William Carlos Williams, Pennsylvania, where he stays with craftsman Wharton Escherick, and New York, where he talks to Theodore Dreiser. There *is* a contemporary writer living in Virginia, Sherwood Anderson, who gets passing mention, but only because Ford mistakes the train announcer's Merion Pa. for Anderson's base in Marion Va. 'Marion Va.? Let's get out and see Sherwood Anderson.... No, Merion, Pa., where the Barnes Collection is' (*GTR* 201). (Ford does not get to see Anderson or the Barnes Collection, Barnes cabling from Geneva in response to a permission request, 'Would rather burn my collection than let Ford Madox Ford see it': *GTR* 208.)

When the subject of Virginia broadens out to the South more generally, *Great Trade Route* becomes more explicit about the role of race in the attempt to forge the connections its title argues for. England emerges momentarily as an alternative, but fades almost immediately as a fiction, even – given its imperialist past – a parallel. Ford is again doubly exiled, the Southern legacy of race finally contributes to his sense of being, and wanting to remain, an outsider.

Twice in *Great Trade Route* reminders of a lost England try to offset the South's racial legacy, although finally they only reinforce the need to confront the contemporary desolate scene that they are a rather wistful attempt to escape – an escape already rejected in Ford's revision of *Ladies Whose Bright Eyes*. One of the examples returns to Gawaine's letter to Lancelot. Towards the end of his U.S. trip Ford is at his southernmost point, Louisiana – along with Maine the most French of the United States. Ford is speaking to his university audience in Baton Rouge of the marketing and distribution of books, but the accompanying commentary that he adds to *Great Trade Route* is on the heritage of the South's racial history. Ford ends it with speculation: 'perhaps it would have been better if I or you or the policemen at the corner had discovered America. I don't think that our first quest would have been a port from which slaves could be exported.... And, if it could only have been Sir Lancelot' (*GTR* 351). In the book's Coda, sailing back to France, he is looking out on and thinking about Africa and again echoes, 'Why *didn't* Lancelot do what Columbus did?' (*GTR* 361). Again, the impossible wish is for a continuity, personal, historical, and mythological, between England, France and the New World.

An idyllic English village scene temporarily displaces the South's racial heritage a few pages earlier in the book, when Ford describes his journey through the southern towns to meet the Tates in Tennessee. Significantly this memory is punctuated by Ford looking out from 'the Tates' balcony' as he reflects on 'how I came here. Perhaps not on this journey. . . On another. . . . I forget' (GTR 348). The view seems 'an earthly near-paradise', although what he recalls of the journey makes clear that it isn't: 'Round the court house in the little town, to the delight of Biala, the square is draped and festooned with friezes of coloured people. . . . I don't like to see coloured people; they spoil the south for me. . . .' (Ford's ellipses, GTR 347). The 'coloured people' are 'draped and festooned' around the square, as if part of a display that insists upon recognition, even celebration, of their role – an exhibition of their role as a vital part of what the South is. Ford affirms that his comments are not based on 'race feeling', and offers his pleasure at seeing 'the shining, ebony, always grinning troops in their scarlet fezzes and slashed faces' in the Mediterranean as a contrasting response. But 'coloured people' counter, 'spoil', any idealistic feudal ideas about the South, as the narrator recognizes. The full engagement with the South's racial past and economic present is made a few paragraphs later via the temporary escape to a fictional England. 'And you go by drab village after drab village with dark people draped on the steps and door steps and before the gauze doors of the stores.' He continues:

> And your chest is oppressed.... And you bundle along and you come to a village that sparkles with white paint... Woodford, I think. And the village green is as green and tidy as a green in English Sussex and bright chintz dresses flit along it.
> And you lift up your heart and you say: 'We're still on the Great Route... And the next village is falling into ruins'. (Ford's ellipses, GTR 348-9).

Momentarily the English village displaces the 'dark people draped on the steps', just as Lancelot being the discoverer of America would have solved the problem of the South's slave heritage – with such alternatives could come the comfortable claim 'we're still on the Great Route'. But Ford's English village is itself a fiction, either a composite of the Woodford of Essex and a village in Sussex (where there is no Woodford), or a village that shifts its location even as he imagines it, in England, and then across continents. The 'white paint' and the triply sounded 'green' of the 'English Sussex' village give way to the 'ruins' of the next village and the sharecroppers, forced from their land and homes. The view from the Tates' balcony, and the recollection of 'how I came here', moves from 'earthly near-paradise' to confronting the realities of the Depression's impact upon both black and white Southerners, and the inadequacy of any feudal myth to alleviate it.

Two important scenes on the voyage back to France confirm Ford's distance from the culture he has just visited, and relate that distance to writing, and to complexities of success and failure. Ford is travelling third class, and describes at one point the view from his lowly regions of the ship, seeing the 'gallery above', where the first class passengers are:

> gorgeous cinema stars, holding their coat-revers together over their throats, hair blowing back in the dawn wind, eyes gazing soulfully into the growing luminosity as if into spotlights. Each with an attendant court of insignificant males, each ignoring all the others and moving with the indifferent, long steps of great waterbirds. (*GTR* 363-64)

Cinema is clearly the art form that contemporary audiences respond to and that the culture rewards financially. Ford does not specify American cinema stars, but the boat has sailed from New York and the language suggests Hollywood. This glimpse of a contemporary elite from which he is excluded ('they are [. . .] far above my head' he writes) turns from cinema stars to fellow writers a little later. Lamenting the discomfort of the voyage, he admonishes himself for not writing to please an audience that could reward him with a berth to rival that of the cinema stars: 'I ought to write my books sufficiently attractively for me to be able to afford the best extra silvergilt sundeck suite on the *Normandie*. . . . I am told many writers can' (*GTR* 393).

Of course the self mocking is – although not completely – tongue in cheek, and Ford has no interest in being a purely commercial writer, but this does not make the distance, and discomfort, any less. But Ford accepts the exile, and isolation, that come from a commitment to books that do more than provide escapist fantasy. Leaving the distant, sunlit deck Ford retreats to 'the dim Jewish quarter of the immense, heaving, roaring, hysterically screaming, pushing, shoving, stinking ship. It is the only quiet spot... a great slice of the ship's hold, dim light coming through rare port holes' (*GTR* 374). For

Ford, two Jewish rabbis whom he sees 'disputing over the colons and full stops of the THORAH' – the only other occupants of the 'large, grey, empty cavern' that he shares with them – 'are responsible for the few glimmers of civilization that here and there gleam weakly in our comity of nations' (*GTR* 382). Significantly, Ford has finally been driven to this subterranean escape by the noise of a group of rowdy American boys who are en route to sing for Mussolini. Ford looks up from his hideaway to see not cinema stars on a sunlit deck, but exiles, 'two old people who have been expelled after forty years from the country we have left... and where they have left every soul of their kin and every soul that they know in the world'. He continues, 'They are expelled whilst the howling boys will be welcomed back after they have sung their hymn of adoration to the dictator' (*GTR* 383).

Ford himself is welcomed back in the final pages of this book, not to England or America but to France – the place of Lancelot's exile. But Ford writes earlier in the book, 'I don't want to become French'. He feels 'mildly American in America, but nothing anywhere else... except when England is playing for the Davis Cup against the United States'. But he asks, 'Why in Hell must there be nations? I don't feel to belong to any nation' (*GTR* 74). But this assertion, early in the account, is just one part of how Ford responds to the journey and experience that this book records. The other is the wish that the concept of nation could be transformed and expanded to connect historically, culturally, and personally the England, United States, and France that figure in this book – with the recognition that while this is possible to imagine, it remains as impossible to achieve as Gawaine's plea to Lancelot. Nevertheless Ford's attempt in this book is at one with his continuing attempts, back to his editing of the *transatlantic review* in the 1920s, and his repositioning of himself as a transnational author in such books as *When the Wicked Man, The Rash Act, Henry for Hugh*, and *Provence*, to see his own identity and his material as transcultural. In such a goal he wants to move 'Englishness' and the best that it can represent, beyond nationality altogether. In *Great Trade Route* the attempt allows him to see knights in Virginia history and on the streets of contemporary New York; it allows him to wish that Lancelot not Columbus had discovered America, and to request that if and when Lancelot returns he bring the Francophile Virginian Jefferson with him. Such a transnational nation would also produce the audience that Ford wished for his books. Such a hope, *Great Trade Route* acknowledges, is rooted – even perhaps lost – in the past.

NOTES

1   Ford, *Great Trade Route* – henceforth *GTR*; New York: Oxford University Press, 1937, p. 88.
2   Lewis Carroll, *Alice's Adventures in Wonderland & Through the Looking-Glass,* New York: Macmillan, 1963, pp. 114-17.

'BUT ONE IS ENGLISH':
FORD'S POETRY 1893-1921

Dennis Brown

Ever since the cultural ascendancy of Movement poetry in the 1950s, and the consolidation of Philip Larkin's reputation, in particular,[1] there has lingered the perception of a basic distinction between English poetic tradition and 'foreign' modernist experimentalism. Writing in 2002, Glyn Maxwell – with L=A=N=G=U=A=G=E poetry in his sights – helped perpetuate this contrast, with a nod to Robert Frost:

> ... two roads diverging, and those two roads are, though worn and cracked with decades of use and abuse, pretty much the same two roads that diverged in the cafés of London and Paris ninety-odd years ago.[2]

Ford Madox Ford (or Hueffer, as he was then) patronised cafés in both capitals. However, being idiosyncratically versatile, Ford managed to find a path between and in touch with both roads. His early verse was written in the late-Victorian era and thereafter traditionalism, with affinities to both Edwardian and Georgian poetry, becomes supplemented by an intensifying pursuit of 'natural' language which is at least proto-modernist. At the same time, with paternal roots in Germany, an admiration for French prose-stylists and a strong interest in Anglo-American relations (Dowell and Ashburnham, for instance), he was never in danger of Little England parochialism. Rather, Ford brought both the resources of native verse-craft and the growing, international aspirations of the modern to bear on his work. And a major theme, drawing on both strands, was the nature of Englishness – an issue on which he wagered his life in the Great War.

In an increasingly multicultural England, where devolution has been a recent political development, and even some solution to the centuries-long Anglo-Irish wrangle seems possible, the topic of Englishness remains very much alive – as publishers have been quick to recognise.[3] England is now, indeed, a 'small island' again and one rich in ethnic diversity as never before. However, when Ford was

establishing his literary career (an era which, for reasons of space, I
have demarcated 1893-1921), the issue of nationality was very
different from that today. The dominant interest then was the
connection between the 'condition of England' in itself and the
exportation of an enforced Englishness within the expansive British
Empire – arguably much the situation the USA finds itself in today.[4]
Where, for Sir Henry Newbolt, England was 'Mother of happy homes
and Empire vast',[5] for Ford it was simply the first – '... give me mead
and a warm hearth-stone,/And a cosy pipe and Dolly'.[6] Ford's verse
shows virtually no interest in 'wider still and wider' Imperialism. His
England rather appears as an extended place-myth[7] of home – the
islanded arena of quasi-Heideggerian 'dwelling'. In essence, it constitutes a fantasy ownership of hearth, region, cultural tradition and
form of language. It is an 'imagined community'[8] – more psychological than political – and this permeates his poetry, even when the
ostensible subject is something quite other.

Ford's early representations of England and Englishness are
expressed in the forms and tones of widely-shared poetic discourse.
He tries out songs, ballads, descriptive pieces, dialogues, personal
lyrics and so forth. The attentive reader can hear echoes of such
mainstream poets as Tennyson and Browning, the Pre-Raphaelites and
Housman, as well as similarities with young contemporaries. In fact,
his titles themselves are indicative of a common practice – 'Song
Dialogue', 'A Night Piece', 'In Adversity', 'A Lullaby', 'The Gipsy
and the Townsman', 'The Peasant's Apology', 'A Ballad of an
Auction', 'The Pedlar Leaves the Bar Parlour at Dymchurch', 'An
Anniversary', 'From the Soil' or 'Wife to Husband'. The 'anxiety of
influence'[9] is here diffused into acculturation within familiar methods
– all in different ways attesting to national preoccupations and native
idioms. Acceptability rather than originality is the aim. Ford's early
poems invoke and convoke a communal consciousness as foundation
of nationality – English, British or whatever the label[10] – within a
particular seasonality – winter, spring and high summer, especially.
Figures tend to be typological – ploughman, townsman, pedlar, gipsy,
parson or auctioneer. There is a William Morris wishfulness as to
social life, where roles are honourable modes of contribution rather
than instruments of oppression. The poems mythologise more than
describe, recycling familiar modes in the process. The poet tends to
become subsumed into the conventions of a verse which is socially
acceptable:

> But the marsh ain'd so lone if you've heered a good song,
> And you hum it aloud as you cater along,
> Nor the stiles half so high, nor the pack so like lead,
> If you've heered a good tale an' it runs in your head. ('The Pedlar...', 13)

Ford's early poetry, then, affirms a shared national awareness – of a largely rural, imaginary community of 'tangled woodland, tarn and town'. It depends heavily on place-myth to naturalise an Englishness which remains unconceptualised as such – a kind of emotive 'given'. Like his contemporaries, he relies on the evocation of landscape, especially that of 'Sussex by the sea', representative figures, recognisable situations and familiar verse-forms. Prior to his more experimental phase, Ford's verse is characterised by formal conventionality. In fact, it is easily assimilated since it is close to oral culture.[11] In this it necessarily lacks the qualities prized by, say, New Criticism – subtlety, complexity, ambiguity, paradoxicality and suggestivity. It has, by contrast the more populist characteristics of orality – simplicity, clarity, traditionality, memorability and regularity. Ford's later work uses more interesting modes of expression, but will leave him somewhat marginalised – a 'Bohemian'. Here Englishness is expressed in terms which bring place-myth and form together in an easily acceptable way. And both operate to create specific 'containers'[12] of national feeling. Place-myth (as in 'From the Soil', 'A Pagan' or 'A Great View') is built up through basic signifying details – 'field' and 'fold', 'upland fallows', 'sea and strand', 'vast marsh [.../ ...] waving plough-lands and willowy closes' – a specifically islanded green and pleasant land. Composition and formal rhythm and rhyme provide the psychic container, creating an aesthetically special space where Englishness can be exercised. In *The Good Society and the Inner World*, Michael Rustin helps explain the mechanism: 'Our experience of responding to cultural forms ... derives from inner unconscious experience and its symbolisation'.[13]

'Midwinter Night' (*From Inland*, 1907) is a convenient poem to indicate how Ford provides containment for a sense of native identity. The poem begins by describing a particular scenario at the seasonal turning-point of bleak mid-winter:

> Now cometh on the dead time of the year:
> Meadows in flood and heaths all barren are.
> Across the downs and black, tempestuous leas
> Blow the dull boomings of deserted seas. (42)

It proceeds to build up a composite package of resonant significations
– cowering birds, howling wind, bell-ringing steeples, lighted hearths,
sleepers awaiting springtime and the Christmas message. A specific
Englishness is rendered in the kind of diction chosen: 'fare'; 'thatch';
'kinship'; 'bell-throats'; 'Lo'; 'hearths'; 'fell'; 'bravely'; 'folds';
'sting' – mainly Old English, knotty and, together, conveying a native
specificity which, say, even a poem in 'Colonial English' would lack.
The raw scenario is islanded from the 'deserted seas' and the 'roofs'
enclose 'golden' interiors providing shelter. Aesthetic enclosure is
provided by the regular, forthright rhythm and rhymes, exercising the
play of difference as simply as in nursery rhyme: 'year/ are';
'leas/seas'; 'watch/thatch'; 'gale/hail' and so on. The somewhat
archaic *'Rest ye: 'tis well'* sets up Christmas glad tidings in terms of
tradition rooted in the Mediaeval world. Like other Victorians, Ford is
helping invent a heritage-as-Christmas. Yet survival is the deeper
psychological theme – as it is in the consolations of nationalism. A
refuge is asserted against the otherness of nature; Spring is promised;
death has lost its sting. The English home, within the English
community on the islanded fortress, contains anxiety as the poem
contains its meanings within the boundaries of metre and rhyme. The
function of the poetry, like the function of the bells' message, is to
render England as a kind of maternal body.[14] In this sense, 'Midwinter
Night', like other such poems, delivers a version of what Antony
Easthope has called 'social phantasy'.[15]

Two further poems, 'A Great View' and 'On the Marsh Road',
use descriptive means to convey the essence of that Englishness which
is diffused throughout Ford's earlier collections. In the first a
panoramic vision of the English countryside is effected by quasi-
filmic technique, moving from West to South, North and then East –
until we see – 'France!' Ford creates a rich sense of the land's solidity
and variability, and also emphasises coastline as boundary of identity:

> [...] For the vast marsh dozes,
> And waving plough-lands and willowy closes
> Creep and creep up the soft south steep.
> In the pallid North the grey and ghostly downs do fold away,
> And, spinning spider threadlets down the sea, the sea-lights dance
> And shake out a wavering radiance. (21)

The view, we are told three times, is 'very like Heaven'. The poem
ends with a 'shimmering' vision of the eastern prospect, rendered

epiphanic with metaphors of femininity as the gaze fades over the channel. A similarly hallucinatory ending is given in 'On a Marsh Road', fading into Housmanesque never-never land. The opening equally conjures up the land's solid presence and specific topography:

> A bluff of cliff, purple against the south [...]
> This wet, clean road; clear twilight held in the pools,
> And ragged thorns, ghost reeds and dim, dead willows. (35)

Both poems, then, use place-myth to suggest an England and Englishness on the threshold of the ineffable – a realm of rich substance, itself containing identity as the poem contains the experience. The effect is to create a kind of Blakean 'Albion' – at once concrete and revelatory; a specific *habitus*[16] unlike any other, which is also a safe psychological haven. Looking ahead, however, such constitutes, for Ford, the 'last of' that kind of England – at least in that kind of way.

For, as *The Soul of London* (1905) indicates clearly, Ford was becoming self-expressively aware that Englishness was changing. The title *Songs From London* (1910) indicates the switch of interest from country to city and, in some of the poems, this is matched by a similar switch from relative timelessness to a restless modernity on the move. In 'Castles in the Fog', for instance, this is demonstrated by an emphasis on the new modes of transportation in an atmospheric urban setting similar to that in T. S. Eliot's 'Preludes' and 'Rhapsody on a Windy Night', written at about the same time:

> *As we come up from Baker Street,*
> *Where Tubes and Trains and 'Buses meet,*
> *There's a touch of frost and a touch of sleet*
> *And mist and mud up Hampstead way*
> *Towards the shutting in of day....* (46)

The essentially transitional nature of the new method is endearingly signalled by the orthography of ''Buses': and a degree of uneasiness is shown even more in the contrast between a modern 'framing' (the italicised beginning and ending) and the small-town medievalism of the main body of the poem. A similar awkwardness is evident in 'June in Town', where there is a contrast between the proto-Betjemanian Metro-Land of 'The Three-Ten at Kilburn' and the evoked 'green hills and daffodils and copses' which have been supplanted. Throughout the first section of the poem, the world of 'paper shops and full 'bus tops' and 'green shades or flowered glades' are brought together in an unsettling conjunction – the past being finally bustled away:

> *And see, and see! 'Tis ten past three above the Kilburn Station*
> *Those maids, thank God! are 'neath the sod and all their generation.* (48)

In the second section, 'Four in the Morning Courage', an 'I' persona mediates the scene, waking early on the longest day of the year, in what may be temporary accommodation (*'that packing case'*), and witnessing a morning coming to consciousness:

> A starling somewhere in the mews, a song-thrush on a broken hat
> Down in the yard the grocers use, all cried: 'Beware! Beware! The Cat'.

It is like a vignette from *The Soul of London* – and could almost be one from, say, Zadie Smith's recent *White Teeth*. In both 'Castles in the Fog' and 'June in Town' the container of Englishness is being both stirred and shaken. Ford, as will be seen, has by no means given up on 'love of one's land', but both land and love are being modified. 1910 was, of course, the year which Virginia Woolf would single out – when 'human character changed'.

However, it was not only the phenomenon of metropolitan modernity that was modifying Ford's representation of Englishness but also his European consciousness and love of travel. There is a significant group of poems which could be entitled 'Home Thoughts from Abroad'. These are mainly to be found in the collections *High Germany* (1912) and *On Heaven and Poems Written on Active Service* (1918). From the context of 'Abroad',[17] England tends to be viewed in two contrastive but frequently intertwining ways: nostalgia for a land of lost content or goodbye to all that. The first is quite overtly expressed in *From Inland*:

> Dear
> What would I give to climb our down [...]
> Beyond our ancient sea-grey town
> The sky-line of our foam-flecked sea. (36-7)

This is, in fact, from an earlier collection, but already Ford is adopting a Browningesque posture of wistful exile – situated in a warmer clime, with 'roe-deer nibbling grapes', but yearning for: 'That recollected, ancient tide'. By contrast, the later 'Süssmund's Address to an Unknown God' uses the persona of 'Carl Eugen Freiherr von

Süssmund' to cast a caustic eye on the vicissitudes of life in literary London. As Ezra Pound uses the mask of the Roman poet in *Homage to Sextus Propertius* (1917) to comment on the 'imbecility' of the British Empire, so Ford employs Süssmund to attack English philistinism and moral earnestness:

> 'Here is a man when times are out of joint
> Who will not be enraged at Edward Morter,
> Parnett or Mosse; who will not to the woes
> Of a grey underworld lend passionate ears
> Nor tear his hair to tatters in the cause
> Of garden suburbs or of guinea pigs
> Injected with bacilli....' (67)

'Süssmund' is accused by his countrymen of being 'a eunuch' – 'morally castrated' – and hence serves also as something of a model for Pound's Hugh Selwyn Mauberley. The verdict on such 'useless' littérateurs is first expressed here by Ford as the opinion of a contemporary English narrowness: 'Give him no management in this great world,/No share in fruity Progress.' This constitutes, of course, Ford's own ironic judgment on what appears to have become a nation of managers.

Ford's celebrated 'On Heaven' is perhaps the poem where his view of England and Englishness is at its bleakest – a rejected world of moral obligations and emotional strangulation. However, there is a catch in the title: if Heaven is the southern France he goes on to describe, then England must be earth – the actual arena of incarnate living. In short, the whole poem is an attractive but somewhat self-indulgent fantasy, with something of the celebratory quality of Lawrence's *Look! We Have Come Through!* about it. Ford's 'working Heaven' – in fact, rather a Bohemian writer's leisure-dream of shaded squares and café tables – is built up as an alternative place-myth. Where England is represented now as 'your Sussex mud/Amongst the frost-bound farms by the yeasty sea', Provence is constructed as a Gauguin/Van Gogh realm of the small-town flâneur, caught in a time-warp of post-impressionist, 'new age' utopianism before the Great War brought early modernism to its very blunt reckoning. Ford paints a charming 'travel-poster' for the good life:

> In the eternal stone of the Alpilles,
> There's this little old town, walled round by the old, grey gardens [...]
> The windows stand open because of the heat of the night

> That shall come.
> And, from each little window, shines in the twilight a light,
> And, beneath the eternal planes [...]
> The Chinese lanthorns, hung out at the doors of hotels,
> Shimmering in the dusk, here on an orange tree, there
> on a sweet-scented lime [....] (104-5)

The poem's narrator awaits his lady-love who is coming in a 'long, red, English racing car'. When she arrives they sit together 'at a little table, under an immense plane', reviewing the past and enjoying the general ambience. Such ambience is presided over by God, who is a sort of Jolly Brown Giant and strolls around with his dog, clapping people on the back and, along with the Virgin Mary, condoning sins of the flesh because they make the world go round. It is a beguiling fantasy of adulterous paradise.

'But one is English'. And Englishness is the world of the living, who appear, in fact, to inhabit a repressive purgatory:

> Heap after heaps, of complications, griefs,
> Worries, tongue-clackings, nonsenses and shame
> For not making good. You see all the coil there was!
> And the poor strained fibres of our tortured brains,
> And the voice that called from depth in her to depth
> In me ... my God, in the dreadful nights,
> Through the roar of the great black winds, through the sound of the sea!
> (102)

In this poem, England appears to be always in winter, with a 'bitter frost' on the very homes and hearths which the earlier poems had made epiphanic of beneficent Englishness. Such houses are now containers of family resentments – 'Eight parents, and the children, seven aunts/And sixteen uncles and a grandmother' – hedged in by 'the broken silver of the English Channel', the 'dreary beaches' lit only by a 'pale', Arnoldian moon. The container has become the 'bad breast'.[18] England now stands for the Reality Principle which the persona seeks to evade: the world of work, obligation, standards. Or, put another way, Englishness now embodies 'the craze to relinquish/What you want most'. However, it is out of the 'blisters and foments' that the dream of heaven is born. In this sense, it is the very integrity and order of England which allows the dream of escape for some kind of 'golden years' Utopia elsewhere. And in the Great War poems Ford will write of the need to defend the English homeland which dreams of heaven.

In 'Footsloggers', a fine and unjustly ignored contribution to poetry of the First World War, Ford is content to use the Tommies' name for that homeland – 'Blighty'. Richard Holmes explains that: 'Blighty was perhaps a corruption of the Hindi *Bilayati*, a foreign country, the Arabic *baladi*, my own country, or the Urdu *belait*, strange or foreign'. And he cites John Brophy and Eric Partridge on its inner meaning: 'a sort of faerie, a paradise which he could faintly remember, a sort of never-never land'.[19] Blighty, then, constitutes a war-time myth of Englishness and serves to name, for one particular nation, the mystery that Ford considers with respect to the desperate Belgian defenders of their homeland in 'Antwerp':[20] 'Was it just love of their land?' In 'Footsloggers' this will become: 'What is love of one's land?' Among other things, Ford's war poetry expresses and explores a core reality about the Great War which the familiar trench-poetry and memoirs have rendered it politically incorrect to contemplate in a positive light – namely, patriotism. However, as Holmes demonstrates in full detail, Englishmen scarcely signed up to fight, endured the rigours and horrors of the front line and, all too often, lost their lives to help in 'inching Field Marshal Haig's drinks cabinet closer to Berlin'.[21] Ford, like several Great War writers, was in a Welsh regiment, and in a poem like 'The Silver Music' Wales is included within Englishness and devotion to its protection:

> Oh I'm weary for the castle,
> And I'm weary for the Wye [...]
> But I must plod along the road
> That leads to Germany. (87)

In 'Nostalgia', the sound of heavy guns, gas-shells and shrapnel are contrasted with an epiphany of homeland: '*But I see the Golden Valley/ Down by Chepstow on the Wye*', and in 'A Solis Ortus Cardine', written from 'Ypres Salient, 6/9/16', the persona addresses civilians he is fighting for: 'Oh quiet peoples sleeping bed by bed/ Beneath grey roof-trees in the glimmering West'. In the next verse he addresses his dead comrades in a similar vein. Unlike the better-known war writers, Ford makes no distinction here between civilians and serving-men, General Staff and front-line soldiers, profiteers and cannon-fodder or the 'old men' and the young. All are part of Englishness: and all the soldier asks is: 'Give us our prayers!'.

'Footsloggers' is dedicated to C. F. G. Masterman – significant-ly the author of *The Condition of England* and organiser of allied literary propaganda in the war.[22] It is in ten sections, followed by a short 'Envoi'. Written in prosy free verse – at times using irregular but insistent rhyme-words – it is an apparently rambling meditation on England and military service, sometimes attaining a heightened, incantatory intensity. It is imagistic in detail, flavoured with colloquialisms and varies wildly in mood – a kind of elaborated free association, using collage methods.[23] At the centre of the poem is 'love of one's land'. The word 'land' is itself important (cf. country, state, kingdom, people, nation or culture), and indicates the environmental basis of Ford's Englishness. However, it is the issue itself which makes this poem stand out, along with David Jones's *In Parenthesis*,[24] from the mainstream of Great War writing. In the later *Parade's End*, and at various points in the poem, Ford articulates the horror and wastage of the front, yet he refuses to treat soldiers as passive victims. In 'Footsloggers' the poetry is not in the pity but in the patriotism.

The first two sections express the central issue in terms of natural phenomena – wave, tornado, flame – and as evocations of passionate emotions – love, madness, asceticism. The next two provide contrastive vignettes of English life to indicate what is 'in the contract' and 'what we die for'. In III the grim reality of Paddington at night is summoned up (non-existent transport, dim lighting, pale faces and 'alcoholic voices'), and IV contrasts this with memories of ceremonies, sing-songs and the woman left behind – a collage of home-life situations which inform the patriotic service. In V there is a resumé of 'love of one's men' similar to one in *Parade's End*:[25]

> You straf them, slang them, mediate between
> Their wives and loves, and you inspect their toe-nails
> And wangle leaves for them [....] (93)

Such love eventually incorporates 'the whole B. E. F in France' – a mirror-image of masculine England, with the same class divisions, counties, towns, even road-signs echoed in ranks, divisions, regiments and trench-names. Hence: 'We bear the State upon our rain-soaked backs'. And in IV the men are seen in the light of historical precedent (Hellas, Nelson, Minden – indices of a native notion of honour and duty). At the end, however, Officer Ford self-consciously merges himself into the unreflecting Tommy – 'But I never had much brain'.

The following four sections use the device of an embarkation train (Cardiff to London) to help join up key themes and scenarios. As in Philip Larkin's later 'Whitsun Weddings', the journey enables the poet to outline a cross-section of England (in this case, 'the West going to the East'). Ford's attention is partly concentrated on what goes on inside the carriage: in VII the bonhomie and gossip among the 'fourteen of us'; in VIII a convivial lunch, with French wine, Russian fowl and American meat, spiced from the Tropics (symbols of a still-great trading-nation); and in IX memories of preparations for the front. The passage commences in a bluff, by-the-way manner – 'I don't know if you know the 1.10 train' – and proceeds at a brisk pace, presided over by a confiding voice. Typical vignettes of Englishness are elicited through the carriage-window:

> Across the counties and over the shires,
> Right over England past farmsteads and byres [...]
> And fields and flowers [...]
> Above the tranquil downs
> And the tranquil towns. (95)

This is not 'stiff upper-lip' stuff – 'bubbles with conversation', 'the talk buzzes on' – but rather high-spirited camaraderie. And in IX there is a sense of the pleasures of leave ('you've been to the Theatre and the Empire') as well as the hectic assembling of equipment, money and luggage necessary. It ends, however, with a chilling awareness of what lies ahead: 'The whine of the shells,/Into the mire and the stress'. And the final destination of the troops is either the Casualty Clearing Station ('C.C.S.'), 'Blighty again' or 'under the sod'.

Section X is considerably the longest one, the most meditative and the most focused on the defence of Englishness. Here again Ford grounds the reflections in place-myth, a *habitus* that could be invaded, as Belgium and France had been. In Geoffrey Hill's 'The Mystery of the Charity of Charles Péguy' (1983), the French mystique of inherit-ance – 'landscape and inner domain' – needs no apology.[26] Nor need there be for Ford's pastoral mythologising of the English equivalent, however recent advertising and pollution have debased the ideal:

> It is because our land is beautiful and green and comely,
> Because our farms are quiet and thatched and homely,
> Because the trout stream dimples by the willow,
> Because the water-lilies float upon the ponds[...]
> And maybe we shall never again
> Plod thro' our mire and the rain [...]
> But we have been borne across this land [...] (97)

The 'Envoi' finally recapitulates the motif and imagery of the first two sections, reminding us that love of our country 'sleeps for a year, for a day' but is irresistible when it breaks out. Such sentiments are commonly held to have become redundant with the death of Rupert Brooke, and jingoistically absurd after Wilfred Owen and Siegfried Sassoon. But that scarcely stands up in the light of England in 1940, and war is not necessarily 'futile' in the light of the Shoah. 'Footsloggers' is an honest poem – honest to the surviving letters of the Great War, to the motivation of the men who fought (in whatever rank) and to Ford himself, whatever his romantic excesses, when he enlisted and served. The aim was to keep England 'inviolate'. There is an overt rape-implication in Ford's diction, and place-myth remains primarily psychological in that sense: yet that is how Belgium and France perceived the thrust and effect of the Schlieffen Plan, and the British Expeditionary Force was witness: '*this* is what we die for.... As we ought'.

In the poem 'Immortality: An Elegy on a Great Poet Dying Abroad' (1920), written soon after the war, Ford looks beyond both 'our land' and the conflicted obligations of military service. It imagines and addresses a poet who has chosen exile from his English homeland, thus presaging the considerable *diaspora* of British writers after 1918 which Fussell describes in *Abroad*, and hinting at a road to be taken by Ford in 1922. It is a disturbingly ambivalent and insistently interrogative poem which negotiates tensions between home allegiances and cosmopolitanism, life and art and the significance of literary immortality. The poem claims the status of 'Elegy', yet while memorialising its subject in coolly descriptive terms, it is in many ways a communication with the dead, which never really resolves its central enigma:

> [...] You, dying so lonely
> Where that foreign river flows
> To its foreign sea [....] (114)

A contrast is set up between the appeal of native Englishness and a felt dedication to an immortalising art which transcends nationality. Yet the poem brings the two together in a way that suggests a single, significant flaw – a lack of commitment to living itself. Rejection of Englishness here is made to appear almost as a negation of life-force in favour of the 'Parnassian' cultivation of pure style – 'contriving your mayflies in amber', as Ford put it in a phrase to be appropriated by Pound.[27] The actual persona of the 'Great Poet' is shadowy, vaguely evoked rather than characterised. Where exactly did he die? What kind of man was he really? Why does his death not strike 'the ear/With any insistence' and yet his 'death made us think about our ends? Who quite are 'we'? The poet is presented as an enigma, and perhaps as an *alter ego*, or even a projection of who the narrator might become. If we equate the narrator with Ford himself (surely a natural reaction), then the poem appears as a rehearsal for Ford's own choice of exile – with the lighter, more parodic *Mister Bosphorus and the Muses* as a bizarre companion-piece.[28]

Yet 'Immortality' seems to make Ford's ultimate decision unlikely. It sets up an opposition between some (lettered?) 'us' and the *unheimlich* option of exiled aestheticism, the former given an aura of 'John Bull' robustness:

> [...] As for us,
> We crave to be remembered, warm, in the flesh;
> If only as those who beat their wives and soaked
> Night-long in taverns; whom the crowing cocks
> Hear staggering homewards; bulbous, veined-nosed,
> Cut-pursey Falstaffs [...]
>
> ... And I have sometimes thought
> That if we, being years-long buried, caused to arise
> In living minds, shapes of our shoulders, say,
> Since once we had great rolling shoulder-blades
> And found some Boswell [....] (113)

The coupling of Falstaff and Dr Johnson sets up English 'normality' against effete, foreign *l'art pour l'art*. The 'dual life' of Ford seems to favour here Lawrentian 'felt life' against Jamesian style, the Englishness of English writing against a global 'imaginary museum'. But the poet has chosen immortality in the latter terms, and may even achieve it, although there is some ambiguity about the worth of his work – 'exquisite words' yet 'unstirred prose/And unstirred verses'. This is an uneasy poem, full of nervy questioning ('why *couldn't* you?') and self-questioning, of reveries and associational vagaries:

> [...] such dyes and such tinctures of gold
> That, incarnadined,
> Not the most disintegrating autumn wind
> [. . .]
> Should have rendered them tenuous [...] (112)

It is difficult, at times, to know simply what the words are saying, and one can see why the poem was not published in any of Ford's Collections. Nevertheless, the poem shows an important tension in Ford's thinking about Englishness and the wider community of culture – and awareness that, for some at least, there is a world elsewhere.

The theme of Englishness has undergone a profound metamorphosis in Ford's poetry from late-Victorian communal traditionalism to personal, pioneering experimentation in the midst of world war and in the war's aftermath. Yet even the war-verse, and the poems written after the war, despite a radical modification in content and form, seeks to preserve, *in extremis*, the essence of a national myth based ultimately on the specificities of *habitus*. In his somewhat valedictory book *England*, Roger Scruton rightly emphasises the importance of place-myth to native awareness at the *fin de siècle* of the twentieth century.[29] Ford's poetry, in this sense, retains an important relevance beyond radical social changes and continuing political struggles. Even in a quite fully multicultural world, *habitus* remains a common reference-point and denominator in a heterogeneous communal experience.

Ford's later poem 'A House' (1921) grounds this denominator in an image which combines natural environment and cultural dwelling. The poem is situated specifically in 'the Sussex Wold' and is diagrammatically basic: 'I resemble/The drawing of a child'. Ford's technique is allegorical, giving choric voice to constituent parts – The House, The Tree, The Dog of the House and so on. It is a basic container of Englishness: likened to a ship and threatened by sea and flood alike – an all-purpose, mothering body. In defiance of the 'othering' theory of nationality,[30] the 'Epilogue' makes the house globally representative – 'all nations'. Native identity is a feature of sheer survival anywhere, and this English house embodies that simple truth: its function is to endure, as it can, and help protect the human species in its passage through time:

> All, all the houses standing beneath the sky
> Shall have very much the same fate as I!
> They shall see the pressing of generations [...]
> And so pass into the hands –
> Houses and lands into the hands
> Of new generations. (138)

The house represents Ford's unpretentious notion of Englishness at its core.

   The pressing of generations becomes speeded up in the condition of late modernity, and Ford's poetry registers much of this process from a national point of view. In particular, the impact of increasing urbanisation and the industrialisation of war rendered largely obsolete a rural myth of 'the old places' and 'waving plough-lands and willowy closes'. At the least, such images must now co-exist with the spreading presence of 'paper-shops and full 'bus tops', with an almost postmodern 'starling in the mews'. The 'soul of London' was, as it were, transmigrating, to invade even small towns and villages. And hard on the heels of such shock of the new comes the even greater, more abrupt and exceptional war-time emergency – 'It isn't just a Tube ride, going to France!' Paradoxically, the Great War both confirmed Ford's sense of a new England of 'endless muddles; endless follies; endless villainies', as he put it in *Parade's End*, and fanned his sense of national identity to white heat:

> Like a tornado [...] that shakes
> The whole being and soul...
> Aye, the whole of the soul. (98)

Such feelings helped induce the lyrical vignettes of English landscape – tellingly evoked through the window of a train speeding its way towards London and the battle-line, and also found expression in the rather manic 'Entertainments' of death's men:[31]

> [...] the song and dance
> Of Battalion concerts, in the shafts of light
> From smoky lamps [...]

> faces lit up
> By inarticulate minds at sugary chords
> From the vamping pianist beneath the bunting:
> 'Until the boys come home!' we sing. (93)

Yet such a sense of social inclusion was scarcely likely to continue after the war itself. As a commentator on social matters, Ford had had his say in prose – whether in book form or in editorial essays for the *English Review* – and would do again, especially in *Parade's End*; yet as post-war poet Ford was increasingly out on a limb – as 'Süssmund's Address' had ironically foreseen. Like his hero

Christopher Tietjens, he was becoming a marginalised spokesman for the 'remnant'[32] – and like later Lawrence, Robert Graves or the Pound of the Hell Cantos, among several others, he eventually chose physical exile – away from the field and fold, flock and stock, hops and copse celebrated earlier in 'A Ballad of an Auction'. The sense of alienation is already embedded in 'Footsloggers':

> But I ask you this:
> About the middle of my first Last Leave,
> I stood on a kerb in the pitch of the night
> Waiting for buses that didn't come
> To take me home.
>   That was Paddington.
> The soot-black night was over one like velvet [...]
> A dim, diaphanous cone of white, the rays
> Of a shaded street lamp, close at hand, existed,
> And then there was nothing but vileness it could show,
> Vile, pallid faces drifted through, chalk white [....] (91-2)

The metropolis has become the city of dreadful night, anticipating the broken images of *The Waste Land*. Englishness ends up in crisis – a desecrated container – and Ford becomes the prophet-abroad – like the 'Great Poet'. Yet his work set a precedent, and remains important in an England of post-Imperial retrenchment, a small island culturally situated somewhere between Europe and North America. Important prose writers such as Peter Ackroyd and Iain Sinclair still extend and expand the spirit of Ford's London-infatuation and the 'condition of England' has remained a live issue in the verse of such post-Larkin poets as Geoffrey Hill, Tony Harrison, John Mole, Peter Reading, Carol Ann Duffy or Glyn Maxwell. The issue which exercised Ford between 1893 and 1921 remains on the current cultural agenda: 'what is love of one's land?'

NOTES

1   Notoriously, Larkin summed up what he disliked as the alliterative trio Picasso, Pound and Charlie Parker.
2   Glyn Maxwell, 'Make it cohere: the deep confusion of the avant-garde', *Times Literary Supplement*, 5 July 2002, p. 5.

3   A short sample of this phenomenon might include Bill Bryson, *Notes from a Small Island*, London: Doubleday, 1995, Jeremy Paxman, *The English: A Portrait of a People*, London: Michael Joseph, 1998, Norman Davies, *The Isles: A History*, London: Macmillan, 1999, Simon Heffer, *Nor Shall My Sword: The Reinvention of England*, London: Phoenix/Orion, 2000 and Andrew Marr, *The Day Britain Died*, London: Profile, 2000. However, new books, not to mention essays, chapters and articles, have continued to be produced. The interest of Ford's own generation in the same issue is signalled by the announcement of the first *Dictionary of National Biography* at Christmas 1882. See Stefan Collini, 'Our Island Story', *London Review of Books*, 20 January 2005, p. 3.

4   See most particularly Paul Kennedy, *The Rise and Fall of the Great Powers: Economic Change and Military Conflict from 1500 to 2000*, New York: 1989 and Niall Ferguson, *Colossus: The Rise and Fall of the American Empire*, New York and London: Allen Lane, 2004 – both, interestingly, written by Britons working in the United States.

5   Quoted by George Walter in 'Loose Women and Lonely Lambs: The Rise and Fall of Georgian Poetry', *British Poetry 1900-50: Aspects of Tradition*, eds. Gary Day and Brian Docherty, Basingstoke: Macmillan, 1995, p. 21.

6   Unless otherwise stated, all quotations from Ford's poems will be referenced to *Ford Madox Ford. Selected Poems*, ed. Max Saunders, Manchester: Carcanet, 1997; here from 'A Pagan', p. 13. Ford quite frequently uses rows of dots in his poetry. Where such are placed in square brackets they indicate my own usage.

7   I have discussed this term in *John Betjeman*, Plymouth: Northcote House, 1999, pp. 40 and 67. It is used to describe the preoccupations of the New Social Geographers of the 1990s – e.g. Rob Shields writes: 'The meaning of particular places is a compendium of intersubjective and cultural interpretations over time', *Places on the Margin: Alternative Geographies of Modernity*, London: Routledge, 1991, p. 25; and Derek Gregory asserts: 'concepts of place, space and landscape have become central to some of the most exciting developments across the whole field of humanities and social sciences', *Maps of Meaning: An Introduction to Cultural Geography*, ed. Peter Jackson, London: Routledge, 1992, p. ix. Of course, Ford *lived* in the landscapes which he mythologises. This undoubtedly provided much of their emotional resonance.

8   See Benedict Anderson, *Imagined Communities*, London: Verso, 1991.

9   See Harold Bloom, *The Anxiety of Influence: A Theory of Poetry*, New York: Oxford University Press, 1973.

10 Maureen Duffy comments: 'I can't think of another state that has so many recognized versions of its name, in itself an indication of a confused identity.... Recent moves towards devolution and the terror of absorption into a federal European state have only highlighted our insecurity and increased our dependence on the myth of olde England'. *England: The Making of the Myth from Stonehenge to Albert Square*, London: Fourth Estate, 2002, p. 2. For Britishness, see Linda Colley, *Britons: Forging the Nation 1707-1837*, London: Vintage, 1996.

11 I am thinking particularly of the discussion in Walter J. Ong, *Orality and Literacy: The Technologizing of the Word*, London: Methuen, 1982.

12 'According to his background a patient will describe various objects as containers, such as his mind, the unconscious, the nation; others as contained, such as his money, his ideas', Wilfred Bion, *Attention and Interpretation*, New

York: Jason Aranson, 1983, p. 122. Bion's work was especially important for the concept. It is similar in psychoanalytic discourse to 'holding': 'Briefly "holding" is a concept used by [D. W.] Winnicott ... to describe the need of the mother to take care of the infant in a devoted manner at least at first, when the infant is utterly dependent and resourceless. [W. R.] Bion ... developed the concept of "containing" in respect of a hypothesis of a mental process, in which elements of primitive psychic experience which cannot be understood by the infant, are fantasised as being projected into the mother. She, by dint of her maturity, is able to bring her understanding to these experiences and being attentive to her infant, facilitates the beginnings of understanding of these experiences in her infant'. D. Colin James, 'The borderline patient...' in *The Practice of Group Analysis*, eds. Jeff Roberts and Malcolm Pines, London: Tavistock/Routledge, 1991, p. 102. Michael Rustin, as will be shown, extends the concept to the cultural sphere.

13 Michael Rustin, *The Good Society and the Inner World,* London: Verso, 1991, pp. 196-7. He continues: 'An educational conclusion which can be drawn from the relevance of psychoanalysis is that it is necessary to create learning settings which give space to the experience of feeling as a primary element of understanding'. In this sense, Ford's early poetry may operate as a means of acculturation into the emotional complex of feeling English.

14 'The internalization in phantasy of the parent-figures will give prominence to their capacity to be satisfactory or unsatisfactory containers, of which mother's body is a powerful and basic image, and a house is a common symbolic transformation in play.' Rustin, *Ibid*, p. 190.

15 See Antony Easthope, *Poetry and Phantasy,* Cambridge: Cambridge University Press, 1989, pp. 40-6. In his book on Englishness Peter Ackroyd states that: 'The idea of a close-knit community (generally withstanding the depradations of a cold and hostile natural world) is central to the English imagination', and he likens it to 'the Anglo-Saxon image of the lighted hall'. See his *Albion: The Origins of the English Imagination,* London: Vintage, 2002, p. 149. This fits 'Midwinter Night' perfectly.

16 A term utilised by Pierre Bourdieu in *Outline of a Theory of Practice*, tr. R. Nice, Cambridge, Mass.: MIT, 1977. *Habitus* is suggestive in English because it suggests both habitation and habit. The Latin root is ultimately from *habeo* which Lewis and Short's *Latin Dictionary* gives as: '*to have*, in the widest sense of the word, *to hold, keep, possess, cherish, entertain, occupy, enclose, contain*'. Such 'possession' is necessarily an ideal. The reality of Englishness is like the Constitution of England which 'is in constant change'. See Walter Bagehot, *The English Constitution*, introduced by R. H. S. Crossman, London: Collins/Fontana, 1971, from the 'Introduction to the Second Edition', 1872, p. 267.

17 Paul Fussell writes interestingly on this place-myth especially with regard to writers who left England in disgust after the Great War – Robert Graves, D. H. Lawrence and Ezra Pound among many others. Ford also exiled himself to France and later the United States. See Paul Fussell, *Abroad: British Literary Travelling between the Wars,* Oxford University Press, 1982.

18 In Kleinian psychoanalysis the nurturative breast is the original 'container', standing for the maternal body. However, the breast may be refused (or disappoint) and there is a 'splitting' between good breast and bad breast which constitutes the basis of future mental polarisations. For a useful guide to the issues

see Hanna Segal, *Klein*, Glasgow: Fontana/Collins, 1979; see also Melanie Klein, *Envy and Gratitude and other Works*, London: Hogarth Press, 1980.

19 See Richard Holmes, *Tommy: The British Soldier on the Western Front 1914-1918*, London: Harper Collins, 2004, p. 495.

20 In Saunders, *Selected Poems*, it is 'In October 1914'. This was its title on first publication in the *Outlook*, 24 October 1914. However in 1915 (*Blast II*) it appeared as 'Antwerp', which seems the more evocative title – despite some of it, as Max Saunders reminded me, being about Charing Cross.

21 The 'Blackadder' joke commented on by Holmes, *Tommy*, p. xviii.

22 See Niall Ferguson, *The Pity of War*, London: Penguin, 1998, p. 223. See also John Chapple, *Documentary and Imaginative Literature 1880-1920*, London: Blandford, 1970, pp. 83-4.

23 Andrzej Gasiorek comments on Ford's collage-technique in *The Soul of London* (see Chapter 4). In the case of 'Footsloggers' it is difficult to know how much conscious control Ford is exercising; James Joyce's last chapter of *Ulysses* ('Penelope') demonstrates how what appears as wild associationism may be a matter of highly controlled technique.

24 I have previously argued for Jones's exceptionality and comparative balance within Great War writing because of his fidelity to serving-men's sense of historical pride and devotion to Blighty. See Dennis Brown, *The Modernist Self in Twentieth-Century English Literature: A Study in Self-Fragmentation*, London: Macmillan, 1989, pp. 66-73.

25 Cf '... men he and Sergeant-Major Cowley had looked after with a great deal of tenderness, superintending their morale, their morals, their feet, their digestions, their impatiences, their desires for women ...', Ford Madox Ford, *Parade's End*, London: Penguin, 1988, p. 296.

26 See Geoffrey Hill, *Collected Poems*, Harmondsworth: Penguin, 1985, p. 188 ff.

27 '*As roses might, in magic amber laid*', Ezra Pound, 'Envoi' (1919) from 'Hugh Selwyn Mauberley (Contacts and Life)' (1920), *Selected Poems*, London: Faber and Faber, 1977, p. 106. As with 'Süssmund's Address', there seems a close thematic unity between 'Immortality' and Pound's much-praised poetic sequence of 1920.

28 Max Saunders has suggested to me that 'Immortality' and 'Mister Bosphorus' represent 'two versions of Ford's farewell to England, played first as tragedy then as farce'. This is surely the case. I have omitted comment on 'Mister Bosphorus And The Muses' here because it is a quasi-dramatic fantasia, very different from the poetry discussed here, and was excluded from Ford's *Collected Poems*, New York: Oxford University Press, 1936. For an appreciation of the poem, see Robert E. McDonough, '*Mister Bosphorus and the Muses*: History and Representation in Ford's Modern Poem', in *History and Representation in Ford Madox Ford's Writings*, ed. Joseph Wiesenfarth, Amsterdam – New York : Rodopi, 2004, pp. 155-162.

29 Roger Scruton, *England: an Elegy*, London: Pimlico, 2001, pp. 7 and 41 especially. Cf. 'English writers and artists, English composers and folk-singers, have been haunted by this sense of place, in which the echoic simplicities of past use and past tradition sanctify a certain spot of ground.' Peter Ackroyd, *Albion*, p 449. The short 'Epilogue' from which this is taken commences with a reference to Ford.

30 For instance, Linda Colley's *Britons*, where the making of British identity is seen
    in relation to France as the 'Other'. Such contrasts may make sense in certain
    historical instances, but a definition by negation is weak, and raises the question
    'How many Others?' Ford's poetry, I am arguing, builds up Englishness in terms
    of positive, local qualities.
31 In *The Soul of London* Ford also uses the technique of the revelatory train-
    window.
32 See Philip Davis's contribution, chapter 1.

CONTRIBUTORS

Christine Berberich is Lecturer in English and European Literature at the University of Derby. She has published articles on Orwell, Waugh, Anthony Powell and Siegfried Sassoon, and has a book under review entitled *Regression and Reaction: Englishness, Nostalgia and the Image of the English Gentleman in the Twentieth Century*. She has research interests in Englishness, masculinity, class, trauma theories and Great War writing and is currently working on two new book projects concerned with Englishness.

Dennis Brown is Emeritus Professor at the University of Hertfordshire. He is the author of *The Modernist Self* (Macmillan, 1989), *Intertextual Dynamics... Joyce, Lewis, Pound and Eliot* (Macmillan, 1990), *The Poetry of Postmodernity* (Macmillan, 1994) and *John Betjeman* (Northcote House, 1999). He is currently working on the interface between literature and psychotherapy.

Philip Davis is a Professor in English at the University of Liverpool. His publications include *The Victorians* in the new Oxford English Literary History Series (2002). His forthcoming books are *Shakespeare Thinking* (Continuum) and the first biography of the novelist Bernard Malamud (Oxford University Press).

Peter Easingwood retired from the post of Lecturer in English at the University of Dundee in 2005. He has a particular interest in twentieth-century English writers who, like Ford, form transatlantic connections, including John Cowper Powys, Wyndham Lewis, Malcolm Lowry and Anthony Burgess.

Andrzej Gasiorek has research interests in modernism, literature and politics, and is Reader in Twentieth Century Literature at Birmingham University. His recent publications include *Wyndham Lewis and Modernism* (2004) and he is co-editing *T. E. Hulme and the Question of Modernism* with Edward Comentale.

Jason Harding is a Senior Lecturer at Åbo Akademi University, Finland. He is the author of *The Criterion: Cultural Politics and Periodical Networks in Interwar Britain* (OUP, 2002) and has published articles in a wide variety of periodicals including the *TLS, LRB, Modernism/Modernity* and the *Cambridge Quarterly*. Most recently, he has contributed the concluding chapter to a forthcoming *Cambridge Companion to Modernist Poetry*.

Sara Haslam is Lecturer in Literature at the Open University, England. She is the author of *Fragmenting Modernism: Ford Madox Ford, the Novel and the Great War* (Manchester University Press, 2002), and editor of Ford's *England and the English* (Carcanet Press, 2003), as well as *Ford Madox Ford and the City*, the fourth volume of International Ford Madox Ford Studies (2005). She has published articles on Ford, Henry James, and modernism, most recently 'The Good Soldier' in the *Blackwell Companion to Modernist Literature and Culture* (2006). Current projects include a book, *Victims of Time and Train: from Victorian invention to Modernist novel*. With pedagogy another of her interests, she has produced an interactive CD-ROM on the poetry of Thomas Hardy.

Nick Hubble, a Research Fellow at the Centre for Suburban Studies, Kingston University, has recently published the book *Mass-Observation and Everyday Life: Culture, History, Theory*. It provides a historical and critical exposition of the Mass Observation research organisation founded in 1937. He has also published articles on a number of writers, including Pat Barker, B. S. Johnson, George Orwell and Christopher Priest.

Anurag Jain is a Ph.D. research student at Queen Mary, University of London. His research project is 'When Art put on Khaki and went into Action': World War I British Propaganda and the Arts.

Karen McDermott acts as an administrator for the Community Team at Hertfordshire County Council. She wrote her MA dissertation on *The Fifth Queen* and is currently considering enrolment for a Ph.D. on Ford and Englishness. She is also very interested in writing a screenplay for *The Fifth Queen*.

Robert E. McDonough is the former Professor of English at Cuyahoga Community College, Cleveland, Ohio. His publications include '*New York Is Not America*, But Then What Is?' in International Ford Madox Ford Studies, vol. 4; '*Mister Bosphorus and the Muses*' in International Ford Madox Ford Studies, vol. 3; and '*The Marsden Case* for the Canon' in *Ford Madox Ford and 'The Republic of Letters'*, ed. Vita Fortunati and Elena Lamberti (Bologna: CLUEB, 2002). He lists his research interest as Ford Madox Ford, especially his poetry and his place in Modernist poetics.

Christopher MacGowan is Chair of Department and Professor of English at the College of William and Mary. He has edited the poetry of William Carlos Williams (New Directions) and the correspondence of Williams and Denise Levertov. He has also published on Williams, Levertov, Sherwood Anderson and Nabokov. His most recent book is *Twentieth Century American Poetry* (Blackwell, 2004).

Donald MacKenzie is a Lecturer in English Literature at the University of Glasgow. He is the author of *The Metaphysical Poets* (Macmillan, 1990) and has edited Kipling's *Puck of Pooks Hill* and *Rewards and Fairies* (Oxford World's Classics, 1993) and co-edited (with Andrew Hook) Scott's *Fair Maid of Perth* for the Edinburgh edition of the Waverley Novels (1990). His current research interests include myths of England (especially in the Edwardian era), romance as a genre and literature and theology.

John Mole is a poet, critic and jazz clarinetist. His most recent poetry collection is *Counting the Chimes: New and Selected Poems 1975-2003* (Peterloo Poets, 2004). He has recently recorded for the Poetry Archive (www.poetryarchive.org).

Ralph Parfect is Programme Manager for the MA 'Cultural and Creative Industries' at King's College London. He has published on Robert Louis Stevenson's unfinished fables, 'The Clockmaker' and 'The Scientific Ape' in *English Literature in Transition*.

Jenny Plastow is Senior Lecturer in Education at the University of Hertfordshire, specialising in Short Courses and Consultancy. She has long experience in education, drama and management. Her Ph.D. was on Ford Madox Ford and Masculinity – conferred in 2000. She has also published various articles, including 'The Feminine at the Front', in *Ford Madox Ford and 'The Republic of Letters'*, ed. Vita Fortunati and Elena Lamberti (Bologna: CLUEB, 2002), and stories; and has written broadcast programmes.

Jörg W. Rademacher currently teaches English, French, History and Italian at two Gymnasia in East Frisia. He is the author of biographies of Oscar Wilde, Victor Hugo and James Joyce. He has also translated biographies of Michael Collins and Hitler, and works by Hugo, Wilde, Franz Hüffer and Ford himself. Most recently, he is the author of a collection of 88 short biographies (including those of Hüffer, Ford and Violet Hunt), entitled *Gelehrtes Münster und Rundum*. He is working on people and places – including Paris and Rome.

Austin Riede is a Ph.D. student in English Literature at the University of Illinois (Urbana – Champaign). He specialises in English Modernism. Areas of his interest include avant-garde arts and literature, postcolonial and film studies and Marxist theory.

Max Saunders is Professor of English at King's College London, where he teaches modern English, European, and American literature. He is the author of *Ford Madox Ford: A Dual Life*, 2 vols (Oxford University Press, 1996), the editor of Ford's *Selected Poems, War Prose*, and (with Richard Stang) *Critical Essays* (Carcanet, 1997, 1999, 2002), and has published essays on Ford, Eliot, Joyce, Rosamond Lehmann, Richard Aldington, May Sinclair, Lawrence, Freud, Pound, Ruskin, and others. He is chairman of the Ford Madox Ford Society.

ABSTRACTS

CHRISTINE BERBERICH 'A Modernist Elegy to the Gentleman? Englishness and the Idea of the Gentleman in Ford's *The Good Soldier*'

Edward Ashburnham was 'very well built, carried himself well, was moderate at the table and led a regular life . . . he had, in fact, all the virtues that are usually accounted English. . . . They were the things that one would set upon his tombstone. They will, indeed, be set upon his tombstone by his widow'. These are the words that, in the opinion of *The Good Soldier*'s narrator Dowell, admirably describe the object of the title, Edward Ashburnham, the good soldier, good sport and quintessential English gentleman. Ford Madox Ford was fascinated with the theme of the 'gentleman' and his decline. His tetralogy *Parade's End* can be seen as a memorial to the 'last Tory gentleman'. This chapter will examine aspects of Englishness in Ford's novel *The Good Soldier*, in particular through the medium of the English gentleman. It will look at the novel from cultural, historical and sociological perspectives and attempt to link it to literary trends of the time: is *The Good Soldier* a forward-looking modernist manifesto, doing away with the cobwebs or a Victorian past? Or is it rather an example of nostalgic harking back to better times? Or is it, in fact, a combination of the two: a modernist elegy?

DENNIS BROWN '"But One is English": Ford's Poetry 1893-1921'

This chapter discusses Ford's poetry written before his 'exile' and traces the way in which Englishness is expressed and interrogated within the parameters of his poetic development from late-Victorian traditionalism into early twentieth-century experimentalism. A particular focus is on the way place-myth – constructed out of both natural topography and cultural habitus – is at the core of Ford's poetic contribution, becoming extended to encompass the realities of a modernising London and tested in the experience of Great War loyalties. 'On Heaven' is given emphasis for its revisionary ambivalence about England and 'Footsloggers' for its important (though marginalised) exploration of patriotism in extremis. Toward the end, the later 'A House' is included to indicate Ford's post-war thoughts from abroad. Overall, Englishness is shown to be idealised yet also rendered contentious – 'But one is English'.

PHILIP DAVIS 'The Saving Remnant'

This essay juxtaposes three motifs as a way of contextualising Ford's ambivalences about Englishness. First, the 'saving remnant' – the dissident few for whose sake Abraham argues against God's destruction of Sodom and Gomorrah. Second, the disguised leader: the example here is Harry disguising himself as one of his subjects before battle in *Henry V*. Third, the figure of the sacrificial scapegoat, exemplified by Sidney Carton's death in Dickens' *A Tale of Two Cities*. These motifs all share a sense of looking back to values that have been neglected, and forwards to a hope that they can be renewed. They are all disguises to rescue a future for the present by means of a suddenly transformed past. Their sense of prophetic isolation, it is argued, are found in Lawrence's Birkin in *Women in Love*; and especially in Ford's creation of the anachronistic figure of Christopher Tietjens in *Parade's End*.

PETER EASINGWOOD '"What I am Always wanting to Say": Ford Madox Ford and the English "Literary Myth"'

The chapter examines several texts by Ford, all of them published within or dealing with the period before 1914. The chosen texts share a novelistic commitment: this consists in a mode of discourse which has elements of a story though the story is not plot-driven as in a novel. Impressions are gathered in a form of notation that allows the narrator to reflect on his approach to the subject and on his own procedure. *The Heart of the Country* and *The Soul of London* explore changes affecting contemporary England and the English and show how such changes bring into question issues of literary representation. *Ancient Lights* and *Return to Yesterday* offer two different versions of the author's experiences as a young man. Each of these texts describes an encounter with an England bound by accepted ideas. Under such conditions, literature can only function as 'literary myth': literary expression is dominated by outworn conventions of style and form.

Ford nevertheless sustains a special insight into the possibility of self-renewal for writers and writing.

ANDRZEJ GASIOREK 'Ford Among the Aliens'

Several related Fordian concerns are explored in this chapter: the difficulty of coming to terms with a London that is a place of personal impressions and knowledges; the contrast between classes; the city's assimilative nature, its capacity to embrace all sorts and kinds of people, whom it remakes as modern cosmopolitan subjects; the ambivalence with which Ford responds to this assimilative process, which eradicates cultural differences and promote a standardisation of the self; the fear of metropolitan anonymity, which may act as cover for the violent criminal or political revolutionary. It asks, finally, what are the implications of all this for Ford's conception of national identity at the turn of the century? The chapter is divided into four sections. The first concentrates on the political context in which Ford was writing, especially with regard to debates about immigration. The second explores a tension in *The Soul of London* between two opposed views of modernity, one stressing its cosmopolitanism, the other emphasising its determinism; it looks at Ford's account of assimilation, in comparison with Conrad's *The Secret Agent*, focusing in particular on the shared trope of cannibalism. The third part challenges David Trotter's *Paranoid Modernism*, which suggests that Ford's antipathy to system may be dated from after the First World War. Finally, Ford's tolerant and humane cultural anarchism is related to his practice of literary collage.

JASON HARDING 'The Englishness of *The English Review'*

This essay explores Ford's cultural construction of 'Englishness' during his editorship of the *English Review*. It examines E. V. Lucas's complaint that the magazine was 'too foreign for its title' in relation to the fraught and sometimes acrimonious collaboration between Ford and Conrad. It will be argued that these difficulties hinged upon finding the 'right accent' in which to address a stolid, English periodical readership. The advanced opinions expressed in Ford's editorials were a provocation to the perceived provincialism and philistinism of a section of his intended audience. These tensions are also viewed in relation to Wells's 'condition of England' novel, *Tono-*

Bungay, and help to explain why, in spite of its undoubted literary merit, Ford eventually lost control of the *English Review*.

SARA HASLAM 'England and Englishness: Ford's First Trilogy'

The chapter provides a discussion of Ford's trilogy *The Soul of London* (1905), *The Heart of the Country* (1906) and *The Spirit of the People* (1907) – published together as *England and the English* in America in 1907. These are significant texts for a variety of reasons. *The Soul of London* provided Ford with his first taste of publishing success. Sections in the chapter focus on the contemporary context, and then the modern context, both with particular reference to ideas about Englishness; further sections are concerned with the biographical background and publication history of the books, and with their technique. Each of these quite different, though linked, volumes is then briefly assessed in terms of its subject matter, prominent tone and/or imagery, and contribution to the debate on Englishness.

NICK HUBBLE 'Beyond Mimetic Englishness: Ford's English Trilogy and *The Good Soldier*'

Displaying sociological insight comparable to that of Georg Simmel and Jürgen Habermas, Ford developed an account of the emergence of a universal social sphere in which everyday experience was broadly shared across classes and showed how this enabled the mass expression of romantic individualism as clerks and office workers spent their weekends emulating the 'Leisured Class'. Ford's desire was not to oppose this 'social mimesis', as David Trotter argues in *Paranoid Modernism*, but to go beyond it as can be seen from a reading of *The Good Soldier*. Dowell's confession that he loved Ashburnham 'because he was just myself' does not signal modernity's collapse into passive imitation, as Peter Nicholls argues in *Modernisms*, but comes as the culmination of a narrative process of remembering, repeating and working-through that enables the imitative fantasy to be acted out as a piece of real life. By showing how the otherwise unexceptional Ashburnham is cast by Dowell's story as a courageous, virile figure, Ford lays bare the narrative trick by which the agency of this textual 'Ashburnham' both derives from and leads to Dowell's own agency and identity as modernist narrator.

ANURAG JAIN 'When Propaganda Is Your Argument: Ford and First World War Propaganda'

This essay discusses Ford's *When Blood is their Argument* and *Between St. Dennis and St. George*, two texts he wrote for the War Propaganda Bureau during the First World War. It situates these texts of propaganda within the larger system of British propaganda and examines how the arguments he makes in these books help to comprise the fight on the cultural front for British war propaganda.

KAREN MCDERMOTT 'The Impressionistic 'Rendering' of Englishness in Ford's *Fifth Queen* Trilogy'

This chapter looks at the ways in which Ford uses the literary 'Impressionism' he had theorised with Joseph Conrad, and in relation to other writers, to construct his *Fifth Queen* trilogy as a fiction of Tudor Englishness. It considers his ideas about fictionality in relation to the 'impressions' of historical evidence and emphasises his almost 'counter-factual' modifications of historical 'facts' in terms of an emergent 'nationalist' mythologisation. Ford's overarching *progression d'effet* is effectively demonstrated, along with his diverse deployments of aesthetic 'techniques' to achieve this. It is argued, then, that the major theme of the *Fifth Queen* trilogy is the nature of a 'modern' Englishness and that 'Impressionism' is the means by which Ford develops it.

ROBERT E. MCDONOUGH 'Escape from Englishness: *The Rash Act* and *Henry For Hugh*'

In *The Rash Act* (1933) and *Henry for Hugh* (1934) Ford Madox Ford examines Englishness (and Americanness) by a comparison of two cousins, distant but almost identical in appearance, and by narrating the experience of the American Henry Martin Aluin Smith while he is taken for the English Hugh Monckton Allard Smith. Henry Martin finds that for him Englishness requires passivity; he spends much of his time as Hugh Monckton supine, abstinent as regards women and alcohol, and almost mute. His experience does not change the hatred of the English he feels required of him as an American, but it does help him become more successful when he resumes his American identity, a successful writer and man of business rather than the impoverished failed investor and cheated writer he had been.

CHRISTOPHER MACGOWAN 'History, Identity and Nationality in Ford's *Great Trade Route*'

Ford Madox Ford's *Great Trade Route* (1937) is a travel book with deep connections to his own sense of physical exile and isolation as a writer. Its account of traveling from France to the United States via an England glimpsed only as a coastline is told through recurring references to Malory's version of Lancelot's exile in France and what was lost by the destruction of Arthur's England. Ford's account of his journey is a self-conscious attempt to unite, through his extension of the Great Trade Route to the New World, his own past, present and possible future with a continuity between France, the England of Arthur, and – particularly – Virginia. But the book finally acknowledges the historical failure of the New World to take up and restore the heritage lost through Lancelot's exile, a failure mirrored in the writer's own return to exile and to an isolation necessary to retain his continuing integrity, and such circumscribed possibilities for his own work as remain to him.

DONALD MACKENZIE 'A Road not Taken: Romance, History and Myth In Ford's *Fifth Queen* Novels'

This chapter places Ford's *Fifth Queen* trilogy in a context of historical romance and historical myth. The kind of romance is that pioneered by Scott in *Kenilworth*. The myth is that of the sixteenth century English Reformation as a Fall from a pristine medieval Catholic society. *Kenilworth* is cited as paradigm not source; but the first section argues that *The Fifth Queen* orchestrates and refines the key features of the kind of historical romance *Kenilworth* initiates: a labyrinthine world of court intrigue; the centring of major historical figures; and a lavish use of historical décor. The second section sketches a brief taxonomy of historical myth, with Reformation and other examples. The final section argues that Ford evokes and rejects – hence the title – the Catholic myth, and that in so doing he both deploys certain generic resources of romance and prepares the way for his major works of the next two decades.

RALPH PARFECT 'Romances of Nationhood: Ford and the Adventure Story Tradition'

This essay analyses ideas of Englishness in Ford's romance novels. Locating these works within a tradition of romance writing in English, the paper focuses first on Ford's collaboration with Joseph Conrad on *Romance* (1903), with its distinct yet distorted echoes of Captain Marryat and Robert Louis Stevenson. The novel of action and adventure, it is argued, enabled Ford and Conrad to present characters with qualities associated in both writers' work with Englishness: courage, self-reliance, pragmatism, loyalty, fairness, and a resistance to systematic critical thought. Yet between the noble English hero John Kemp and characters of Spanish, Irish, and middle- and working-class English descent there are affinities as well as differences, and discourses of racial superiority, which are here understood within the context of imperial ideology, are thus contested and relativised. The essay also considers how another, very different, appropriation of the romance tradition by Ford, the *Fifth Queen* trilogy (1906-08), not only regenders the English adventure hero by taking for its protagonist a feisty Katharine Howard, but also reconceives Englishness by making of the Machiavellian Thomas Cromwell a paradoxically alien English villain.

JENNY PLASTOW 'Englishness and Work'

Throughout his life Ford Madox Ford regarded work as a specific against despair. This chapter considers the influence on him of Thomas Carlyle and his doctrine of work, through the agency of Ford's two revered father-figures, Ford Madox Brown, a prodigious worker, and William Morris, famous for his energy and versatility. Ford's own interest in work, and his view of the effect of work on the individual, is considered through readings of his earlier writing.

JÖRG W. RADEMACHER 'Ford Madox Ford's Englishness as Translated into German in *Some Do Not . . .* and *No More Parades*'

The Englishness shown by Christopher Tietjens resembles a mental image presented by Ford in his non-fictional *England and the English* trilogy. Just as he reconstructs German civilisation in his post-war fiction, today's translator redefines an historical state of Englishness in German. Using the opening and ending of *Some Do Not* . . . (1924) and *No More Parades* (1925), this chapter discusses the German texts and makes suggestions about how to annotate them for newcomers to Ford. English and German, languages of Germanic origin, transfused with Latin syntax and Romance vocabulary, are parallel worlds. Whoever wishes to create similar effects in his translation needs to follow the run of Ford's syntax, which means that neither *Parade's End* nor Ford's œuvre can be considered from an isolated point of view but require an overall and international perspective.

AUSTIN RIEDE 'The Decline of English Discourse and the American Invasion in *The Good Soldier* and *Parade's End*'

Ford's two most canonized works reflect the political and cultural tensions between the entrenched ideologies of England and the emerging imperial inclinations of the US in the early decades of the twentieth century. The respective protagonists of these novels, Edward Ashburnham and Christopher Tietjens, are quintessential taciturn Tories with feudalist views, set adrift in the decadence of the twentieth century. Both pay dearly for their lack of ability, or volition, to compromise their anachronistic values, and both leave the sites of their power, their estates, open to occupation by loquacious Americans. These symbolic displacements demonstrate that, for Ford, relations between England and its commonwealth and ex-colonies were defined by differing patterns of discourse, and that the English values of 'playing the game' (i.e., conforming rigidly) and not 'talking about things' had been over-extended in the pursuit of empire, and were threatened by the emergence of the US as a possible economic threat and imperial competitor.

ABBREVIATIONS

The following abbreviations have been used for works cited several times, whether in the text or in the notes. The list is divided into two alphabetical sections: works by Ford and by others. A full list of abbreviations to be used in future volumes can be found on the Ford Society website.

(i) Works by Ford

In most cases publication details given here are of first editions only. Contributors referring to a different edition have specified which one in the first endnote citing it.

AL	*Ancient Lights* (London: Chapman & Hall, 1911)
BSDSG	*Between St. Dennis and St. George: A Sketch of Three Civilisations* (London: Hodder and Stoughton, 1915)
CA	*The Critical Attitude* (London: Duckworth, 1911)
Call	*A Call* (London: Chatto & Windus, 1910)
CW	*Critical Writings of Ford Madox Ford*, ed. Frank MacShane (Lincoln: University of Nebraska Press, 1964)
FMB	*Ford Madox Brown* (London: Longmans, Green, 1896)
FQ	*The Fifth Queen: And How She Came to Court* (London: Alston Rivers, 1906) – first part of *The Fifth Queen* trilogy (London: Penguin, 1999)
FQC	*The Fifth Queen Crowned* (London: Eveleigh Nash, 1908) – third part of *The Fifth Queen* trilogy (London: Penguin, 1999)

GS   *The Good Soldier* (London: John Lane: The Bodley Head, 1915)

GTR   *Great Trade Route* (New York: Oxford University Press, 1937; London: Allen & Unwin, 1937)

HC   *The Heart of the Country* (London: Alston Rivers, 1906) – second part of *England and the English* trilogy (Manchester: Carcanet, 2003), ed. Sara Haslam

HH   *Henry for Hugh* (Philadelphia: J. B. Lippincott, 1934 [published only in the USA])

Holbein   *Hans Holbein* (London: Duckworth, 1905; New York: Dutton, 1905)

JC   *Joseph Conrad* (London: Duckworth, 1924; Boston: Little, Brown, 1924)

LF   *Letters of Ford Madox Ford*, ed. Richard M. Ludwig (Princeton, NJ: Princeton University Press, 1965)

LP   *Last Post* (London: Duckworth, 1928) – fourth part of *Parade's End* Tetralogy

MC   *The Marsden Case* (London: Duckworth, 1923)

MCSU   *A Man Could Stand Up* – (London: Duckworth, 1926) – third part of *Parade's End* Tetralogy

MI   *Memories and Impressions,* ed. Michael Killigrew (Harmondsworth: Penguin, 1979)

NE   *No Enemy* (New York: Macaulay, 1929) [written 1919, published only in USA in Ford's lifetime]; ed. Paul Skinner (Manchester: Carcanet, 2002)

NMP   *No More Parades* (London: Duckworth, 1925) – second part of *Parade's End* Tetralogy

PE	*Parade's End* (Harmondsworth: Penguin Modern Classics, 1982)
PS	*Privy Seal* (London: Alston Rivers, 1907) – second part of *The Fifth Queen* trilogy (London: Penguin, 1999)
RA	*The Rash Act* (New York: Ray Long & Richard R. Smith, 1933; London: Jonathan Cape, 1933)
Romance	*Romance*, with Joseph Conrad (London: Smith Elder, 1903; New York: McClure, Phillips, 1904)
RY	*Return to Yesterday* (London: Victor Gollancz, 1931; also Manchester: Carcanet, 1999)
SDN	*Some Do Not . . .* (London: Duckworth, 1924) – first part of *Parade's End* Tetralogy
SL	*The Soul of London* (London: Alston Rivers, 1905) – first part of *England and the English* trilogy (Manchester: Carcanet, 2003), ed. Sara Haslam
SP	*The Spirit of the People* (London: Alston Rivers, 1907) – third part of *England and the English* trilogy (Manchester: Carcanet, 2003), ed. Sara Haslam
TR	*Thus to Revisit* (London: Chapman & Hall, 1921)
WBTA	*When Blood is Their Argument* (New York & London: Hodder & Stoughton, 1915)

(ii) Ford Novels in Translation

MTN	*Manche tun es nicht – Some Do Not . . .* trans. Joachim Utz (Berlin: Eichborn, 2003)
KPM	*Keine Paraden mehr – No More Parades* trans. Joachim Utz (Berlin: Eichborn, 2004)

(iii) Works by Others

1900 *1900: A Fin-de-Siècle Reader,* eds. Mike Jay, Michael Neve (London: Penguin, 1999)

D Bram Stoker, *Dracula*; ed. Maurice Hindle (Harmondsworth: Penguin, 1993)

History James Anthony Froude, *History of England from the Fall of Wolsey to the Defeat of the Spanish Armada* (London: Longmans, Green and Co., 1910)

PA Jack London, *The People of the Abyss* (1903) (London: Pluto, 1998)

Paranoid Modernism David Trotter, *Paranoid Modernism: Literary Experiment, Psychosis, and the Professionalization of English Society* (Oxford: Oxford University Press, 2001)

Porter *Myths of the English*, ed. Roy Porter (Cambridge: Polity Press, 1992)

SA Joseph Conrad, *The Secret Agent* (Harmondsworth: Penguin, 1975)

Saunders Max Saunders, *Ford Madox Ford: A Dual Life*, Two Volumes (Oxford: Oxford University Press, 1996)

WW H. G. Wells, *The War of the Worlds* (London: J. M. Dent, 1998)

Returning (to) Communities

Theory, Culture and Political Practice of the Communal

Edited by Stefan Herbrechter and
Michael Higgins

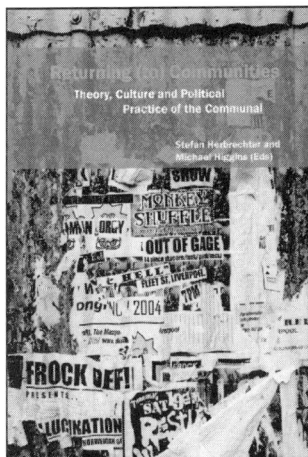

Returning (to) Communities offers an innovative collection of examples and case studies into what has become a hotly disputed topic. The chapters present a wide-ranging series of interventions into the new debates over the concepts and practices of "community" and the communal. For this book, scholars have been gathered from across Europe and Australia as well as from the United States, and several contributors are involved in community practice. *Returning (to) Communities* is essential reading to researchers and students in social policy, sociology, ethnic studies, cultural analysis, media studies, and across all of the social sciences and humanities concerned with the communal and the collective.

Amsterdam/New York, NY,
2006 404 pp.
(Critical Studies 28)
Bound € 82 / US$ 107
ISBN-10: 9042018984
ISBN-13: 9789042018983

USA/Canada:
295 North Michigan Avenue - Suite 1B Kenilworth, NJ 07033,
USA. Call Toll-free (US only): 1-800-225-3998
All other countries:
Tijnmuiden 7, 1046 AK Amsterdam, The Netherlands
Tel. +31-20-611 48 21 Fax +31-20-447 29 79
Please note that the exchange rate is subject to fluctuations

Rodopi

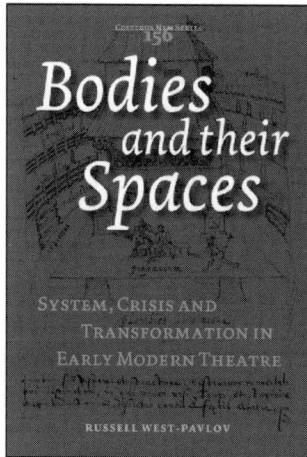

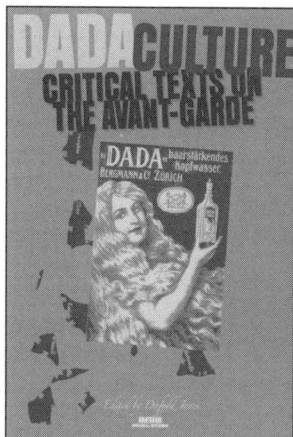

The Invention of Politics in the European Avant-Garde (1906-1940)

Edited by Sacha Bru and
Gunther Martens

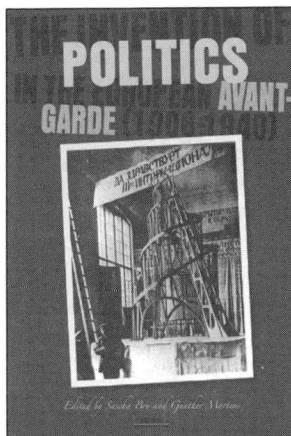

POLITICS
IN THE EUROPEAN
AVANT-
GARDE (1906-1940)

Edited by Sacha Bru and Gunther Martens

In 1906, for the first time in his life, F.T. Marinetti connected the term 'avant-garde' with the idea of the future, thus paving the way for what is now commonly called the 'modernist' or 'historical avant-garde'. Since 1906 the ties between the early twentieth-century European aesthetic vanguard and politics have been a matter of debate. With a century gone by, *The Invention of Politics in the European Avant-Garde* takes stock of this debate. Opening with a critical introduction to the vast research archive on the subject, this book proposes to view the avant-garde as a political force in its own right that may have produced solutions to problems irresolvable within its democratic political constellation. In a series of essays that combine close readings of texts and plastic works with a thorough knowledge of their political context, the book looks at avant-garde works as media producing political thought and experience. Covering the canonised avant-garde movements of Futurism, Expressionism, Dadaism and Surrealism, but also focussing on the avant-garde in Europe's geographical outskirts, this book will appeal to all those interested in the modernist avant-garde.

Amsterdam/New York, NY,
2006 290 pp. (Avant-Garde
Critical Studies 19)
Bound € 60 / US$ 75
ISBN-10: 9042019093
ISBN-13: 9789042019096

USA/Canada:
295 North Michigan Avenue - Suite 1B Kenilworth, NJ 07033,
USA. Call Toll-free (US only): 1-800-225-3998
All other countries:
Tijnmuiden 7, 1046 AK Amsterdam, The Netherlands
Tel. +31-20-611 48 21 Fax +31-20-447 29 79
Please note that the exchange rate is subject to fluctuations

Rodopi

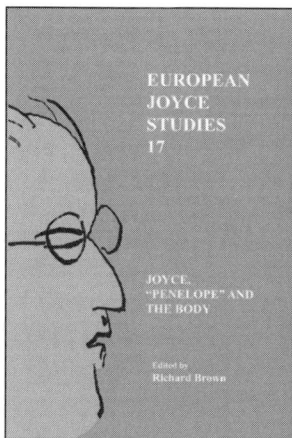

Waiting for Pushkin

Russian Fiction in the Reign of Alexander I (1801-1825)

Alessandra Tosi

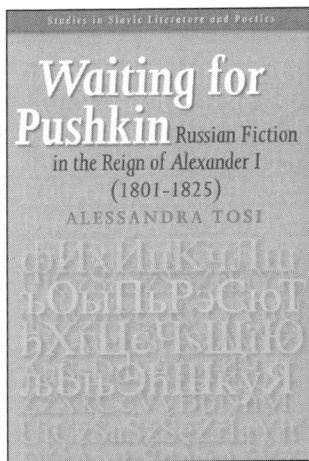

Studies in Slavic Literature and Poetics

Waiting for Pushkin Russian Fiction
in the Reign of Alexander I
(1801-1825)
ALESSANDRA TOSI

Waiting for Pushkin provides the only modern history of Russian fiction in the early nineteenth century to appear in over thirty years.

Prose fiction has a more prominent position in the literature of Russia than in that of any other great country. Although nineteenth-century fiction in particular occupies a privileged place in Russian and world literature alike, the early stages of this development have so far been overlooked.

By combining a broad historical survey with close textual analysis the book provides a unique overview of a key phase in Russian literary history. Drawing on a wide range of sources, including rare editions and literary journals, Alessandra Tosi reconstructs the literary activities occurring at the time, introduces neglected but fascinating narratives, many of which have never been studied before and demonstrates the long-term influence of this body of works on the ensuing "golden age" of the Russian novel.

Waiting for Pushkin provides an indispensable source for scholars and students of nineteenth-century Russian fiction. The volume is also relevant to those interested in women's writing, comparative studies and Russian literature in general.

Amsterdam/New York, NY,
2006 429 pp.
(Studies in Slavic
Literature and Poetics 44)
Paper € 85 / US$ 106
ISBN-10: 9042018291
ISBN-13: 9789042018297

USA/Canada:
295 North Michigan Avenue - Suite 1B Kenilworth, NJ 07033,
USA. Call Toll-free (US only): 1-800-225-3998
All other countries:
Tijnmuiden 7, 1046 AK Amsterdam, The Netherlands
Tel. +31-20-611 48 21 Fax +31-20-447 29 79
Please note that the exchange rate is subject to fluctuations

Rodopi

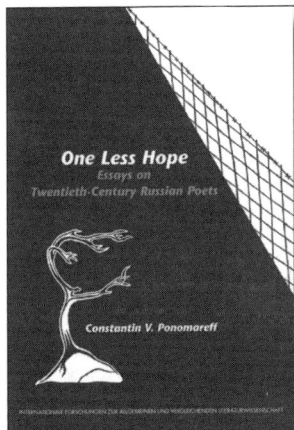

Montaging Pushkin

Pushkin and Visions of Modernity in Russian Twentieth–Century Poetry

Alexandra Smith

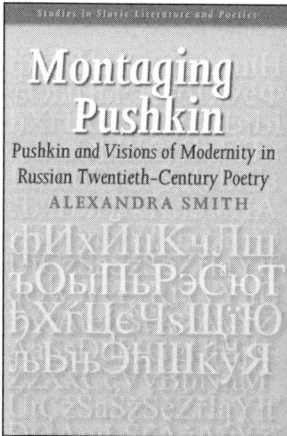

Amsterdam/New York, NY, 2006 361 pp.
(Studies in Slavic Literature and Poetics 46)
Paper € 72 / US$ 90
ISBN-10: 9042020121
ISBN-13: 9789042020122

Montaging Pushkin offers for the first time a coherent view of Pushkin's legacy to Russian twentieth-century poetry, giving many new insights. Pushkin is shown to be a Russian forerunner of Baudelaire. Furthermore it is argued that the rise of the Russian and European novel largely changed the ways Russian poets have looked at themselves and at poetic language; that novelisation of poetry is detectable in the major works of poetry that engaged in a creative dialogue with Pushkin, and that polyphonic lyric has been achieved. Alexandra Smith locates significant examples of Pushkin's cinematographic cognition of reality, suggesting that such dynamic descriptions of Petersburg helped create a highly original animated image of the city as comic apocalypse, which followers of Pushkin appropriated very successfully even as far as the late twentieth century. Montaging Pushkin will be of interest to all students of Russian poetry, as well as specialists in literary theory, European studies and the history of ideas.

"Smith's thesis is both startling and original: that Pushkin, for all his Mozart-like fluidity and perfection, can be productively read as a poet of pain and violence. His reflex was to respond to the totalizing, authoritative public landscape of his era with an equally severe but specifically private, individualizing, disciplined set of demands on the Poet. The recurring attention that later generations have paid toward those aspects of Pushkin's life and texts governed by the private right to resist or to initiate violence (his duel, his struggles with the bureaucracy, his failed pursuit of service with honour) suggest that this mythologeme is among the most productive in Pushkin's astonishing legacy"
CARYL EMERSON (A. Watson Armour III University Professor of Slavic Languages and Literatures, Chair of the Slavic Department, Professor of Comparative Literature at Princeton University)

"Smith's innovative study offers a wonderful analysis of how cinematographic editing and polyphony are detected in Russian twentieth-century poetry ... It views Pushkin as a "référence obligée" of contemporary urban poetry"
VÉRONIQUE LOSSKY (Professor Emeritus of Russian Literature at the Université de Paris-Sorbonne IV)

USA/Canada:
295 North Michigan Avenue - Suite 1B Kenilworth, NJ 07033, USA. Call Toll-free (US only): 1-800-225-3998
All other countries:
Tijnmuiden 7, 1046 AK Amsterdam, The Netherlands
Tel. +31-20-611 48 21 Fax +31-20-447 29 79

Please note that the exchange rate is subject to fluctuations

Rodopi

Sartre's *Nausea*

Text, Context, Intertext

Edited by Alistair Rolls and Elizabeth Rechniewski

Sartre's *Nausea*
Text, Context, Intertext

FAUX

Twenty-five years after his death, critics and academics, film-makers and journalists continue to argue over Sartre's legacy. But certain interpretations have congealed around his iconic text *Nausea*, tending to confine it within the framework provided by the later philosophical work, *Being and Nothingness*. This volume opens up the text to a range of new approaches within the fields of English and Comparative Literature, as well as Philosophy and French Studies, under the headings : 'Text', 'Context', and 'Intertext': the textual strategies at work within the novel; the literary, cultural and philosophical context of its production; and the intertextual web within which it is situated.

This volume will interest a wide public of teachers, students and all those who want to reconsider Sartre's legacy in the twenty-first century.

Amsterdam/New York, NY,
2006 VII-213 pp.
(Faux Titre 273)
Paper € 44 / US$ 55
ISBN-10: 904201928X
ISBN-13: 9789042019287

USA/Canada:
295 North Michigan Avenue - Suite 1B Kenilworth, NJ 07033,
USA. Call Toll-free (US only): 1-800-225-3998
All other countries:
Tijnmuiden 7, 1046 AK Amsterdam, The Netherlands
Tel. +31-20-611 48 21 Fax +31-20-447 29 79
Please note that the exchange rate is subject to fluctuations

Rodopi

Intermediality in Theatre and Performance

Edited by Freda Chapple and
Chiel Kattenbelt

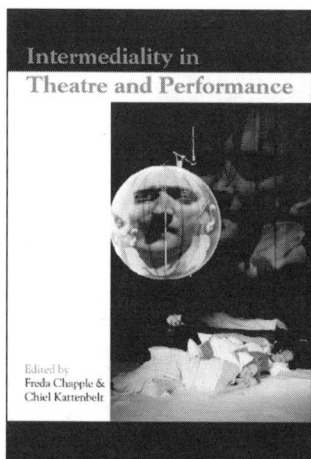

rodopi

Orders@rodopi.nl—www.rodopi.nl

Intermediality: the incorporation of digital technology into theatre practice, and the presence of film, television and digital media in contemporary theatre is a significant feature of twentieth-century performance. Presented here for the first time is a major collection of essays, written by the *Theatre and Intermediality Research Group* of the *International Federation for Theatre Research*, which assesses *intermediality in theatre and performance*. The book draws on the history of ideas to present a concept of intermediality as an *integration of thoughts and medial processes*, and it locates intermediality at the *inter-sections situated in-between* the performers, the observers and the confluence of media, medial spaces and art forms involved in performance at a particular moment in time. Referencing examples from contemporary theatre, cinema, television, opera, dance and puppet theatre, the book puts forward a thesis that the intermedial is a space where the boundaries soften and we are *in-between and within a mixing of space, media and realities, with theatre providing the staging space for intermediality*. The book places theatre and performance at the heart of the 'new media' debate and will be of keen interest to students, with clear relevance to undergraduates and post-graduates in Theatre Studies and Film and Media Studies, as well as the theatre research community.

Amsterdam/New York, NY,
2006 266 pp.
(Themes in Theatre 2)
Paper € 54 / US$ 70
ISBN-10: 9042016299
ISBN-13: 9789042016293

USA/Canada:
295 North Michigan Avenue - Suite 1B Kenilworth, NJ 07033,
USA. Call Toll-free (US only): 1-800-225-3998
All other countries:
Tijnmuiden 7, 1046 AK Amsterdam, The Netherlands
Tel. +31-20-611 48 21 Fax +31-20-447 29 79
Please note that the exchange rate is subject to fluctuations